Library of
Davidson College

LEGAL RESPONSIBILITIES AND RIGHTS OF PUBLIC ACCOUNTANTS

*This is a volume in the
Arno Press collection*

DIMENSIONS OF ACCOUNTING THEORY AND PRACTICE

Advisory Editor
Richard P. Brief

*See last pages of this volume
for a complete list of titles*

LEGAL RESPONSIBILITIES AND RIGHTS OF PUBLIC ACCOUNTANTS

WILEY DANIEL RICH

ARNO PRESS
A New York Times Company
New York • 1980

344.73
R499 l

Editorial Supervision: Brian Quinn

Reprint Edition 1980 by Arno Press Inc.
Reprinted from a copy in the Duke University Library

DIMENSIONS OF ACCOUNTING THEORY AND PRACTICE
ISBN for complete set: 0-405-13475-4
See last pages of this volume for titles.

Manufactured in the United States of America

85-0689

Library of Congress Cataloging in Publication Data

Rich, Wiley Daniel, 1895-
  Legal responsibilities and rights of public
accountants.

  (Dimensions of accounting theory and practice)
  Reprint of the ed. published by American Institute
Pub. Co., New York.
  Originally presented as the author's thesis, Colum-
bia University.
  Bibliography: p.
  1. Accountants--Legal status, laws, etc.--United
States. 2. Accountants--Legal status, laws, etc.--
Great Britain. I. Title. II. Series.
KF2920.R5 1980   344.73'01761657   80-1514
ISBN 0-405-13539-4

LEGAL RESPONSIBILITIES
AND RIGHTS
OF PUBLIC ACCOUNTANTS

LEGAL RESPONSIBILITIES AND RIGHTS OF PUBLIC ACCOUNTANTS

BY WILEY DANIEL RICH

PUBLISHED BY
AMERICAN INSTITUTE PUBLISHING CO., INC.
NEW YORK, N. Y.

COPYRIGHT, 1935,
AMERICAN INSTITUTE PUBLISHING CO., INC.

Printed in the United States of America by
J. J. LITTLE AND IVES COMPANY, NEW YORK

TO

JUDGE AND MRS. O. S. LATTIMORE

PREFACE

THIS book is a comprehensive treatment of case and statutory law applicable particularly to public accountants. The first chapter is concerned with the public accountant's liability for negligence, libel and fraud. The three remaining chapters involve the law relative to the public accountant's certificate, the accountant as an expert witness and some special rights of public accountants.

In the development of the subjects, primary emphasis has been placed upon the case law in England and America. I am reasonably sure that every appeal case in England prior to July, 1933, and every appeal case in America prior to February, 1935, has been taken into consideration in the preparation of this work. A limited search of the English law books leads me to believe that no important appeal case on the responsibilities of auditors arose in England during the period from July, 1933, to January, 1935. While the English decisions cited in the treatise have been colored somewhat by the English companies acts, the portions of such opinions reported have to do in the main with common-law principles. The English companies acts have been reviewed only so far as has been necessary to afford a proper interpretation of the English case law presented. The American state and District of Columbia statutes on public accountants have been summarized under appropriate titles. While these summaries have been supported principally by citations to *Certified Public Accountant Laws of the United States,* published by the American Institute of Accountants in 1930, I found from a close search of state and District of Columbia statutes as of July, 1933, that the summaries were as applicable in 1933 as in 1930. The United States statutes affecting directly public accountants have been reviewed to January 1, 1935.

I wish to acknowledge my indebtedness to: Professors James L. Dohr and Roy B. Kester of Columbia University for their criticisms and suggestions as to organization and content of the treatise; Professors I. P. Hildebrand, R. W. Stayton, W. P. Keeton, and A. W. Walker of the University of Texas School of Law for conferences on unsettled questions of law; Walter A. Staub, partner of Lybrand, Ross Brothers & Montgomery, A. P. Richardson, Editor of the *Journal of Accountancy,* J. M. B. Hoxsey of New York Stock Exchange, and Professor Chester F. Lay of the University of Texas School of Business Administration for materials furnished; and my wife for her untiring efforts in helping me with the manuscript.

WILEY DANIEL RICH.

Hardin-Simmons University,
Abilene, Texas, 1935.

CONTENTS

	PAGE
CHAPTER I. LIABILITY OF THE PUBLIC ACCOUNTANT FOR NEGLIGENCE, FRAUD AND LIBEL	3
I. INTEREST IN THE PUBLIC ACCOUNTANT'S LIABILITY FOR NEGLIGENCE AND FRAUD	3
II. NATURE OF NEGLIGENCE	4
Failure to Exercise Due Care	4
Breach of Duty	7
Injury	9
Proximate Cause of Injury	10
III. LIABILITY OF THE PUBLIC ACCOUNTANT FOR NEGLIGENCE TO HIS CLIENT	12
Relation of the Accountant-client Contract to the Public Accountant's Liability for Negligence . .	12
Duty of the Public Accountant to Inquire into the Substantial Accuracy of Accounting Reports .	17
Duty of the Public Accountant to Exercise Reasonable Care to Show the Whole Truth as to Value of Assets Represented by the Balance-sheet . .	19
The Auditor's Duty Relative to Stock-in-trade .	29
Duty of the Public Accountant to Verify the Inventory of Securities	35
The Duty of the Public Accountant to Verify Cash	39
The New York Stock Exchange on the Public Accountant's Duty to Make a Proper Verification of Cash	47
Duty of the Public Accountant Relative to Secret Reserves	48
Inference of Negligence on the Part of the Public Accountant	54

		PAGE
	Contributory Negligence on the Part of the Client	57
	Liability of the Public Accountant to His Client for Negligent Disclosure of Confidential Communications	60
IV.	LIABILITY OF THE PUBLIC ACCOUNTANT TO HIS CLIENT FOR LIBEL	64
V.	LIABILITY OF THE PUBLIC ACCOUNTANT TO THIRD PARTIES FOR NEGLIGENCE AND FRAUD	66
	The Public Accountant Not Liable to Third Parties for Mere Negligence	66
	The Public Accountant Liable to Third Parties for Fraud	68
	Liability of the Public Accountant to Third Parties for Misrepresentation under the United States Securities Act	76
	Liability of the Public Accountant to Third Parties for Misrepresentation under the United States Securities Exchange Act of 1934	86
VI.	EXTENSION OF THE AMBIT OF NEGLIGENCE RATHER THAN THAT OF FRAUD TO COVER THE PUBLIC ACCOUNTANT'S LIABILITY TO THIRD PARTIES FOR INNOCENT BUT NEGLIGENT MISREPRESENTATION	88
	Meaning of Fraud	88
	The Negligence Formula as a Mode of Extending the Public Accountant's Liability to Third Parties for Mere Negligence	94
VII.	CRIMINAL LIABILITY OF THE PUBLIC ACCOUNTANT FOR FRAUD	100
	Case Law on the Public Accountant's Liability for Fraud	100
	The Public Accountant's Criminal Liability for Fraud under Statutes	109
CHAPTER II. LAW AND THE CERTIFIED PUBLIC ACCOUNTANT'S CERTIFICATE		111
	Issuance of Certified Public Accountant's Certificate	111

	PAGE
Recognition of a Certified Public Accountant's Certificate Issued by Another State or a Foreign Country	113
Illegal Issue and Illegal Assumption of the Certified Public Accountant's Certificate or Membership in an Established Accounting Fraternity	120
Liability of a Publisher Who Falsely Advertises One as a Certified Public Accountant	129
Cancellation of a Certified Public Accountant's Certificate	130
The Reissuance of a Certified Public Accountant's Certificate Which Has Been Cancelled	133
Restriction of the Practice of Public Accounting to Persons Who Hold the Certified Public Accountant's Certificate	134

CHAPTER III. THE ADMISSIBILITY OF THE PUBLIC ACCOUNTANT'S EXPERT TESTIMONY IN COURT 142

General Nature of Expert Testimony	142
English Law Relative to the Admissibility of an Accountant's Expert Testimony	143
American Law Relative to the Admissibility of an Accountant's Expert Testimony	144
The Admissibility of Accounting Records as Evidence	144
Admissibility of an Expert Accountant's Statements and Schedules of Voluminous and Multifarious Books	153
Admissibility of Expert Testimony of an Accountant	154
The Parol-evidence Rule and the Expert Accountant's Testimony	155
The Accountant's Expert Testimony Not Barred by the Rules of Hearsay or Primary Evidence	158
Custody of Records	161
Authenticity of Records	168

Contents

PAGE

A Certified Public Accountant's Certificate Not a Prerequisite to Qualification as an Expert Witness in Matters of Accounting 173

Credibility of Witness 174

Confidential Communications Between Public Accountant and Client 175

Preparation of a Part of Audit by Assistants Not a Bar to Admission of Expert Accountant's Testimony 182

An Expert Bookkeeper's Testimony Advisory, Not Binding 183

Conclusions of an Expert Accountant 184

Accountant's Right to Refresh His Memory from Records 193

CHAPTER IV. SOME SPECIAL RIGHTS OF PUBLIC ACCOUNTANTS . 194

Champerty 194

Ownership of Working Papers 203

The Accountant's Lien Upon His Employer's Books 205

Rights of the Public Accountant Under United States Bankruptcy Act 210

Expenses of Audit in Addition to Personal Services of Accountant 221

Nature of Accountant's Services Affect Reasonableness of Charges 222

Auditing Contracts with Corporations and Governmental Agencies 222

Power of Practitioners of Public Accountancy to Incorporate 223

APPENDIX. RULES OF PROFESSIONAL CONDUCT OF THE AMERICAN INSTITUTE OF ACCOUNTANTS 225

TABLE OF CASES 229

TABLE OF STATUTES 233

BIBLIOGRAPHY 235

LEGAL RESPONSIBILITIES
AND RIGHTS
OF PUBLIC ACCOUNTANTS

Chapter I

LIABILITY OF THE PUBLIC ACCOUNTANT FOR NEGLIGENCE, FRAUD AND LIBEL

THE development of the law on the liability of the public accountant for negligence, fraud and libel is unfolded in this chapter under main divisions as follows:

I. Interest in the public accountant's liability for negligence and fraud.
II. Nature of negligence.
III. Liability of the public accountant to his client for negligence.
IV. Liability of the public accountant to his client for libel.
V. Liability of the public accountant to third parties for negligence and fraud.
VI. Extension of the ambit of negligence rather than that of fraud to cover the public accountant's liability to third parties for innocent but negligent misrepresentation.
VII. Criminal liability of the public accountant for fraud.

I

INTEREST IN THE PUBLIC ACCOUNTANT'S LIABILITY FOR NEGLIGENCE AND FRAUD

In "boom" periods, in which business enterprises are led to believe that prosperity abounds, the public accountant has rarely been held accountable for the negligent character of his services; but whenever a business depression has occurred, public accountants, with other classes in the business community, have been brought to task for the wide-spread distress. Out of the fire of business and public reaction against public accountants in each business depression of the last half century there have been wrought in England and America the greatest legal developments of the responsibilities of public accountants.

As in preceding economic depressions, there has been prevalent during the past few years of dislocations of trade and industries a keen public and professional interest in the duties of public accountants. The public has sought to surround investments in business with greater safeguards by means of placing more responsibilities upon the accounting profession. Several cases, the United States securities act of 1933, as amended in 1934, and the United States securities exchange act of 1934, dealing with negligence and fraud of public accountants, have thus far resulted.

II

NATURE OF NEGLIGENCE

"Negligence has been defined to be either the non-performance or the inadequate performance of a legal duty. The existence of a duty to plaintiff, omission to perform it or performance in an improper or inadequate manner and injury to him resulting therefrom, are essential to the maintenance of an action for negligence." [1] In negligence there is no wrongful intent. Negligence is unreasonable conduct, in violation of a legal duty owed to the plaintiff, resulting directly in injury to the plaintiff. Every action for negligence must be based upon all the following elements: (1) a failure to exercise due care; (2) a breach of duty; (3) an injury; (4) defendant's act a proximate cause of the plaintiff's injury.

FAILURE TO EXERCISE DUE CARE

The tests which courts have advanced for determining the lack of due care or the existence of negligence have been many. The early decisions and writings upon negligence generally divided the subject into gross, ordinary, and slight negligence, depending upon

[1] *Newton Auto Salvage Co.* v. *Herrick* (supreme court of Iowa, 1927) 212 N. W. 680.

the amount of care required in the particular circumstances.[2] Thus, according to this school of thought, slight negligence is the want of great diligence; gross negligence is the want of slight diligence; ordinary negligence is the want of a moderate amount of diligence. For example, persons who employ dangerous agencies, such as guns and explosives, may be held liable for slight negligence for such persons are required to use a very high degree of care. A gratuitous bailee, i.e., one who takes custody of a chattel solely for the benefit of the bailor, is liable only for gross negligence, for such a person owes a duty to the owner of the chattel to exercise only a slight degree of care. An ordinary bailee for hire may be held liable for ordinary negligence if he fails to use a moderate amount of care with reference to the chattel. While the theory of three degrees of negligence commands the support of some of the best courts in the country and is to be found in a few statutes, it is undesirable and leads to confusion.

The better and more recent view of negligence holds that "the law imposes but one duty in such cases, and that is the duty to use due care; and the law recognizes only one standard by which the quantum of care can be measured, and that is the care which a person of ordinary prudence would exercise under like circumstances." [3] The test should be what a reasonable person would have done or would have omitted to have done in the particular set of circumstances. The test of the existence of negligence is, not what the defendant thought was wise, but whether an ordinarily careful and reasonable person would have thought the particular course of action was wise and would have acted as did the defendant. Again, in different language, the test of the existence of negligence is whether a reasonable person would have foreseen injury to the plaintiff and then acted as did the plaintiff in the circumstances. The juror or the judge furnishes the standard of an ordinary reasonable man. If the particular circumstances involve special skill, technique or scientific learning, the defendant must have conducted

---

[2] 29 Cyc. 415-426. Burdick's *Law of Torts*, 1926, pp. 510-513.
[3] *Union Traction Co. v. Berry* (supreme court of Indiana, 1919) 188 Ind. 514, 121 N. E. 655, 124 N. E. 737; American Law Institute, *Restatement of the Law of Torts*, T. D. No. 4, 1929, secs. 165-171.

himself as other persons of the same profession or calling would have done in the same circumstances.[4]

As a requisite to the existence of negligence in a breach of duty there must have been an unreasonable risk of injury to the plaintiff. In determining whether or not a risk was unreasonable, as viewed by an ordinary prudent man in the position of the defendant at the time the alleged act of negligence occurred, the magnitude of the risk must be balanced against the utility of the particular conduct, and, if the risk exceeded the utility, the conduct was negligent.[5] If a reasonable person would have deemed the defendant's conduct to involve too great risk as compared to the utility that might be derived from the act, then negligence was existent. In considering the reasonableness of the risk it is not sufficient to show that the chances of no injury were greater than the chances of injury, for, where there was probability of injury from the conduct, the conduct was negligent, unless it was sufficiently useful to offset the risk of injury. A person rushing in front of a speeding train to rescue a child is not assuming an unreasonable magnitude of risk in view of the great utility involved, namely, the saving of the child's life.[6] On the other hand, a person would assume an unreasonable amount of risk if he should rush before a rapidly moving train to save a cat. The risk would be too great as compared to the utility. Money in a business is a legal object of utility. It has been held that a business owner is not required to incur an unreasonable

[4] *Chapman v. Walton,* 10 Bing. 57, 131 Reprint 826 (1833). Note: "Every man who offers his services to another and is employed, assumes the duty to exercise in the employment such skill as he possesses with reasonable care and diligence. In all those employments where peculiar skill is requisite, if one offers his services, he is understood as holding himself out to the public as possessing the degree of skill commonly possessed by others in the same employment, and if his pretensions are unfounded, he commits a species of fraud upon every man who employs him in reliance on his public profession. But no man, whether skilled or unskilled, undertakes that the task he assumes shall be performed successfully, and without fault or error; he undertakes for good faith and integrity, but not for infallibility, and he is liable to his employer for negligence, bad faith or dishonesty, but not for losses consequent upon mere errors of judgment." (Cooley on *Torts,* third edition, volume II, p. 1386.)

[5] Note: In the determination of the reasonableness of conduct in negligence cases, courts rarely state that the comparison of the utility with the risk of injury of an act is the basis of decision; yet, in reality such comparison is the underlying principle of substantially all the decisions on negligence. (The American Law Institute, explanatory notes on torts, tentative draft No. 4, 1929, p. 7.)

[6] *Eckert v. Long Island R.R. Co.,* 43 N. Y. 502 (1871).

amount of expense in taking precautions against injury.[7] He must take such precautions as the business can afford. In other words, in view of all the circumstances, he must balance the risk of injury against the utility of money required to take precautions. He is not negligent as long as he does not take an unreasonable risk in order to save the cost of precautions.

The distinction between the existence of negligence as a matter of fact and the existence of negligence as a matter of law deserves consideration.[8] The determination of reasonableness or unreasonableness of conduct is an inference from data. If the inference of reasonableness or unreasonableness of conduct can not be governed by a precedent, but must be made on the basis of the factual data in terms of the common experience of the lay jurors, the question of negligence is said to be one of fact. On the other hand, if general rules of law can be applied to a set of facts from which only one inference may be drawn, the question of negligence is one of law. If the circumstances of a case in which a decision is made are so peculiar that a similar case will never arise again, no precedent is established; but if the circumstances are such as commonly happen, the decision affords a precedent, and whenever a new set of facts arises similar to the precedent, the court will rule that, if the jury finds such a set of facts to exist, there is negligence per se, that is, negligence as a matter of law. For example, it is negligence as a matter of law for one to point a gun at another person and pull the trigger, even though the actor believes the gun to be unloaded.[9]

Breach of Duty

Liability for a negligent act can exist only where the act was done in breach of a duty owed to the plaintiff. One's legal duty and moral duty may not be the same. One is morally bound to rescue a stranger from drowning, but he owes no legal duty to do so. One's legal duty to exercise care may arise from the express terms of a contract or from legislation, but generally it grows out of

---

[7] Henry T. Terry, "Negligence," 29 *Harvard L. Rev.* 46.
[8] Cooley on *Torts*, vol. II, pp. 1428-1438. Henry T. Terry, "Negligence," 29 *Harvard L. Rev.* 50.
[9] Henry T. Terry, "Negligence," 29 *Harvard L. Rev.* 50.

common-law implications from a contractual relationship or from other circumstances.[10]

One's duty to use care, arising from the express terms of a contract, may be as varied as it is possible to make different contracts. Where a negligent act is nothing more than a breach of the express terms of a contract, the action for recovery must be brought on the contract and not in tort.[11] The public accountant's duty to use care in the accountant-client relation as affected by the terms of the auditing contract is given extended treatment in a subsequent part of this volume.

There are great variations in the duty of care as imposed by legislation. Where an act in breach of a statute becomes both a public and a private wrong, American courts uniformly hold that the public and the party aggrieved have concurrent remedies.[12] The public wrong is sought to be cured through indictment; the private wrong is sought to be remedied through tort action. But, where an act is a public wrong, courts do not always hold that there exists also a private wrong. If a statute requires an affirmative act, as in the case of a municipality placing its own duty upon citizens to keep snow off sidewalks abutting the property of such citizens, the violation of the statute would not be negligence per se—the defendant would owe to the person injured no duty to perform the affirmative act. On the other hand, it has been held by many courts that the commission of an act forbidden by statute constitutes negligence per se, and that damages should be allowed where the defendant's act was a proximate cause of the injury to the plaintiff. This type of holding would seem to be sound. If a statute prohibits certain conduct, it is because that conduct has been found dangerous to society. It is fair to presume that an ordinary reasonable person would not engage in conduct dangerous to society and that one who does so may be guilty of negligence. If society has seen fit to protect itself by prohibiting certain conduct, it would be logical to conclude that such conduct would also violate the defendant's common-law duty to exercise care to the particular

[10] 29 Cyc. 424, 425.
[11] Burdick's *Law of Torts*, pp. 46, 47.
[12] Ibid., pp. 42-46.

LIABILITY FOR NEGLIGENCE, FRAUD AND LIBEL

person or class of persons protected by the statute. Some courts, however, have held that liability for negligence does not necessarily follow the breach of a prohibitory statute and that under police ordinances there is no implied power to create tort liability.[13] The English companies acts and the United States securities act of 1933 have placed specific responsibilities upon public accountants to exercise due care to particular classes of persons.

Whatever legal duty the defendant may owe to the plaintiff is to be found principally in the common-law implications requiring a person to conduct himself in such a manner as not to injure another's person or property.[14] This duty of care owed to others may be implied from a contract, or it may be implied from many other circumstances. The defendant's duty to use due care does not extend to the world in general, but only to the particular plaintiff or the definite class of persons to which the plaintiff belongs. The defendant owes a duty of care only to those persons who might reasonably be expected to be endangered by the risk taken by the defendant.[15] For example, one driving a car down a street owes a duty of careful driving to all those pedestrians and motorists who might reasonably be expected to be injured by his reckless driving. But if the driver should negligently collide with a car containing bombs and thereby set off an explosion which injured office workers in adjacent buildings, he would not be liable to such persons—he would have owed those persons no duty of careful driving, for it would not have been reasonably expected that his negligent driving would injure persons in adjacent buildings.

INJURY

The plaintiff's action for negligence must be founded upon an injury to his person or property. If the plaintiff does nothing more than to prove an injury, with the other elements essential to an action for negligence, he can recover only substantial damages. It behooves the plaintiff to prove the actual monetary loss resulting

---

[13] Burdick's *Law of Torts*, p. 45.
[14] 29 Cyc. 424, 425.
[15] Harper on *Torts*, pp. 165-170.

from the injury if he would obtain proper redress for defendant's negligent conduct.[16]

PROXIMATE CAUSE OF INJURY

The defendant's liability to the plaintiff for negligence is dependent upon proof that the defendant's negligent act was the direct cause of the plaintiff's injury. The direct cause of injury has been interpreted to mean a substantial factor in producing the alleged damage.[17] An act is a direct cause if it is a substantial part of the causative antecedents, if it is one of several substantial factors. If the plaintiff's injury would not have happened without the defendant's negligent act, the defendant's act was a direct cause of the plaintiff's injury. If the injury would have occurred regardless of the defendant's negligent act, the defendant's conduct was not the actual cause of the injury. Before the defendant's act can be said to have been the actual cause of the alleged damage, the effect of the act must have had an appreciable continuation, either down to the very moment of injury, or, at least, down to the setting in motion of the final active injurious force which immediately produced the damage.

A review of a few cases on direct causation of injury is in order. Direct causation of injury was held to have existed where the defendant with a boat negligently ran into a group of piles in a stream, whereby force communicated from one pile to another finally created a wedge between two piles so as to injure plaintiff who was caught within the wedge.[18] In another case where the defendant negligently left in the highway a truck loaded with iron slabs in such a way that some of the iron could easily slide off the truck, and a third person wrongfully moved the truck and unintentionally let slabs of iron fall off and injure plaintiff, it was held that the defendant's act was a direct cause of the plaintiff's injury.[19] A child was negligently sold gun powder by the defendant. With its parent's knowledge the child placed the powder in a cupboard; and later, after the child was handed the powder by

[16] Ibid., pp. 283-287.
[17] Burdick's *Law of Torts*, pp. 32-38.
[18] *Hill* v. *Winsor*, 118 Mass. 251 (1875).
[19] *Lane* v. *Atlantic Works*, 111 Mass. 136 (1872).

its parent, the child used the powder and thereby sustained an injury. The court held in this case that the active effect of the defendant's conduct was so slight that no cause of action arose.[20] Where a client who was interested in a corporation wrote to the defendant accountant a libelous letter concerning two officers of the company, and the accountant negligently left the letter where a third person found it and communicated it to the company officers, the court held that the accountant's act was not a direct cause of the client plaintiff's damages sustained from having been sued by the officers, that the chain of causation between the accountant's negligent act and the plaintiff's loss was broken by the wrongful conduct of the third person.[21] As shown by these cases, it is not always easy to determine whether or not a particular act was the cause of an injury. If the defendant negligently induced a third person's act, which was the immediate cause of the plaintiff's injury, the defendant is generally held to have caused directly the injury. But, on the other hand, where a third person intervened to break the chain of causation between the commission of the negligent act and the happening of the injury, courts hold that the act was not the direct cause of the injury.

The defendant's reasonable ability to foresee risk of injury to the plaintiff as a test to determine whether an act was the proximate cause of the injury deserves consideration. The majority of American courts hold that before a finding that a negligent act was the proximate, direct, or substantial cause of an injury can be justified, it must appear that the injury was the natural and probable consequence of the negligent act, and that the injury ought to have been foreseen by the defendant in the light of the attending circumstances.[22] Under this rule courts hold that defendant must have been able reasonably to foresee injury to the plaintiff or to the class of persons to which plaintiff belonged. The defendant is not charged with prevision of injury to persons in general but only those in the class threatened by the risk taken by the defendant. A railroad company negligently failed to keep its stock-

[20] *Carter* v. *Towne*, 103 Mass. 507 (1870).
[21] *Weld-Blundell* v. *Stephens*, page 60, post.
[22] Burdick's *Law of Torts*, pp. 38-41. Henry T. Terry, "Negligence," Harvard Law Review Association, *Selected Essays on the Law of Torts*, p. 263.

pen in repair. A passing train, as a result of the engineer's negligence, frightened plaintiff's cattle enclosed within the pen. The stampeded cattle injured not only themselves, but the plaintiff while he was attempting to make the gate secure. The court imputed to the defendant railroad company ability to foresee the property loss, that is, the injury to the cattle, but refused to charge the defendant with prevision of the personal injury to the plaintiff.[23]

III

LIABILITY OF THE PUBLIC ACCOUNTANT TO HIS CLIENT FOR NEGLIGENCE

Relation of the Accountant-client Contract to the Public Accountant's Liability for Negligence

Robert H. Montgomery, in his address before the International Congress on Accounting, 1933, London, had this to say about the scope of the public accountant's employment: [24]

> "In determining whether or not an auditor has been guilty of negligence, it is necessary to consider specifically what he was employed to do. A client can not expect a detailed audit where the auditor was engaged to make merely a balance-sheet audit. The auditor should be careful, however, to obtain definite written instructions to which he can refer and to limit his statements and certificates to the matters of which he has actual knowledge.
>
> "Sometimes after a balance-sheet audit, specifically requested in writing, has been made and the report rendered, it is discovered that petty defalcations have been going on for a long time. It is natural for the client, in such a case, to criticize the auditor, but if the latter has specific instructions to which he can refer, he can clearly show that the detection of the small theft was not within the scope of the audit.
>
> "The scope of the employment can not be determined simply from the compensation paid, though in a doubtful case the amount of compensation would be some evidence of the character of employ-

---

[23] *T. & P. Ry. Co.* v. *Bigham*, 90 Tex. 223, 38 S. W. 162 (1896).
[24] R. H. Montgomery, *The Auditor's Responsibility in Relation to Balance-sheets and Profit-and-loss Accounts*, p. 3.

LIABILITY FOR NEGLIGENCE, FRAUD AND LIBEL 13

ment. An auditor may undertake to perform for one hundred dollars work for which the reasonable compensation is one thousand dollars. He will, nevertheless, be held to have agreed to exercise the skill of his calling in the work which he agreed to do."

A public accountant's liability for negligence will usually involve a breach of duty emanating from a contract. A breach of a contract may or may not be the result of negligence. If the plaintiff's right which had been invaded by the defendant was created solely by the agreement of the parties, the plaintiff is limited to an action for breach of contract. On the other hand, if the invaded right of the plaintiff was created by law, the plaintiff may sue in tort. The distinction between a cause of action resulting from an invasion of a right created solely by contract and a cause of action resulting from an invasion of a right created solely by law was clearly set forth by the supreme court of Alabama: "Take for illustration the contract of a carpenter to repair a house partly decayed or defective. The implications of his contract are that he will bring to the service reasonable skill, good faith and diligence. If he fail to do the work or leave it incomplete the remedy, and the only remedy, against him is ex contractu. Suppose in the attempted performance he, by his want of skill or care, destroys, damages and needlessly wastes the materials furnished by the hirer; or suppose that in making the needed repair he did it so unskillfully or carelessly as to damage other portions of the house—this is tort, for which the contract furnished the occasion. The contract is mere inducement, and the action is on the case." [25] Between the extreme situations, first, where negligent conduct is merely an invasion of a right created by agreement, and, second, where negligent conduct is merely an invasion of a right created by law, a numerous and extensive class of cases involves negligent conduct which is both a breach of duty created by contract and a breach of duty created by law.[26] The plaintiff in such cases may elect to sue in either contract or tort. For example, the bailee of a horse, which is injured through the bailee's negligence, may be sued either for

[25] *Insurance Co.* v. *Randall*, 74 Ala. 170 (1883). In accord: *Junker* v. *Forbes* (C.C.A., 1891) 45 Fed. 840; *Royce* v. *Oakes*, 20 R. I. 252, 38 A. 371, 39 L. R. A. 845 (1898).
[26] Burdick's *Law of Torts*, pp. 46-48.

breach of his contract to treat the horse with ordinary care or for breach of his legal duty so to treat the horse.[27] Wherever the plaintiff is entitled to sue in either contract or tort, generally it is to his advantage to sue in tort (trespass on the case for negligence). The plaintiff is entitled to substantial damages without proof of actual damage if he bases his claim on negligence; but if he sues in contract, he can recover only a nominal sum, unless he proves his actual damage. It is also true that, if the plaintiff bases his claim on negligence, he can attach defendant's property prior to judgment. The plaintiff can not attach defendant's property prior to judgment where his action is brought in contract. On the other hand, it may be more advantageous to the plaintiff to sue in contract because the proof of the cause of action can be effected more easily in assumpsit than in tort.[28] Obviously, it would generally be better for the public accountant if he were charged with a breach of contract than if he were charged with negligence for the same offense.

Of course, a definite contract reduced to writing will save many difficulties in the accountant-client relation, but not all. If the public accountant merely fails to perform the duties intended by the contract—as where he fails to perform the audit at all or fails to bring to the task he has undertaken a reasonable amount of skill, good faith and diligence—he can be held liable only in contract. If the auditor carries out the terms of the auditing contract, express or implied in fact, but in so doing violates a duty implied by law, he can be held liable only in tort. For example, if an auditor should, inadvertently and without any wrongful intention, divulge to a third person a client's trade secret which was learned, not in the audit, but incidentally from a conversation with an employee of the client, the auditor would be liable to his client only in tort (for negligence). In most cases where a public accountant is guilty of negligence to his client his negligence amounts to a breach of duties created by the intentions of the parties to the auditing contract and also his common-law duties implied from the contract and other circumstances. For example, it is submitted

---

[27] *Pelton* v. *Nichols,* 180 Mass. 345, 62 N. E. 1 (1902).
[28] Burdick's *Law of Torts,* pp. 50, 51.

LIABILITY FOR NEGLIGENCE, FRAUD AND LIBEL

that, where an auditor has undertaken a detailed audit, if the auditor in verifying the cash-disbursements record fails to test the genuineness of cancelled cheques, he can be held liable for loss resulting from his negligence either on the ground of negligence or for breach of contract. In every contract rights and obligations are created either by the intentions of the contracting parties or by implications of the law from the circumstances. The public accountant and his client would intend nothing about verification of cancelled cheques at the time of making the contract for a detailed audit. But, on the other hand, a court would imply a duty on the part of the auditor to verify cancelled cheques in a detailed audit for the client—the court would imply the obligation of the auditor to afford justice in the circumstances. Hence, a failure to test the genuineness of cheques would be a breach of a phase of the contract implied by law and would give to the client a right to sue in contract (in assumpsit). This breach of a duty implied by law would also give rise to an action in tort.

On February 24, 1933, a group of the largest accounting firms of New York addressed to President Richard Whitney of the New York Stock Exchange a letter relative to the scope of the auditor's employment. The letter was signed by: Arthur Anderson & Co.; Barrow, Wade, Guthrie & Co.; Deloitte, Plender, Griffiths & Co.; Haskins & Sells; Lybrand, Ross Bros. & Montgomery; Peat, Marwick, Mitchell & Co.; Price, Waterhouse & Co.; Touche, Niven & Co.; Arthur Young & Co. Two paragraphs of the letter read as follows:

> "We fully recognize the importance of defining the responsibility of auditors and of bringing about a proper understanding on the part of the investing public of the scope and significance of financial audits, to the end that their importance should not be underrated nor their protective value exaggerated in the minds of investors. This is the more necessary because the problem of delimiting the scope of audits or examinations is essentially one of appraising the risks against which safeguards are desirable in comparison with the costs of providing such safeguards. The cost of an audit so extensive as to safeguard against all risks would be prohibitive; and the problem is, therefore, to develop a general scheme of examination of accounts

under which reasonably adequate safeguards may be secured at a cost that will be within the limits of a prudent economy. The position was clearly stated by a partner in one of the signatory firms in 1926 as follows:

" 'In any such work we must be practical; it is no use laying down counsels of perfection or attempting to extend the scope of the audit unduly. An audit is a safeguard; the maintenance of this safeguard entails an expense; and this expense can be justified only if the value of the safeguard is found to be fully commensurate with its cost. The cost of an audit so extensive as to be a complete safeguard would be enormous and far beyond any value to be derived from it. A superficial audit is dangerous because of the sense of false security which it creates. Between the two extremes there lies a mean, at which the audit abundantly justifies its cost.' "

The statement to the New York Stock Exchange is founded on solid legal principles. Of course, if an auditor expressly agrees to check every item in an entire set of books, he will generally be held liable for failing to do so. In the absence of an express agreement covering in detail every sort of review and verification which it would be possible to make, the question arises: How far must the audit extend in view of the requirements for safeguards and the amount of compensation inuring to the auditor? In other words, how much risk of errors may be taken as compared to the utility accruing to the public accountant in the form of audit fees? It is well-established law that if the defendant assumed an unreasonable amount of risk as compared to the utility of his act, he was negligent; and, if his conduct violated a duty owed the plaintiff and resulted directly in injury to the plaintiff, he is liable.[29] It would not be expected that the accountant should take no risk at all as compared to his compensation; neither would it be expected that the accountant should take no precautions at all against errors. The accountant is expected to assume a reasonable amount of risk of error as compared to his compensation. The test of reasonableness of the accountant's assumption of risk as compared to his compensation is how much risk other skilled professional accountants would have taken in the same set of circumstances.

[29] Henry T. Terry, "Negligence," 29 *Harvard L. Rev.*, pp. 40-54.

LIABILITY FOR NEGLIGENCE, FRAUD AND LIBEL

DUTY OF THE PUBLIC ACCOUNTANT TO INQUIRE INTO THE SUBSTANTIAL ACCURACY OF ACCOUNTING REPORTS

The first important English court decision on the duties of an auditor [30] was rendered by Justice Sterling of the chancery division in 1887. This case, *Leeds Estate Building and Investment Company v. Shepherd*,[31] extended the auditor's duties to inquiry into the soundness, not merely the mathematical accuracy, of the figures included in the balance-sheet.

The articles of association of the Leeds Estate, Building and Investment Company entitled the directors and manager to a bonus in proportion to the amount of profits available for dividends. It was to the interest of these officers to report profits as high as possible. And that is what they did; they overstated the assets of the balance-sheet so as to show a profit available for dividends. The auditor, elected by a vote of the stockholders, accepted without any inquiry whatever the reports of the manager and directors and certified the accuracy of the balance-sheet which included a profit-and-loss account. Dividends were illegally paid out of capital as a result of the inaccurate statement. The stockholders brought an action for damages against the auditor and other officers of the company. Justice Sterling held:

> "It was in my opinion the duty of the auditor not to confine himself merely to the task of verifying the arithmetical accuracy of the balance-sheet, but to inquire into its substantial accuracy, and to ascertain that it contained the particulars specified in the articles of association (and consequently a proper income and expenditure account), and was properly drawn up, so as to contain a true and correct representation of the state of the company's affairs."

The principle of the *Leeds Estate Building and Investment Co. v. Shepherd* case seems too obvious to the modern accountant to re-

---

[30] Note: "The sphere of accountancy is strictly limited to work of a constructive nature upon the books and accounts of a business or undertaking and involves little liability beyond that of an agent to his principal, while that of the auditor is confined to the criticism of accounts already prepared and submitted to him for certification and report; and therein lies the whole essence of his liability." (Grainger, W. H., "The Duties, Obligations and Liabilities of Auditors," *The Accountant*, London, 1923, volume 68, p. 521.)

[31] (1887) 36 Ch. D. 787.

quire statement; yet, this early decision laid a foundation stone upon which many cases rest. The auditor certainly falls short of his duty if he stops at merely verifying the arithmetical accuracy of the balance-sheet. Proving the accounting equation upon which the balance-sheet is based is not enough. The auditor must reasonably test the genuineness of the representation and amount of each item on the balance-sheet.[32]

[32] Under the English companies acts the auditor is an officer of the company and directly responsible to the stockholders by whom he was elected. While the English cases are colored with the auditor's duties as set forth in the companies acts, it is generally true that the principles laid down in such decisions find general application in the common law. The English accountants' attitude toward the auditor's duties was colorfully portrayed in an address before a meeting of chartered accountants during the economic depression of the middle nineties:

"In conclusion, I would remark that it is impossible for an auditor to check in detail, in a few days, work which it has taken a large staff twelve months to do. An audit is really an examination by an expert in accounts resembling the diagnosis of a skilled physician. His wide experience and knowledge of affairs enable him by a careful examination to form an opinion as to the financial soundness of the business and to say whether the balance-sheet gives a truthful account of the state of the institution. The expert may be mistaken, for he is neither omniscient nor infallible. Many a man has been told by a physician that he has not six months to live, and yet has survived for a score of years; but eminent physicians still have a large practice, and rightly so. Much depends on the experience, the judgment and the character of the expert you have called in. He observes how the books are kept, suggests precautions against fraud, points out in what way the accounts can be arranged so that the working of the business can be facilitated and its operations controlled, and forms an opinion whether the liabilities are stated at too little or the assets put down at too much. Subsequent visits enable him to keep the accounts on right lines, if his advice be followed. If through negligence on his part loss is sustained, he is liable for damages. If he is not merely negligent but is guilty of wilfully shutting his eyes to the truth; if when the truth lay under his hand he abstained from finding it out, not from mere negligence, but from the wilful determination not to inquire, then he may be liable to imprisonment. If he has been auditor of a company, and it is wound up, he may, as an officer of the company, be examined as to the manner in which he performed his duties, and unless he has full notes of his audit, to which he can refer, and an able counsel, it may go hardly with him. If through want of care on his part a dividend has been paid out of capital, he may have to refund as damages 50 or 100 times the amount of the modest fee he has been paid. If, owing to any report of his, a dividend has not been paid, and alarm is in consequence occasioned amongst the shareholders or customers, and the company comes to a premature end, he runs the risk of being sued for damages for having by his report caused the suspension of a concern which was perfectly sound. He is between Scylla and Charybdis and needs a clear brain and a stout heart, for the responsibility of auditors is a reality; but so far as the members of the Institute of Chartered Accountants are concerned, I think I may safely say that they intend to face that responsibility, and to perform the duty that is laid upon them without fear and without favor." (Theodore Gregory, "The Responsibilities of Auditors," *The Accountant*, London, 1894, volume 20, p. 957.)

Liability for Negligence, Fraud and Libel

Duty of the Public Accountant to Exercise Reasonable Care to Show the Whole Truth as to Value of Assets Represented by the Balance-sheet

Perhaps the world's greatest single legal development in defining the duties of the public accountant with respect to a proper showing of the values of assets on the balance-sheet was made by the English court of appeal in 1895 in the case *In re London and General Bank*.[88]

The London and General Bank was a limited company formed for the purpose of lending to and otherwise assisting certain building companies called the "Balfour" group. The bank's profits consisted of interest and commissions derived from loans to the "Balfour" group.

For some years prior to the action in this case the greater part of the capital of the bank had been advanced to four of the "Balfour" companies on securities which were insufficient and difficult of realization. The defendant, Theobald, had been auditor of the company since 1882, and had in his reports to the directors repeatedly called their attention to the precarious financial position of the bank, which became more evident year by year. His reports to the shareholders took the form of a certificate or memorandum written on the balance-sheet for the year; and in the earlier years contained a statement to the effect that in his opinion the balance-sheet exhibited a correct view of the position of the bank. But for the year 1891 this statement was omitted from Mr. Theobald's report to the shareholders.

The report to the directors for 1891 was submitted on February 3, 1892. In the balance-sheet of that date the most important asset was £346,975, put down as "Loans to customers and other securities." The report, also, contained a detailed statement calling the directors' serious attention to the unsatisfactory nature of such loans and securities and the difficulty of their realization in the following sentences:

"The gravity of the situation is enhanced by the fact, as we believe it to be, that the board is in many cases powerless to decline

[88] (1895) 2 Ch. 673.

further help because they are powerless to realize. We beg also respectfully to point out that the quarters from which the bank obtains by far the larger proportion of its business are such that the constitution of the bond must make it difficult, if not impossible, to obtain a sufficiently independent opinion upon many vital questions which have to be decided in the management." The auditors concluded the report to the directors with the observation: "We can not conclude without expressing our opinion unhesitatingly that no dividend should be paid this year." This last sentence, however, the auditor was persuaded by the chairman of the board to omit before the report was officially laid before the directors. The report contained this postscript: "We do not wish it to be understood that we consider all the accounts in the schedule unsecured, but as a whole the capital therein represented is locked up."

In contrast with this report to directors, the certificate signed by the auditor and laid before the shareholders at their annual meeting was as follows: "We have examined the above balance-sheet and compared it with the books of the company; and we certify that it is a correct summary of the accounts therein recorded. The value of the assets as shown on the balance-sheet is dependent upon realization." The report to the shareholders as originally drawn contained this additional sentence: "And on this point we have reported specifically to the board." But this sentence, at the request of the chairman of the board, was withdrawn before the report was presented to the meeting of shareholders.

The favorable report of the auditor to the shareholders induced them to declare a dividend. The shareholders believed they were paying dividends out of profits of the bank; but, as a matter of fact, the shareholders were disbursing invested capital in the form of dividends. For this conduct it was contended by the shareholders that the auditor was guilty of misfeasance. Hence arose this action on the part of the shareholders to recover from the auditor, Theobald, the sum paid out as dividends.

The holding in this case that the auditor was guilty of misfeasance doubtless could have been sustained on the basis of common law. However, the English companies acts played a part in the decision. The relevant sections follow:

Liability for Negligence, Fraud and Libel

By subsection 1 of section 7 of the companies act of 1879, a banking company registered after that date was required to have its accounts audited by an auditor elected annually by the stockholders.

By subsection 5 of the 7th section of the companies act of 1879, "Every auditor shall have a list delivered to him of all books kept by the company, and shall at all reasonable times have access to the books and accounts of the company; and any auditor may, in relation to such books and accounts, examine the directors or any other officer of the company."

By subsection 6 of the 7th section of the companies act of 1879, "the auditor or auditors shall make a report to the members on the accounts examined by him or them and on every balance-sheet laid before the company in general meeting during his or their tenure of office; and in every such report shall state whether, in his or their opinion, the balance-sheet referred to in the report is a full and fair balance-sheet properly drawn up, so as to exhibit a true and correct view of the state of the company's affairs, as shown by the books of the company."

On a former appeal of this case judgment was given on the preliminary point whether the auditor of a banking company were an officer of the company within the 10th section of the companies act of 1890, and it was held that the auditor was an officer within the meaning of the act and if guilty of misfeasance might be made liable in damages under that section.

Lord Justice Lindley delivered the opinion of the court:

"* * * In connection with these articles (the charter), and in order to save repetition, it should be stated that by the articles of this bank it is the duty of the directors, and not of the auditors, to recommend to the shareholders the amounts to be appropriated for dividends (clause 98), and it is the duty of the directors to have proper accounts kept, so as to show the true state and condition of the company (clause 103). Lastly, it is for the shareholders, but only on the recommendation of the directors, to declare a dividend (clause 115). It is impossible to read s. 7 of the companies act, 1879, without being struck with the importance of the enactment that the auditors are to be appointed by the shareholders, and are to report to them directly, and not to or through the directors. The object of this enactment is obvious. It is evidently to secure to the shareholders independent and reliable information respecting the true financial position of the company at the time of the audit. * * * It is no part of an auditor's duty to give advice, either to directors or shareholders, as to what they ought to do. An auditor has nothing to do with the prudence or imprudence of making loans with or without security. It is nothing to him whether the business of a company is being conducted prudently or imprudently, profitably or unprofitably. It is nothing to him whether dividends are properly or improperly declared, provided he discharges his own duty to the shareholders. His business is to ascertain and state the true financial position of the company at the time of the audit, and his duty is confined to that. But then comes the question, How is he to ascertain that position? The answer is, By examining the books of the company. But he does not discharge his duty by doing this without inquiry and without taking any trouble to see that the books themselves show the company's true position. He must take reasonable care to ascertain that they do so. Unless he does this his audit would be worse than an idle farce. Assuming the books to be so kept as to show the true position of a company, the auditor has to frame a balance-sheet showing that position according to the books and to certify that the balance-sheet presented is correct in that sense. But his first duty is to examine the books, not merely for the purpose of ascertaining what they do show, but also for the purpose of satisfying himself that they show the true financial position of the company. This is quite in accordance with the decision of Stirling, J. in *Leeds Estate Building and Investment Co.* v. *Shepherd*, (1887) (36 Ch. D. 787). An auditor, however, is not bound to do more than exercise reasonable care and skill in making inquiries and investigations. He is not an insurer; he does not guarantee that the books do correctly show the true position of the company's affairs; he does not even guarantee that his balance-sheet is accurate according to the books of the company. If he did, he would be responsible for error on his part, even if he were himself deceived without any want of reasonable care on his part, say, by the fraudulent concealment of a book from him. His obligation is not so onerous as this. Such I take to be the duty of the auditor: he must be honest—i.e., he must not certify what he does not believe to be true, and he must take reasonable care and skill before he believes that what he certifies is true. What is reasonable care in any particular case must depend upon the circumstances of that case. Where there is nothing to excite suspicion very little inquiry will be reasonably sufficient, and in practice I believe business men select a few cases at haphazard, see that they are right and assume that others like them are correct also. Where suspicion is aroused, more care is obviously necessary; but, still, an auditor is not bound to exercise more than reasonable care and skill, even in a case of suspicion, and he is perfectly justified in acting on the opinion of an expert where special knowledge is required. Mr. Theobald's evidence satisfies me that he took the same view as myself of his duty in investigating the company's books and preparing his balance-sheet. He did not content himself with making his balance-sheet from the books without troubling himself about the truth of what they showed. He checked the cash, examined vouchers for payments, saw that the bills and securities entered in the books were held by the bank, took reasonable care to ascertain their value, and in one case obtained a solicitor's opinion on the validity of an equitable charge. I see no trace whatever of any failure by him in the performance of this part of his duty. It is satisfactory to find that the legal standard of duty is not too high for business purposes and is recognized as correct by business men. The balance-sheet and certificate of February, 1892 (i.e., for the year 1891), was accompanied by a report to the directors of the bank. Taking the balance-sheet, the certificate, and report together, Mr. Theobald stated to the directors the true financial position of the bank, and if this report had been laid before the shareholders Mr. Theobald would have completely discharged his duty to them. Unfortunately, however, this report was not laid before the shareholders, and it becomes necessary to consider the legal consequences to Mr. Theobald of this circumstance. A person whose duty it is to convey information to others does not discharge that duty by simply giving them so much information as is calculated to induce them, or some of them, to ask for more. Information and means of information are by no means equivalent terms. Still, there may be circumstances under which information given in the shape of a printed document circulated amongst a large body of shareholders would, by its consequent publicity, be very injurious to their interests, and in such a case I am not prepared to say that an auditor would fail to discharge his duty if, instead of publishing his report in such a way as to insure publicity, he made a confidential report to the shareholders and invited their attention to it and told them where they could see it. The auditor is to make a report to the shareholders, but the mode of doing so and the form of the report are not prescribed. If, therefore, Mr. Theobald had laid before the shareholders the balance-sheet and profit-and-loss account, accompanied by a certificate in the form in which he first prepared it, he would perhaps have done enough under the peculiar circumstances of this case. I feel, however, the great danger of acting on such a principle; and in order not to be misunderstood I will add that an auditor who gives shareholders means of information instead of information respecting a company's financial position does so at his peril and runs the very serious risk of being held judicially to have failed to discharge his duty.

"In this case I have no hesitation in saying that Mr. Theobald did fail to discharge his duty to the shareholders in certifying and laying before them the balance-sheet of February, 1892, without any reference to the report which he laid before the directors and with no other warning than is conveyed by the words, 'The value of the assets as shewn on the balance-sheet is dependent upon realization.' The most important asset on that balance-sheet is put down as 'Loans to customers and other securities,' £346,975, and on these a full and detailed report was made to the directors showing the very unsatisfactory state of these loans and securities, and it is impossible to read the oral evidence, the report of Balfour and Brock, dated December 22, 1891, and the report of the auditor to the directors of February 3, 1892, without coming to the conclusion that the entry of that large sum as a good asset without explanation was unjustifiable. It is a mere truism to say that the value of loans and securities depends on their realization. We were told that a statement to that effect is so unusual in an auditor's certificate that the mere presence of those words was enough to excite suspicion. But, as already stated, the duty of an auditor is to convey information, not to arouse inquiry, and, although an auditor might infer from an unusual statement that something was seriously wrong, it by no means follows that ordinary people would have their suspicions aroused by a similar statement if, as in this case, its language expresses no more than any ordinary person would infer without it. But Mr. Theobald relies on the fact that he was induced to omit from his certificate all reference to the report which he made to the directors because Mr. Balfour, the chairman, promised to mention that report in his speech to the shareholders, and he did so. But, although Mr. Balfour twice alluded to the report, he did so in such a way as to avoid attracting attention to it.

The second time he mentioned it was after a dividend had been declared and when a motion to reappoint the auditors was before the meeting. The truth is that not a word was said to convey to the shareholders the substance of the information contained in the report or to induce them to ask any question about it. The balance-sheet and profit-and-loss account were true and correct in this sense—that they were in accordance with the books. But they were, nevertheless, entirely misleading, and misrepresented the real position of the company. Under these circumstances I am compelled to hold that Mr. Theobald failed to discharge his duty to the shareholders with respect to the balance-sheet and certificate of February, 1892. Possibly he did not realize the extent of his duty to the shareholders as distinguished from the directors, and he unfortunately consented to leave the chairman to explain the true state of the company to the shareholders instead of doing so himself. The fact, however, remains, and can not be got over, that the balance-sheet and certificate of February, 1892, did not show the true position of the company at the end of 1891, and that this was owing to the omission by the auditor to lay before the shareholders the material information which he had obtained in the course of his employment as auditor of the company, and to which he called the attention of the directors.

"But then it is contended that, even if this be so, there was after all no payment of dividend out of capital, and further that, even if there was, still that such payment was not the natural or immediate result of Mr. Theobald's certificate and of the accounts which he prepared. Whether the payment was made out of capital or not is a question of fact. The payment was professedly made out of profits made by the bank, by charging its customers with interest and commission on loans and discount. The books showed such profits; but the question is, Where did the money come from with which the dividends were paid? The money came from cash at the bankers' or in hand; but this cash could not be properly treated as profit, and the directors and auditors knew this perfectly well. This part of the case has been most carefully investigated by the learned judge whose decision we are reviewing and, after attending closely to the observations of counsel on the reasonings and conclusions contained in the judgment appealed from, I see no reason whatever for dissenting from them. On the contrary, I entirely agree with the learned judge in saying that the profits for the year 1891 never really existed except on paper, and that, to use his words, 'whatever may be the right line to draw as to when profit not received may be carried to profit for the purpose of the annual revenue account, it is plain that there was not justification for so doing in the present case.' The real truth is that the assets of the bank were put down in the balance-sheet at far too high a figure, and this entry, though not misleading if explained (as it was to the directors), was seriously misleading in the absence of explanation. Mr. Theobald says that he regarded the assets of the bank as only locked up; but his report and the schedule to it go far beyond this. The value of the principal asset depended on the probability of the Balfour group of companies and some of the other large borrowers repaying their loans. They were financing each other; their indebtedness to the bank had increased largely during the year; the securities held by the bank for these loans were, to say the least, to a great extent of very doubtful value; and yet the total amount due to the bank in respect of these loans is inserted in the balance-sheet as a good asset, without any deduction and without a word of explanation to the shareholders. We know now that those assets have realized a comparatively small sum, and we were very properly warned against the danger of doing injustice by being wise after the event. But, disregarding the result of realization, and attending only to what was known to the auditors in February, 1892, the entry in the balance-sheet of the sum of £346,975 as a good asset was wholly unjustifiable, unless explained. We are now in a position to understand the true meaning of the passage contained in the auditors' report to the directors of February 3, 1892, and which runs thus: 'We can not conclude without expressing our opinion unhesitatingly that no dividend should be paid this year.' I find it impossible to treat this as a statement by the auditors that there are profits divisible amongst the shareholders, but that the auditors can not recommend a dividend. I can only regard the passage as meaning that there are no funds out of which a dividend can properly be paid, and therefore no dividend ought to be paid this year. A dividend of 7 per cent. was, nevertheless, recommended by the directors, and was resolved upon by the shareholders at a meeting furnished with the balance-sheet and profit-and-loss account certified by the auditors, and at which meeting the auditors were present, but silent. Not a word was said to inform the shareholders of the true state of affairs. It is idle to say that these accounts are so remotely connected with the payment of the dividend as to render the auditors legally irresponsible for such payment. The balance-sheet and account certified by the auditors, and showing a profit available for dividend, were, in my judgment, not the remote, but the real operating cause of the resolution for the payment of the dividend which the directors improperly recommended. The auditors' accounts and certificate gave weight to this recommendation, and rendered it acceptable to the meeting. It was wholly unnecessary for the official receiver to call a shareholder to say that he was induced by the auditors' certificate to concur in the resolution to pay a dividend. As to this part of the case res ipsa loquitur."

The duty which the auditor owed to the shareholders of the London and General Bank emanated from the companies acts; yet, in view of the fact that the auditor was elected by the shareholders, it would seem that the auditor's duty would have been held not different under contract and in the absence of the statute providing that the auditor owed as an officer a duty to state to the shareholders the true financial condition of the business. In other words, it would appear that all the principles laid down in this case are applicable at common law.

Following the *Leeds Estate Building and Investment Company v. Shepherd* case, supra, the *London and General Bank* case held that an auditor is in duty bound to ascertain and state the true financial position of his client's business at the time of the audit. In ascertaining the financial condition of the business, the auditor must go beyond the mere showing of the books; he must exercise reasonable care to ascertain whether or not the books themselves show the true financial position of the business. Yet, the auditor is not an insurer; he does not guarantee that the books show the true financial position of his client's business. As a matter of fact, it is impossible to know the true financial position of an unliquidated enterprise. An auditor is bound only to exercise reasonable care and skill in making inquiries and investigations to determine whether the records and the balance-sheet correctly show the financial condition of the business. The test of the reasonableness of the amount of care and skill exercised by the auditor in making inquiries and investigations is the amount of care and skill other members of the profession would have made in the same circumstances. It is not enough that the auditor determine for himself the correct values of items on the balance-sheet.

He must show the true values of the balance-sheet items in unequivocal terms. The auditor must not stop at stating in his report to his client the means of information which will show correct values of the assets represented on the balance-sheet; he must clearly state the values of assets to the best of his knowledge after he has exercised a reasonable amount of care and skill in determining such values.

In the instant case it was also held that, since the stockholders of the bank used the auditor's balance-sheet prior to declaring a dividend upon recommendation of the board of directors, proof of negligence of the auditor in overstating the values of the assets of the bank was sufficient to fix the auditor's liability to the stockholders for injury resulting from payment of dividends out of capital. It was not necessary to prove that the false balance-sheet induced the stockholders to declare the dividends out of capital. The court held that proof of the circulation of printed copies of the balance-sheet among the stockholders was sufficient evidence from which to infer that the defendant's negligent audit was the proximate cause of the stockholders' injury. The principle of res ipsa loquitur (the thing speaks for itself) was applied in holding defendant's negligence, not the remote, but the real operating cause of the stockholders' loss.

Ordinarily, in actions for negligence the plaintiff must prove by direct evidence that the defendant committed a specific act of negligence, and that the defendant's negligence was the proximate cause of the plaintiff's injury. But such proof may be dispensed with where the proven circumstances were such as to make it possible to infer a negligent act on the part of the defendant, and that the defendant's negligent act was the direct cause of the plaintiff's injury. This rule, res ipsa loquitur, applies where the instrumentalities causing the injury were under the control of the defendant and the nature of the case was such that in the ordinary course of events no injury would have resulted without negligence.[34] In this case the court did not infer from the circumstances the existence of negligence, for the defendant's specific act of negligence, the preparation and certification of the false balance-sheet,

[34] Burdick's *Law of Torts*, pp. 515-517; Cooley on *Torts*, p. 1425.

was proven by direct evidence. It was not necessary for the court to determine whether the preparation of the balance-sheet was under the control of the auditor or not. The court merely inferred that no injury would have happened except for the defendant's negligence and, therefore, that the proven negligence was the proximate cause of the injury.

It would seem that in most instances a dividend would not be declared by the directors of a corporation unless the auditor's report would justify such a dividend. If the auditor's report gives assets at inflated values as a result of the auditor's negligence, and the directors, after receiving such report, declare a dividend injurious to the business of the corporation, it should be held that the circumstances attendant upon the injury were of such a character as to justify an inference that the auditor's negligence caused the injury.

The principles laid down in *In re London and General Bank* are unimpeachable. The case has been followed in many decisions and should be followed in future decisions under like conditions.

The Auditor's Duty Relative to Stock-in-trade

The auditor's duty relative to a proper showing of the value of stock-in-trade on the balance-sheet was set forth by the English court of appeal, 1896, in the oft-quoted case of *In re Kingston Cotton Mill Company*.[35] The facts of the case follow:

For several years prior to 1894 the defendant auditors were the official auditors of the Kingston Cotton Mill Company. In their capacity as company auditors the defendants audited the company's records and prepared balance-sheets as of the close of each of those years. The auditors included in each of such balance-sheets a certificate that the balance-sheet gave a correct view of the financial condition of the Kingston Cotton Mill Company at the date of the particular balance-sheet. The stockholders relied upon these several balance-sheets and paid out dividends for each of the four years preceding 1894. Each of these balance-sheets overstated the financial condition of the company. The result was that the dividends were paid out of invested capital. The company became in-

[35] (No. 2), (1896) 2 Ch. D. 279.

solvent and went into the hands of a liquidator in 1894. To restore the estate's losses from the payment of these improper dividends the liquidator brought an action against the company auditors for negligence under s. 10 of the English companies act of 1890, which provided for the liability of company auditors to the company for losses resulting from their failure to use reasonable care and skill in representing the financial condition of the company.

The alleged negligent conduct of the defendant auditors consisted in the auditors' failure to disclose an overstatement of the company's stock of cotton yarn. The auditors did not look into the manager's figures for the cotton-yarn inventories on the dates of the balance-sheets. They simply accepted the manager's certificate that the inventory sheets showed correctly the values and quantities of cotton yarn on hand. The auditors placed in their balance-sheets immediately preceding the figures for the inventories the words, "As per manager's certificate." The auditors had access to figures for the beginning inventories, the cost of purchases and the cost of sales. They could have easily tested the accuracy of the manager's figures for stocks; but they did not. The court in the following language refused to hold the auditors liable for negligence in overstating inventories:

"* * * The auditors did not profess to guarantee the correctness of this item. They assumed no responsibility for it. They took the item from the manager, and the entry in the balance-sheet showed that they did so. I confess I can not see that their omission to check his returns was a breach of their duty to the company. It is no part of an auditor's duty to take stock. No one contends that it is. He must rely on other people for details of the stock-in-trade on hand. In the case of a cotton mill he must rely on some skilled person for the materials necessary to enable him to enter the stock-in-trade at its proper value in the balance-sheet. In this case the auditors relied on the manager. He was a man of high character and of unquestioned competence. He was trusted by everyone who knew him. The learned judge has held that the directors are not to be blamed for trusting him. The auditors had no suspicion that he was not to be trusted to give accurate information as to the stock-in-trade on hand, and they trusted him accordingly in that matter. But it is said they ought not to have done so, and for this reason. The stock journal showed the quantities—that is, the weight in pounds—of the cotton and yarn at the end of each year. Other books showed the quantities of cotton bought during the year and the quantities of yarn sold during the year. If these books had been compared by the auditors they would have found that the quantity of cotton and yarn in hand at the end of the year ought to be much less than the quantity shown in the stock journal, and so much less that the value of the cotton and yarn entered in the stock journal could not be right, or at all events was so abnormally large as to excite suspicion and demand further inquiry. This is the view taken by the learned judge. But, although it is no doubt true that such a process might have been gone through, and that, if gone through, the fraud would have been discovered, can it be truly said that the auditors were wanting in reasonable care in not thinking it necessary to test the managing director's return? I can not bring myself to think they were, nor do I think that any jury of business men would take a different view. It is not sufficient to say that the frauds must have been detected if the entries in the books had been put together in a way which never occurred to any one before suspicion was aroused. The question is whether, no suspicion of anything wrong being entertained, there was a want of reasonable care on the part of the auditors in relying on the returns made by a competent and trusted expert relating to matters on which information from such a person was essential. I can not think there was. The manager had no apparent conflict between his interest and his duty. His position was not similar to that of a cashier who has to account for the cash which he receives, and whose own account of his receipts and payments could not reasonably be taken by an auditor without further inquiry. The auditor's duty is not so onerous as the learned judge has held it to be. The order appealed from must be discharged with costs.

"* * * But in determining whether any misfeasance or breach of duty has been committed, it is essential to consider what the duties of an auditor are They are very fully described in *In re London and General Bank*, (1895) 2 Ch. D. 673, to which judgment I was a party. Shortly, they may be stated thus: It is the duty of an auditor to bring to bear on the work he has to perform that skill, care, and caution which a reasonably competent, careful and cautious auditor would use. What is reasonable skill, care and caution must depend on the particular circumstances of each case. An auditor is not bound to be a detective, or, as was said, to approach his work with suspicion or with a foregone conclusion that there is something wrong. He is a watch-dog, but not a bloodhound. He is justified in believing tried servants of the company in whom confidence is placed by the company. He is entitled to assume that they are honest, and to rely upon their representations, provided he takes reasonable care. If there is anything calculated to excite suspicion he should probe it to the bottom; but in the absence of anything of that kind he is only bound to be reasonably cautious and careful.

"In the present case the accounts of the company had been for years falsified by the managing director, Jackson, who subsequently confessed the frauds he had committed. It is only, however, just to him to say that they were not committed with a view of putting money in his own pocket, but for the purpose of making things appear better than they really were and in the hope of the company ultimately recovering itself. Jackson deliberately overstated the quantities and values of the cotton and yarn in the company's mills. He did this for many years. It was proved that there is great waste in converting cotton into yarn, and the fluctuations of the market in the prices of cotton and yarn are exceptionally great. Jackson had been so successful in falsifying the accounts that what he had done was never detected or even suspected by the directors. The auditors adopted the entries of Jackson and inserted them in the balance-sheet as 'per manager's certificate.' It is not suggested but that the auditors acted honestly and honestly believed in the accuracy and reliability of Jackson. But it is said that they ought not to have trusted the figures of Jackson, but should have further investigated the matter. Jackson was a trusted officer of the company in whom the directors had every confidence; there was nothing on the face of the accounts to excite suspicion, and I can not see how in the circumstances of the case it can be successfully contended that the auditors are wanting in skill, care or caution in not testing Jackson's figures.

"It is not the duty of an auditor to take stock; he is not a stock expert; there are many matters in respect of which he must rely on the honesty and accuracy of others. He does not guarantee the discovery of all fraud. I think the auditors were justified in this case in relying on the honesty and accuracy of Jackson and were not called upon to make further investigation. It is not unimportant to bear in mind that the learned judge has found the directors justified in relying on the figures of the managing director.

LIABILITY FOR NEGLIGENCE, FRAUD AND LIBEL   33

"The duties of auditors must not be rendered too onerous. Their work is responsible and laborious, and the remuneration moderate. I should be sorry to see the liability of auditors extended any further than in *In re London and General Bank,* (1895) 2 Ch. D. 673. Indeed, I only assented to that decision on account of the inconsistency of the statement made to the directors with the balance-sheet certified by the auditors and presented to the shareholders. This satisfied my mind that the auditors deliberately concealed that from the shareholders which they had communicated to the directors. It would be difficult to say this was not a breach of duty. Auditors must not be made liable for not tracking out ingenious and carefully laid schemes of fraud when there is nothing to arouse their suspicion, and when those frauds are perpetrated by tried servants of the company and are undetected for years by the directors. So to hold would make the position of an auditor intolerable. The appeal will be allowed.

"* * * It is said that it is easy to be wise after the event. In former years when the stock journal was correctly entered the alterations in value in a year were frequently very considerable. The increase in the years now in question did not excite any suspicion in the directors. Why should it in the auditors? They had no reason to distrust the manager. Moreover, he had, or was supposed to have, taken the stock which was actually on the premises at the date to which the balance-sheets referred. The auditors could not do this. The only book from which they could obtain information as to the quantities received in the year, other than the stock journal, was a book called the 'invoice guard book,' in which were pasted the invoices received with goods supplied. But this was not necessarily accurate. Invoices received might have been omitted. Goods might in some cases have been received without invoices. Were the auditors bound to enter upon an investigation which could not bring out an accurate result in order to test the truth of a statement by the manager which no one had any reason to discredit?"

In the *Kingston Cotton Mill Company* case it was held that it is no part of an auditor's duty to take stock. This holding was made in reference to a set of facts in which the auditor had no reason to suspect dishonesty on the part of the manager who certified the amount of stock-in-trade, and in which the auditor clearly showed in the balance-sheet that the figures for the value of the inventory were obtained from the manager. It was also held that, in the absence of suspicion of dishonesty, the auditor has no duty to check by means of book figures the value of inventories as given by a competent officer of the business.

There are important dicta in one of the opinions in the decision with respect to the auditor's duty to use care. An auditor, according to the dicta, is charged with a duty to perform his work with such care, skill and caution as a reasonably careful and cautious auditor would use in the particular circumstances. The auditor is not expected to enter upon his work with suspicion or a foregone conclusion that there is something wrong. He is, according to this case, entitled to rely upon employees who have been trusted by his client, provided the auditor takes reasonable care. The opinion doubtless does not mean that the auditor should accept blindly statements of trusted employees of the client. The auditor would be derelict in his duty if he should accept his client's trusted employee's certificate of a cash count where it was at all feasible for the auditor to count the cash. A reasonable amount of care would require a thorough investigation of circumstances which ordinarily would excite suspicion.

The *Kingston Cotton Mill Company* case is sound in principles; it has been followed in other decisions; and it should be followed in future decisions in similar circumstances, even where the auditor's duties arose only from contract.[36]

The professional attitude of public accountants towards assuming responsibility for the showing of the value of inventories has been expressed as follows: [37]

"The Bradford Chartered and Incorporated Accountants at a joint meeting * * * resolved:

"'(1) That this meeting is of opinion that professional accountants are unable to express reliable opinions upon the market values of stock-in-trade.

"'(2) That it is not within the functions of a professional accountant or auditor to value stocks, and therefore those practising ac-

---

[36] Note: A holding in agreement with *In re Kingston Cotton Mill Company* is to be found in *Henry Squire, Cash Chemist, Ltd.,* v. *Ball, Baker & Co.* (C.A., 1911) 106 L. T. 197, 28 T. L. R. 81.

[37] Grainger, W. H., "The Duties, Obligations, and Liabilities of Auditors," *The Accountant*, 1923, volume 68, p. 521.

LIABILITY FOR NEGLIGENCE, FRAUD AND LIBEL 35

countants represented at this meeting are not prepared to undertake responsibilities of this nature, or to give certificates as to the value of the said stocks, which might deprive auditors of the protection to which they are entitled under judicial ruling laid down in the *Kingston Cotton Mills* case.'"

When a client hires an auditor to review his books, generally he does not expect that the auditor will take stock. Auditors generally do not have the specialized knowledge of merchandise requisite to a proper valuation of a stock of goods. Besides, the client, in most instances, would be unwilling to pay the fees necessary to justify the auditor's taking stock.

The auditor should be required to take stock only in case he expressly agreed to do so. In the usual auditing contract, it would be unreasonable to require the auditor to take stock. If the implications of law should place upon the auditor the duty to take stock, an onerous burden would be thrust upon him; the cost of safeguards would be too great as compared to his compensation. The auditor is entitled to assume a reasonable amount of risk of error with respect to the value of inventories in comparison with the utility of his compensation.[38]

DUTY OF THE PUBLIC ACCOUNTANT TO VERIFY THE INVENTORY OF SECURITIES

The common-law liability of the public accountant to verify the inventory of securities for his client was set forth by the English court of appeal, *In re City Equitable Fire Insurance Co., Ltd.*,[39] 1924. The facts of the case follow:

The City Equitable Fire Insurance Co., carrying on a large international business in fire and marine insurance, had occasion to buy and sell securities in great amounts through Ellis & Co., a brokerage firm. The company's managing director, Bevan, was also a partner in the brokerage firm of Ellis & Co., and he caused enormous sums of the company's money to be kept on deposit with the firm for the purpose of dealing in securities. During 1921 and the two preceding years the accounts the company maintained

---
[38] Note: See page 6, ante.
[39] (1925) Ch. 407, 40 T. L. R. 853, 94 L. J. (Ch.) 445, 133 L. T. 520.

with Ellis & Co. showed much larger amounts of money and securities than were really with the firm. Bevan had improperly taken the funds through his brokerage firm, and had concealed his dishonesty through a false showing of the company's accounts with Ellis & Co. In auditing the company's records for 1921 and the two preceding years the auditors, Lepine and partner, made no further investigation of the securities supposed to be in the custody of Ellis & Co. than to obtain a certificate of custody from one of the firm partners. At the close of each of the three years the figures as thus certified were in agreement with the company's accounts and were used in the company's balance-sheet certified by the auditors. Soon after 1921 the company went into bankruptcy; and the receiver brought an action for negligence against the auditors to recover a huge loss sustained from dealings with Ellis & Co. The court refused judgment to the receiver under a provision in the company's charter relieving company officers from liability to the company for unwillful negligence. The court's decision on the propriety of the auditors' acceptance of Ellis & Co.'s certificate of securities held for the company follows:

"* * * Banks in ordinary course do hold certificates of securities for their customers; it is part of their business to do so, and therefore certificates in the hands of bankers are in their proper custody, and if a bank is a reputable bank, you may legitimately accept the certificate of that bank, because it is a business institution in whose custody you would expect both to find and to put securities, and also it is respectable; but the fact that it calls itself a bank does not seem to me to conclude the matter either one way or the other. On the other hand, it may be said that it is the duty of an auditor not to take a certificate as to possession of securities, except from a person who is not only respectable—I should prefer to use the word 'trustworthy'—but is also one of that class of persons who, in the ordinary course of their business, do keep securities for their customers. It may be said that a stockbroker does not, in the ordinary course of his business, keep securities for his customers, and therefore he is ruled out, because the auditor ought not to accept, from a person of that class, whether he be respectable or not, a certificate that he has securities in his hands. Now, accepting the rule as so stated, that it is right to find the securities in the hands of a bank, whose business it is to hold securities, and applying the proviso that the bank must be one that is trustworthy, it seems to me that the rule may, prima facie, be a right one to follow; but it is going too far to say that, under no circumstances, may you be satisfied with a certificate that securities are in the hands of a stockbroker, because it seems to me that, in the ordinary course of business, you must, from time to time, and you legitimately may, place in the hands of stockbrokers securities for the purpose of their dealing with them in the course of their business. With a large institution like the City Equitable Co., with a very considerable number of investments to make and securities to sell, it may well be that, for the convenience of all parties, it may have been a useful method of business, even if it be examined with the most exiguous care, for the directors to have decided that they would, in the interests of their business, leave securities of a considerable amount in the hands of their stockbrokers, who, I suppose, at that time held a position not less trustworthy or respected than the City Equitable Co. itself. I do not wish in any way, by anything that I say, to discharge the auditors from their duties as laid down in the *Kingston Cotton Mill* case; far less do I wish to discharge them from their duty of seeing that securities are held, and accept the certificate that they are so held from a respectable, trustworthy and responsible person, be that person a bank or an individual; but in applying my mind to the facts of this case, I am not content to say that, simply because a certificate was accepted otherwise than from a bank, therefore there was necessarily so grave a dereliction of duty as to make the auditors responsible. In my opinion it is for the auditor to use his discretion and his judgment, and his discrimination as to whom he shall trust; indeed that is the right way to put a greater responsibility on the auditors.

"If you merely discharge him by saying he accepted the certificate of a bank because it was a bank, you might lighten his responsibility. In my view, he must take a certificate from a person who is in the habit of dealing with and holding securities, and whom he, on reasonable grounds, rightly believes to be, in the exercise of the best judgment, a trustworthy person to give such a certificate. Therefore, I by no means derogate from the responsibility of the auditor—I rather throw a greater burden upon him; but at the same time, I throw a burden upon him in respect of which the test of common sense and business habits can be applied, rather than impose on him a rigid rule which is not based on any principle either of business or common sense.

"So we come to the responsibility which the learned judge finds, and I think rightly, falls upon Mr. Lepine. Now what is that? He finds that, in respect of these securities, Mr. Lepine did what he ought not to have done, by accepting from Ellis & Co. a statement of the securities which they, at that time, declared that they held. The learned Judge says: 'In my judgment, not only did Mr. Lepine commit a breach of his duty in accepting, as he did, from time to time the certificate of Ellis & Co. that they held large blocks of the company's securities, but he also committed a breach of his duty in not either insisting upon those securities being put in proper custody, or in reporting the matter to the shareholders.' As I have said, the learned judge also finds that, in what he did Mr. Lepine acted honestly and in all good faith, 'holding the mistaken belief as to what his duty was.' I agree with the learned judge. It seems to me that Mr. Lepine has made a mistake, and a grave mistake. In justification of him it may be said that every artifice was brought into play in order to deceive him, and to maintain the apparent responsibility and trustworthiness of Ellis & Co. But that does not discharge him from having put aside what I described to counsel for the appellant as the rule of the road applied with the proviso as to business rules and common sense. Therefore Mr. Lepine would, prima facie, be liable in respect of that dereliction of duty."

The *City Equitable Fire Insurance Company* case placed upon the auditor with respect to verification of the inventory of securities in the hands of a custodian for the client no further duty than to obtain from the custodian a certificate that he has in his possession certain securities belonging to the auditor's client, provided the custodian ordinarily keeps securities for customers and is trustworthy. Banks will generally meet the requirements for such custodians. Stock-brokerage firms or other institutions may meet the two qualifications. If the auditor uses less care in proving the inventory of securities in the hands of another person than that involved in obtaining a certificate of possession from a person who is in the habit of dealing with and holding securities, and whom the auditor, on reasonable grounds, rightly believes to be, in the exercise of the best judgment, a trustworthy person to give such certificate, the auditor may be held liable to his client for loss resulting proximately from the auditor's negligence.

The responsibility placed upon auditors by the *City Equitable Fire Insurance Company* case is reasonable. The case has been followed in other decisions; and it should be followed in future decisions under like conditions.

Duty of the Public Accountant to Verify Cash

The earliest English case dealing directly with the auditor's duties in regard to ascertaining the validity of cash payments was decided by the court of appeal in 1899. This case, *Thomas v. The Corporation of Devonport*,[40] was an action in which Thomas sought compensation for audit services rendered in his character of elective auditor of the borough and also for audit services rendered to the sanitary authority of that town. The opinion reads:

> "But language was used [in the lower court] which, in my view, suggests too narrow a judgment of what the proper duties of the elective auditor are. I do not subscribe to the doctrine that his sole duty is to see whether there are vouchers, apparently formal and regular, justifying each of the items in respect of which the authority seeks to get credit upon the accounts put before the auditors for audit. I think that is an incomplete and imperfect view of the duties of the auditors. I think an auditor is not only entitled, but justified and bound to go further than that, and by fair and reasonable examination of the vouchers to see that there are not amongst the payments so made payments which are not authorized by the duty of the authority, or contrary to the duty of the authority, or in any other way illegal or improper. If he discovers that any such improper or illegal payments appear to have been made, his duty will certainly be to make it public by report to the authority itself, and the burgesses who create that authority."

Unquestionably it is the duty of an auditor in a review of cash disbursements to scrutinize the paid vouchers to ascertain whether the payments were properly authorized or not. In the absence of circumstances indicating wrongful conduct on the part of the authority to whom has been delegated the power to approve dis-

[40] (1900) 1 Q. B. 16.

bursements, the auditor would not be negligent in accepting as correct payments evidenced by properly signed vouchers. On the other hand, if circumstances should be such as to excite suspicion that the executive authorized to approve the payments of vouchers had abused his power, or if the circumstances would seem to indicate that the executive's approval of disbursements had in particular instances been fraudulently procured, the auditor would be required to report the matter to the proper authority—a failure to do so would constitute negligence on the part of the auditor.

While the facts of *Thomas* v. *The Corporation of Devonport* are peculiar, the principles of the decision are sound and have been applied in other decisions concerned with auditors' duties in the verification of disbursements.[41]

Fox and Son v. *Morrish, Grant, and Co.*[42] is the most recent English case on the auditor's duty to verify cash. The case was reviewed by the king's bench division in 1918. Justice A. T. Lawrence, delivering the opinion, said:

> "The liability of the defendants turned on what they were employed to do. It had been urged by the defense that Mr. Grant was not employed to audit the accounts, and was therefore not responsible for the documents which he prepared. It was true that he was not employed as auditor fully and generally, but he was employed under a specific engagement, as the result of an interview between the plaintiffs and the defendants under which he was to check the books, and it was understood that it was not to be a full audit. There was no requirement on the part of the plaintiffs that the defendants should verify everything. The question was whether Mr. Grant was wanting in due care and skill in the performance of his duty, in not having in any way checked the amounts appearing in the cashbook as 'cash in hand' and 'at the bank.' He made out his balance-sheets without taking any steps to ascertain whether those figures were correct. It turned out that Cranston, a dishonest clerk of the plaintiffs, ingeni-

---

[41] The English court of appeal in *Cuff* v. *London and County Land and Building Company, Limited,* (1912) 1 Ch. 440, 81 L. J. (Ch.) 426, 19 Mans. 166, 106 L. T. 285, (1912) W. N. 40, 28 T. L. R. 218, seemed to imply that, where auditors in auditing the books of a real-estate company failed to investigate the counterfoils of rent receipts issued to tenants, the auditors would be liable for negligence.

[42] 35 T. L. R. 126, 63 S. J. 193.

ously seeing that the bank passbook was not investigated, took advantage of that and played upon it.

"The eminent accountants who had been called as witnesses on both sides endeavored to give evidence as favorable as possible to the defendants. They had tried to mitigate the severity of the standard laid down by Mr. Matthews; but they did not achieve complete success. They had to admit that in the preparation of balance-sheets the cash at the bank and in hand must be stated, and in stating it one must either look at the passbook or get a certificate from the bankers; or if that was not done the client must be told that had not been done. That was the real gravamen of the case as far as the defendants were concerned. Mr. Grant did not tell the plaintiffs that he was not doing this. He frankly admitted that he never had, as he was not bound to do so under the retainer. As to that, he was wrong. He agreed that the object of having a balance-sheet drawn up was that Mr. Fox might know what his business position was; and it was impossible for him to know how matters stood without knowing what was the result in cash. All business was conducted for the purpose of producing cash. There was not a single word in the retainer, or anything which passed between the parties, which relieved Mr. Grant from seeing that the cash was accurately stated in the balance-sheet. If the passbook had been looked at it would have been found that what was stated to be at the bank was not at the bank; and if the bank passbook had been examined it would have been found that the figures in the books had been inserted by Cranston.

"There was a clear default of duty on the part of Mr. Grant; though it was natural and easy for him to slip into it at the time. But there was nothing in the arrangement made which discharged him from the duty of seeing that when he made a statement on his balance-sheet there was a foundation for it. It was a positive statement which was intended to be acted upon."

Fox and Son v. *Morrish, Grant, and Company* held that an auditor in undertaking a balance-sheet audit is duty bound to exercise reasonable care to verify the amount of cash on hand and in the bank. The auditor is derelict in duty if he states in his client's balance-sheet that "cash at the bank" is a certain amount without having ascertained the correctness of the figures from a bank certificate or from an investigation of the client's passbook. Likewise, the auditor is negligent if he states in his client's balance-sheet that "cash on hand" is a certain amount without having taken any steps to ascertain the correctness of the figures. Though the decision does not so state, the auditor or one of his employees should count the "cash on hand." The auditor is not justified in accepting the cashbook figures for cash, nor in accepting from his client's employee figures for the count of "cash on hand"—unless, of course, the auditing contract expressly provided that the auditor would not be required to verify the showing of cash, and the balance-sheet clearly showed that the figures for "cash on hand" had not been verified. Dicta in the case imply that the auditor might have been relieved of liability had he stated in the balance-sheet that cash had not been verified. The underlying principles of the decision are sound and should be followed in future decisions involving similar facts.

The leading American case on the liability of the public accountant for negligence in failing to detect embezzlement is the famous *City of East Grand Forks* v. *Steele* [43] case decided by the supreme court of Minnesota in 1913. This case was an action for breach of an auditing contract to conduct a skillful and diligent investigation of the plaintiff's records to disclose any defalcations which might have existed. The opinion reads in part as follows:

"The defendants, representing themselves to be expert accountants, and able to detect any irregularities in the transactions of the city officers, contracted with the city to investigate and audit the books, accounts and financial transactions of the city and of its officers for the year 1908, and especially the books, accounts, and financial transactions of the city clerk, for the sum of $150. The city clerk, in addition to his ordinary duties as clerk, was also employed to collect money due the city for electric lights, water and sewer assessments and licence fees and had given a surety bond to secure the faithful performance of these additional duties. The investigation of these collections, and of whether they had been properly accounted for, was included in the duties of the defendants. They made the investigation and audit, and in February, 1909, reported to the city that all books and accounts had been correctly kept and all funds properly

---

[43] 141 N. W. 181, 121 Minn. 296, 45 L. R. A. (N. S.) 205, Ann. Cas. 1914 C, 720. See *Smith* v. *London Assurance Corporation*, (1905) 96 N. Y. S. 820, 109 App. Div. 882.

accounted for. Plaintiff, believing they had made a correct report and had properly performed their work, paid them the full contract price therefor.

"In December, 1909, defendants again contracted with the city to make a similar investigation and audit, concerning both the years 1908 and 1909, for the sum of $500. They made such an investigation and audit and reported the result thereof. Plaintiff, still believing that they had made a correct report and had properly performed their work, paid them the full contract price for this second audit. In fact, the clerk had embezzled the sum of $1,984.26 during the year 1908, and the further sum of $5,339 during the year 1909 and prior to the investigation made by the defendants. The defendants failed to discover and disclose these defalcations, by reason of incompetence and negligence. They were discovered and disclosed by an investigation made by the state examiner immediately after defendants had completed their second audit. If in making their first audit defendants had discovered and reported the defalcation then existing, it could have been recovered from the surety company, and the clerk would have been removed from office, and his subsequent embezzlement could not have occurred. The surety company became insolvent before the investigation made by the state examiner, and the amount of the defalcations of the clerk has been wholly lost to the city.

"This is not an action in tort, but an action to recover damages for breach of contract. As said by Justice Mitchell in *Whittaker* v. *Collins,* 34 Minn. 299, 25 N. W. 632, 57 Am. Rep. 55 (an action brought to recover for the negligence of a physician): 'Where the action is not maintainable without pleading and proving the contract, where the gist of the action is the breach of the contract, either by malfeasance or nonfeasance, it is in substance, whatever may be the form of the pleading, an action on the contract. * * * The foundation of the action is the contract, and the gravamen of it its breach.'

"The rule governing liability for breach of contract is given in the syllabus to *Sargent* v. *Mason,* 101 Minn. 319, 112 N. W. 255, as follows: 'In an action for damages for breach of contract, the defaulting party is liable only for the direct consequences of the breach, such as usually occur from the infraction of like contracts, and within the contemplation of the parties when the contract was entered into as likely to result from its nonperformance.'

"To recover damages, not naturally and necessarily resulting from a breach of the contract, on the ground that such damages were within the contemplation of the parties when making the contract, it is said in *Liljengren F. & L. Co.* v. *Mead,* 42 Minn. 420, 44 N. W. 306, that 'there must be some special facts and circumstances, out of which they naturally proceed, known to the persons sought to be held liable, under such circumstances that it can be inferred from the whole transaction that such damage was in the contemplation of the parties, at the time of making the contract, as the result of its breach, and that the party sought to be charged consented to become liable for it.' This rule is well established.

"The damages claimed on account of the losses resulting from the defalcations of the clerk and the insolvency of his surety are too remote to be recovered, without showing the existence of special circumstances, known to defendants, from which they ought to have known that such losses were likely to result from a failure to disclose the true condition of affairs. Such losses are neither the natural nor the proximate consequences of the failure of defendants to make a proper audit. Neither are any facts shown from which it may be inferred that a loss from either of these causes was or ought to have been contemplated, when the contract was made, as likely to result from a breach of duty on the part of defendants.

"If, at the making of the contract and in the light of the knowledge then possessed by them, the parties had taken thought as to what consequences might reasonably be expected to result from its breach, there is nothing set forth in the complaint from which we can say that they ought to have foreseen or to have contemplated that the clerk was likely to commit a crime, or that his surety was likely to become bankrupt, and thereby entail financial loss upon the city. There may be circumstances under which the negligence of an expert accountant may make him liable for losses, as where he is employed to determine the amount that should be exacted from a surety for the default of his principal; but the facts alleged in the complaint do not bring this case within any such rule.

"Defendants represented themselves as expert accountants which implied that they were skilled in that class of work. In accepting employment as expert accountants, they undertook, and the plaintiff had the right to expect that in the performance of their duties they would exercise the average ability and skill of those engaged in that branch of skilled labor. They were employed to ascertain, among other things, whether any irregularities had occurred in the financial transactions of the city clerk, and, if so, the nature and extent of such irregularities. If, from want of proper skill, or from negligence, they did not disclose the true situation, they failed to perform the duty which they had assumed and failed to earn the compensation which plaintiff had agreed to pay them for the proper performance of such duty.

"The work of an expert accountant is of such technical character and requires such peculiar skill that the ordinary person can not be expected to know whether he performs his duties properly or otherwise, but must rely upon his report as to the thoroughness and accuracy of his work. The full contract price having been paid in the belief, induced by defendants' report, that such report disclosed fully and accurately the condition of the city's accounts, the city is entitled to recover back the amounts so paid, upon proving that, through the incompetence or the negligence of defendants, the report was in substance misleading and false."

In the *City of East Grand Forks* v. *Steele* case it is possible that the judge, when he held that the auditor was incompetent and negligent in failing to disclose the defalcations of the city clerk, had in mind specific acts or omissions committed by the auditor in the course of the audit of cash collections. But, in view of the context of the opinion, it is more probable that the judge found the existence of negligence from the fact that the auditor contracted to bring to his task that degree of professional skill and diligence necessary to uncover defalcations and then failed to disclose the irregularities of the city clerk. When a public accountant as such enters into an auditing contract he expressly or impliedly agrees to give to his client such skill and diligence as reasonably prudent, skillful, and diligent public accountants would give in the circumstances.[44] After having entered into such a contract, the auditor would be guilty of negligence if he should fail to exercise the care, skill and diligence which other professional accountants normally would have furnished in the circumstances.

The auditor contracted to investigate and audit the client's books for the purpose of discovering any irregularities that may have existed during the audit period. The auditor's negligence in failing to discover the defalcations amounted to nothing more than an

[44] *Smith* v. *London Assurance Corporation*, 96 N. Y. S. 820, 109 App. Div. 882, would seem to support the holding in *City of East Grand Forks* v. *Steele*.

invasion of the client's rights which had been created solely by the auditing contract. The auditor's negligence was not an invasion of any right of the client, created by implications of the law. Hence, the gist of the cause of action was a breach of the contract, and by well-established law the remedy had to be limited to an action in contract. Since the cause of action could be in contract only, the damages, in accordance with well-settled legal principles, had to be limited to such losses as the contracting parties, at the time of making the agreement and in the light of the knowledge then possessed by them, might have reasonably contemplated would follow naturally from a breach of the contract. The court held that the defendant in the light of knowledge possessed at the time of the making of the contract was not chargeable with ability to foresee losses resulting from embezzlement by the city clerk and bankruptcy of the surety company subsequent to the audit, and, therefore, was not liable for such losses. The court held that the only damages resulting directly from the auditor's breach of contract were the loss of the service fees which had been remitted to the auditor.

If the auditor's negligent conduct had been a breach of a duty implied by law and the action had been brought in tort, the damages would have been such losses as the auditor might reasonably have foreseen, at the time of the commission of negligence and in the light of circumstances existing at that moment, would result naturally and directly.[45] Though the case was decided on the basis of a breach of contract, the court stated that the loss resulting from the defalcation of the clerk and the insolvency of his surety subsequent to the audit was neither the natural nor the proximate consequence of the failure of the defendant to make a proper audit. Had the cause of action been brought in tort for negligence, it would seem that the proper inference to be drawn from the opinion would lead to the conclusion that the court would have held the defendant's negligence not to constitute a reasonably discernible or direct cause of the loss from defalcation of the clerk and bankruptcy of the clerk's surety, both of which occurred subsequent to the audit. Without knowledge of the clerk's dishonesty and without information relative to the financial condition of the

[45] Burdick's *Law of Torts*, pp. 39-41.

clerk's surety a reasonably prudent, skillful and diligent auditor would not have foreseen as resulting from his negligence losses from defalcation of the clerk and insolvency of his surety.

The *City of East Grand Forks* v. *Steele* decision is based upon well-settled legal principles. It has been followed in other cases; and it may well be accepted as the law with respect to the particular circumstances.

The New York Stock Exchange on the Public Accountant's Duty to Make a Proper Verification of Cash

On October 24, 1933, J. M. B. Hoxsey, executive assistant of the New York Stock Exchange committee on stock list, addressed to the governing committee of the exchange a letter which reads in part as follows:

> "Your committee is satisfied that the detailed scrutiny and verification of the cash transactions of large companies can most efficiently and economically be performed by permanent employees of the corporation, particularly today, when bookkeeping is to so large an extent done by mechanical means, and that it would involve unwarranted expense to transfer such work to independent auditors or to require them to duplicate the work of the internal organization. Your committee, however, feels that the auditors should assume a definite responsibility for satisfying themselves that the system of internal check provides adequate safeguards and should protect the company against any defalcation of major importance. Unless so satisfied, the auditors should make clear representations on this point —in the first place, to the management, and in default of action by the management, to the shareholders. Your committee also suggests that this limitation on the scope of the audit, though an entirely proper one, should be specifically mentioned in the common form of audit report."

In the absence of an express contract relieving the auditor of the detailed scrutiny and verification of cash transactions, it is extremely doubtful that courts would excuse an auditor from such verification work, even in large companies where bookkeeping is done chiefly by mechanical means and where the auditor has used reasonable care in satisfying himself that the system of internal check provides adequate safeguards against defalcations. The common law, in a detailed audit, places upon the auditor the duty to make the detailed scrutiny and verification of all cash receipts and disbursements necessary to uncover irregularities and defalcations, and to ascertain the correctness of the cash balance. The common law, in a balance-sheet audit, places upon the auditor the duty to prove the correctness of the figures for the cash balance by means of a count of the "cash on hand," and an investigation of the client's bank pass-book, or of the bank's certificate, showing the client's "cash at the bank." [46] The limitation of the scope of the cash audit as suggested by the New York Stock Exchange could be made safely only where the auditing contract expressly provides for such limitation and where the audit report clearly mentions the limited extent of the verification of cash.

DUTY OF THE PUBLIC ACCOUNTANT RELATIVE TO SECRET RESERVES

The American courts have not ruled on the public accountant's liability with respect to secret reserves. There are two outstanding English cases on the point. One case, *Newton v. Birmingham Small Arms Company, Limited*,[47] dealt with the auditor's duty to his client, the stockholders, in regard to hidden reserves. This case is reported below. The other case which involved the criminal liability of the auditor of the Royal Mail Steam Packet Company is given later under the subject "Criminal liability of the public accountant for fraud."

The stockholders of the Birmingham Small Arms Company in February, 1906, passed a resolution which authorized the directors to set aside out of profits a secret reserve fund which the directors could invest as they saw fit. The directors were bound to disclose the particulars of this inner reserve fund to the company auditors; but the company auditors were prohibited from revealing any information whatever about the secret fund to the stockholders or otherwise. Newton, the plaintiff stockholder in this case, sought a court order to prevent the enforcement of such resolution. After

---

[46] Note: See "Duty of the Public Accountant to Verify Cash," page 39, ante.
[47] (1906) 2 Ch. 378, 1906 W. N. 146.

reviewing the English companies acts and ruling that secret reserve funds could be maintained under such acts, the court held:

> "The special resolutions in the present case provide that the balance-sheet shall not disclose the internal reserve fund. It must, therefore, omit on the assets side of the balance-sheet the assets which make up the amount standing to the credit of that fund and the contra item—namely, the credit balance of the fund—on the liability side. The result will be to show the financial position of the company to be not so good as in fact it is. If the balance-sheet be so worded as to show that there is an undisclosed asset, whose existence makes the financial position better than that shown, such a balance-sheet will not, in my judgment, be necessarily inconsistent with the act of parliament. Assets are often, by reason of prudence, estimated, and stated to be estimated, at less than their probable real value. The purpose of the balance-sheet is primarily to show that the financial position of the company is at least as good as there stated, not to show that it is not or may not be better. The provision as to not disclosing the internal reserve fund in the balance-sheet is not, I think, necessarily fatal to these special resolutions. The act, however, provides that the auditors shall report to the shareholders on the accounts examined by them. These auditors will examine, amongst others, the accounts of the internal reserve fund. A principal question in this case, I think, is whether it is a compliance with these words of the act that the auditors shall report that they have examined the accounts as to the internal reserve fund, that they are satisfied with them, and that the funds have been employed in the manner authorized by the company's regulations, or whether there will be default in complying with the act if they do not go on to say how the fund has been employed. In my judgment such a report would be a sufficient report within the act if the auditor is bona fide satisfied that in making this report, and nothing further, he is truly reporting as to 'the true and correct view of the state of the company's affairs.' But the special resolutions do not stop there. They provide that it shall be the duty of the auditor not to disclose any information with regard to this fund to the shareholders or otherwise. It is, I think, inconsistent with the act of parliament that the auditor shall be bound, even when he thinks that the true state of the company's affairs is affected by facts relating to the internal reserve fund, to withhold all information with regard to the same from the shareholders. If, for instance, the directors had in-

vested the internal reserve fund upon investments which might involve the company under certain circumstances in enormous loss, the act, I think, requires that the auditor shall be at liberty and be bound to report that fact. In reporting upon the accounts submitted to them the auditors do not, of course, report as to the details of accounts to which they find no cause to take exception. Their duty is to call attention to that which is wrong, not to condescend upon all the details of that which is right. It is, I think, competent to the statutory majority of the shareholders to say that as to particular items of their business it is to the interest of the corporation that there shall be secrecy, and that the auditors, who must for the purposes of their audit know all such details, shall not, unless their duty under the statute requires it, disclose such details to the members. There is no suggestion in this case that these clauses are intended to be used for any other than a legitimate purpose. Those who are engaged in commerce are familiar with the fact that undue publicity as regards the details of their trade, or as to their financial arrangements, may often be very injurious to traders, having regard to the rivalry of competitors in trade, to complications sometimes arising from strained relations between capital and labor, and the like. There are legitimate reasons for ensuring secrecy to a proper extent. It is not, I think, necessary, nor, having regard to the great utility of these acts, is it desirable, to expose persons who trade under these acts to the necessities of a publicity from which their competitors are free, unless such publicity is required to ensure commercial integrity. I am not disposed to look too closely for reasons why I should find clauses such as these to be inconsistent with the act if I see that the true purpose of the act is satisfied. I think, however, these special resolutions go too far. Any regulations which preclude the auditors from availing themselves of all the information to which under the act they are to make as to the true and correct state of the company's affairs, are I think, inconsistent with the act."

The *Newton* v. *Birmingham Small Arms Company* case held that under the company act of 1900 the company auditor was not required to show in the balance-sheet items which the directors desired to keep secret from the stockholders, provided the auditor stated in his certificate that he had examined the accounts as to the internal reserve fund, and that he was satisfied with them. But it was held that if the auditor, through his investigation of internal reserve accounts, found that the directors had abused the privilege of managing the secret fund, the auditor was obligated to report that which was wrong. The court relieved the auditor of the duty to disclose secret reserves on the theory that such secrecy is often essential to the proper management of the company. The allowance of secret reserves was based on the proposition that a disclosure of inner reserves might reveal to competitors of the business information which would be injurious to the client, or that such a disclosure might inspire labor to strike for higher wages. While no case has ruled on secret reserves under the companies acts passed subsequent to the act of 1900, since all the subsequent acts, including the consolidating companies act of 1929, have required the company auditor to state whether or not the balance-sheet shows the true and correct financial position of the company and have not expressly prohibited secret reserves, it would appear that the decision of the *Newton* v. *Birmingham Small Arms Company* case could have been rendered under any of these subsequent acts as well as under the act of 1900.

It would seem that the court was in error in holding that an auditor may fail to disclose a secret reserve in the balance-sheet and yet comply with the company act of 1900 which required that the auditor should state whether the balance-sheet exhibited a correct view of the condition of the company's financial affairs. Such a compliance with the act can not logically be explained by the proposition that "the purpose of the balance-sheet is primarily to show that the financial position of the company is at least as good as there stated, not to show that it is not or may not be better." The *London and General Bank* case, supra, and several other decisions have held that a balance-sheet showing assets at a higher value than their real worth does not present truly the financial condition of the business. Showing less than the real value of the property is as far from the truth as showing more than the real value of the property.

There is some justification for permitting secret reserves on the ground that it may become necessary for the corporate management to follow a conservative program with respect to the payment of dividends, and that the withholding of the payment of dividends becomes well nigh impossible where the stockholders know the full worth of the business. Yet, under American common law the managing director of a corporation may work great loss to stockholders through the maintenance of secret reserves. According to the majority view of American courts a director may purchase from a stockholder shares of stock in the company without revealing to the shareholder secret reserves.[48] There would be much less risk of loss to stockholders through the maintenance of secret reserves under the minority view of the American courts, which holds that a corporate director is a quasi-trustee of the stockholders and under obligation to disclose inner reserves to a stockholder prior to purchasing shares of the corporation from such stockholder.[49] This minority view has the support of eminent author-

[48] "Directors' Liability to Individual Shareholders and to the Corporation," 45 Harvard Law Review 1389 (1931); Board v. Reynolds, 44 Ind. 509 (1873); Deaderick v. Wilson, 8 Baxter 107 (Tenn., 1874).

[49] Note: The minority view was clearly set forth by the supreme court of Georgia in 1903 in the following language: "All the authorities agree that he (director) is trustee for the company, and in his capacity as such he serves the interests of the entire body of stockholders, as well as those of the individual shareholder, who usually can not sue in his own name for wrongs done the company by the officer. . . . No process of reasoning and no amount of argument can destroy the fact that the director is, in a most important and legitimate sense, trustee for the stockholder. . . . Not a strict trustee, since he does not hold title to the shares, not even a strict trustee who is practically prohibited from dealing with his cestui que trust, but a quasi-trustee as to the shareholder's interest in the shares. If the market or contract price of the stock should be different from the book value, he would be under no legal obligation to call special attention to that fact, for the stockholder is entitled to examine the books, and this source of information, at least theoretically, is equally accessible to both. It might be that the director was in possession of information which his duty to the company required him to keep secret; and, if so, he must not disclose the fact even to the shareholder, for his obligation to the company overrides that to an individual holder of stock. But if the fact so known to the director can not be published, it does not follow that he may use it to his own advantage and to the disadvantage of one whom he also represents. The very fact that he can not disclose prevents him from dealing with one who does not know and to whom material information can not be made known. If, however, the fact within the knowledge of the director is of a character calculated to affect the selling price, and can, without detriment to the interest of the company, be imparted to the shareholder, the director, before he buys, is bound to make a full disclosure. In a certain sense the information is a quasi-asset of the company, and the shareholder is as much entitled to the advantage of that sort of an asset as to any other regularly entered on the list of the company's holding. If the officer should purposely conceal from a stockholder information as to the existence of valuable property belonging to the company and take advantage of this concealment, the sale would necessarily be set aside. The same result would logically follow where the fact giving value to the stock was of a character which

ity;[50] and it is thought by no less an authority on corporation law than Dean I. P. Hildebrand of the University of Texas law school that the doctrine making a director a quasi-trustee of stockholders will be accepted by the majority of American courts within a decade.

But the wisdom of allowing inner reserves or the duty to reveal such reserves to stockholders of the American corporation is no business of the public accountant—under common law. Certainly, if a director is not, by the weight of authority, a quasi-trustee of stockholders under obligations to disclose to them secret reserves prior to the purchase of their shares, the auditor who contracts independently with the directors would have no fiduciary relationship with the stockholders and would not be obligated to disclose secret reserves to them by means of the balance-sheet prepared from his audit. Even if courts should follow the minority view, making a director a quasi-trustee under obligations to disclose secret reserves to a stockholder prior to the purchase of his shares, the auditor would owe no common-law duty to a stockholder to reveal secret reserves in the balance-sheet prepared from an audit of the company. If the minority view should be followed, in the absence of circumstances indicating that a director intended to use the auditor's report to induce a stockholder to sell shares of stock to the director for himself or for the corporation, the auditor would not be charged with negligence in failing to report secret reserves. It has been held—*City of East Grand Forks* v. *Steele,* supra—that an auditor is not chargeable with ability to foresee dishonest conduct on the part of a trusted employee of a business.

could not formally be entered on the record. Where the director obtains the information giving added value to the stock by virtue of his official position, he holds the information in trust for the benefit of those who placed him where this knowledge was obtained, in the well-founded expectation that the same should be used first for the company and ultimately for those who were the real owners of the company. The director can not deal on this information to the prejudice of the artificial being which is called the corporation, nor, on any sound principle, can be permitted to act differently towards those who are not artificially but actually interested." (*Oliver* v. *Oliver,* 118 Ga. 362, 45 S. E. 232.) See also: *Strong* v. *Repide,* 213 U. S. 419 (1909); *Stewart* v. *Harris,* 69 Kan. 498, 77 P. 277, 66 L. R. A. 261 (1904).

[50] A. A. Berle, "For Whom Corporate Managers Are Trustees," 45 *Harvard Law Review* 1365 (1932).

Inference of Negligence on the Part of the Public Accountant

The burden of showing no negligence is placed upon the auditor where the client has proved damages to have resulted from an incorrectly stated balance-sheet, according to the case, *In re Republic of Bolivia Exploration Syndicate, Limited*,[51] decided by Justice Astbury of the English chancery division in 1913. The opinion in part reads:

> "Now, there are some legal matters which an auditor must obviously know, as there are others which it is equally obvious he could not be held responsible for not knowing, and it may not always be easy to say in which category any particular case falls. I think that auditors of a limited company are bound to know or make themselves acquainted with their duties under the articles of the company whose accounts they are appointed to audit and under the companies acts for the time being in force; and that when it is shown that audited balance-sheets do not show the true financial condition of the company and that damage has resulted, the onus is on the auditors to show that this is not the result of any breach of duty on their part. The authorities, however, are not very clear as to what, if any, is the liability of auditors of a limited company for including or passing in accounts audited by them sums paid by the company or its directors prior to the audit, and which, by reason of the want of authority in the regulations of the company or non-compliance with some statutory provision of the companies acts, ought not in the particular circumstances to have been paid, nor, if any liability would otherwise exist, what is sufficient by way of warning or identification in the audited accounts for the necessary information to be expressly conveyed by the auditors to the company in order to free them from further responsibility."

In this case, where the plaintiff liquidator had merely proved an incorrect balance-sheet prepared by the defendant auditor, and financial loss resulting therefrom, the court inferred from such circumstances that negligence not only existed but also resulted directly in the loss which was the basis of complaint. Negligence is regularly inferred from proof of injury in a certain class of cases

---

[51] (1914) 1 Ch. D. 139, (1913) W. N. 329, 30 T. L. R. 78, 58 S. J. 321, 83 L. J. (Ch.) 235, 21 Mans. 67, 109 L. T. 741, 110 L. T. 141.

LIABILITY FOR NEGLIGENCE, FRAUD AND LIBEL 55

where the defendant has been required by contract or statute to do something safely. This rule of presumption of negligence, res ipsa loquitur, on the part of the defendant is ordinarily limited to cases of absolute duty, or an obligation practically amounting to that of an insurer. Wherever the defendant is required to exercise the highest care and skill with regard to the safety of some one else, res ipsa loquitur (the thing speaks for itself) applies—negligence and the injury resulting directly therefrom are presumed.[52] Thus, when a common carrier's passenger is injured the common carrier is presumed to have caused the injury through negligent conduct. The common carrier may rebut the inference of negligence by proof that the injury arose from an accident which the utmost skill, foresight and diligence could not have prevented. As far as proof of the existence of negligence and the loss resulting therefrom is concerned, the *Republic of Bolivia Exploration Syndicate, Limited,* case puts the company auditor in the class of persons required by statute or contract to do a thing safely. While the English companies acts place upon the company auditor a duty to render a balance-sheet which gives the true financial position of the company, according to the best of his information and the explanations given him and as shown by the books, it would seem that the court went too far in the present case in presuming negligence merely from the failure to comply with the statute. In the *London and General Bank* case, supra, after specific acts of negligence in the preparation of the balance-sheet had been proven by direct evidence, the court presumed that the defendant auditor's negligence was the proximate cause of the loss which resulted from the declaration of dividends out of capital subsequent to the circulation of copies of the balance sheet among the stockholders who declared the dividends. In the English case, *Henry Squire, Cash Chemist, Limited,* v. *Ball, Baker & Co.,* 106 L. T. 197, 28 T. L. R. 81, it was held that, where a money-lender hired an auditor to investigate a borrower's books in order that the money-lender might ascertain the wisdom of advancing a loan to the borrower prior to the making of the loan which resulted in a loss to the money-lender, the money-lender would have to prove specific

[52] Burdick's *Law of Torts*, pp. 514-516.

negligence on the part of the auditor and that such negligence was the proximate cause of the money-lender's loss before he could recover.

In rare instances negligence has been presumed where the defendant's duty was not absolute but arose in the ordinary course of business. In cases of this sort it is essential that it shall appear that all the elements of the occurrence were within the exclusive control of the defendant, and that the result was so far out of the usual course that there is no fair inference that it could have been produced by any other cause than negligence of the defendant. For example, negligence was presumed where sparks escaped from a fire pot (which was used in repairing a roof) and set fire to the building.[53] It would seem that an auditor is rarely, if ever, in such exclusive control of the audit that he could be presumed to have been negligent where his reports have been proven incorrect. The client's employees generally have access to the records during the audit, and may change, substitute or otherwise manipulate the records. The employees may divert cash deposits or securities so as to render an incorrect showing of the client's financial affairs. The auditor does not assume the responsibility of verifying every entry in the entire set of records, even in a detailed audit. It may easily happen that the balance-sheet prepared from an audit is incorrect through no lack of reasonable care and skill of the auditor. Inferring negligence on the part of the auditor merely from an incorrect report is placing an onerous and unjustifiable burden upon the auditor and should not be countenanced by the courts.

Where negligence in the preparation of a balance-sheet has been proven by direct evidence, in some circumstances the inference that the loss resulted proximately from such defective balance-sheet may well be made. For example, where it has been proved that an auditor was negligent in preparing a balance-sheet which understated the worth of his client's business, and the client immediately after such audit sold his business at a loss, a court would be justified in inferring that the auditor's negligence was the proximate cause of his client's loss.

[53] Cooley on *Torts*, third edition, volume II, pp. 1415-1428.

Liability for Negligence, Fraud and Libel

Contributory Negligence on the Part of the Client

The supreme court of New York in 1925 rendered a strong decision, *Craig v. Anyon*,[54] which defines the responsibility of the public accountant for negligence where the client is guilty of contributory negligence. In this case the defendant auditors had for many years audited the books of the plaintiff brokerage firm. As a part of their audit contract with the plaintiffs, the defendants had originally agreed to calculate the indebtedness of customers on open account, and to "supervise, superintend and send out" statements of account to the customers of the plaintiffs. The defendants never performed this part of their audit contract; and in failing to do so, the court found, they were guilty of negligence. The plaintiffs knew from year to year that the defendants had not lived up to their agreement with respect to their audit of customers' accounts, and did nothing about it. In fact, the plaintiffs refused to allow statements of account to be sent to customers.

Furthermore, the plaintiffs entrusted the entire management and control of the commodities department of their brokerage business to an employee named Moore. Moore had complete charge of the records of the department; he was margin clerk, whose duty it was to decide what margin should be maintained, and he had full supervision of buying and selling for customers. The plaintiffs took no trouble at all to investigate the work of Moore; they simply relied upon him with an unquestioning faith to carry on the work of the commodities department. The defendant auditors also trusted Moore. In these circumstances Moore was able to manipulate the account of a customer, Zabriskie, so as to effect the loss. Zabriskie's original margin with the firm was only $200; but in the course of a few years under the direction of Moore the plaintiffs paid out to Zabriskie $123,689.04 without once investigating the credit position of Zabriskie or making an examination of his account to see whether anything was due him. These payments to Zabriskie were improper; and they constituted the loss which the plaintiffs contended was a direct result of the negligence of the defendant auditors. The defendants argued that the loss resulted

[54] 208 N. Y. S. 259, 212 App. Div. 55. (Affirmed in the court of appeals of New York, 1926, 152 N. E. 431, 242 N. Y. 569.)

from the contributory negligence of the plaintiffs. A portion of the opinion reads:

> "There is no doubt in this case that plaintiffs could have prevented the loss by the exercise of reasonable care, and that they should not have relied exclusively on the accountants.
>
> "We think the damages can not be said to flow naturally and directly from defendants' negligence or breach of contract. Plaintiffs should not be allowed to recover for losses which they could have avoided by the exercise of reasonable care.
>
> "The plaintiffs, in effect, contend that defendants are chargeable with negligence because of failure to detect Moore's wrongdoing, wholly overlooking the fact that although they were closely affiliated with Moore, who was constantly under their supervision, they were negligent in failing properly to supervise his acts or to learn the true condition of their own business and to detect his wrongdoing."

In the *Craig* v. *Anyon* case the court held that the defendant auditors were excused from liability for their negligent audit because of the contributory negligence on the part of the client brokerage firm. The court held that the plaintiffs' own contributory negligence was a substantial cause of the loss resulting from fraudulent payments to a customer of their brokerage firm. The conduct of the plaintiffs amounting to negligence consisted of several specific acts of omission and commission. It was deemed by the court that the plaintiffs failed to use reasonable care when they placed the defalcator in complete charge of all the transactions and accounting for the commodities department of their brokerage firm and later exercised no control or supervision over him whatsoever. It was also thought by the court that there was a lack of due precaution on the part of the plaintiffs in that they refused to allow the defendant auditors to superintend and send out certain statements of account to customers in accordance with an auditing contract formed in prior years. Moreover, the plaintiffs were aware of the fact that the defendants were not even calculating the liability of the customers on open contract, at the time of each audit, and did nothing about it. This negligence of the plaintiffs, the court held, was the direct cause of their loss. Had the plaintiffs exercised due care, according to the opinion, the loss would not have occurred. In other words, the defendants' negligent audit was not the direct cause of the plaintiffs' loss. The chain of causation between the defendants' negligent audit and the plaintiffs' loss was broken by a criminal act—made possible by the plaintiffs' negligence—of the defalcator, so that there was not present that sequential relation between the negligent audit and the plaintiffs' loss which is required to make an act the direct cause of an injury. The defendants were not expected to foresee that a trusted employee of their clients would take advantage of their negligent audit and effect their clients' loss.

The tests for the existence of contributory negligence are the same as those for the existence of negligence upon which it is sought to establish a claim for damages. By the great weight of authority in England and America " 'the onus of proving affirmatively that there was contributory negligence, on the part of the person injured, rests, in the first instance, upon the defendant, and in the absence of evidence tending to that conclusion, the plaintiff is not bound to prove the negative in order to entitle' him to recover." [55] Wherever contributory negligence is shown to have been a substantial cause of the plaintiffs' loss, it affords a complete bar to the plaintiff's recovery at common law. According to the United States supreme court, "the general accepted and most reasonable rule of law applicable to actions in which the defense is contributory negligence may be thus stated: Although the defendant's negligence may have been the primary cause of the injury complained of, yet an action for such injury can not be maintained if the proximate and immediate cause of the injury can be traced to the want of ordinary care and caution in the person injured; subject to this qualification, which has grown up in recent years, that the contributory negligence of the party injured will not defeat the action, if it be shown that defendant might, by the exercise of reasonable care and prudence, have avoided the consequences of the injured party's negligence." [56] By this authority it is possible for the plaintiff to defeat the defense of contributory

---

[55] Burdick's *Law of Torts*, pp. 520-521.
[56] *Grand Trunk Railway Co.* v. *Ives*, 144 U. S. 408, 429, 12 Sup. Ct. 679, 36 L. Ed. 485 (1892).

negligence by showing that no injury would have resulted from his own negligence if the defendant had acted with reasonable care and prudence. Such a showing would, of course, establish the fact that the plaintiff's negligence was not the proximate cause of his injury.[57]

In the light of the well-settled law on contributory negligence it must be concluded that the *Craig* v. *Anyon* case is correctly decided. The finding of the existence of negligence on the part of the plaintiffs, and the determination that the plaintiffs' loss would not have occurred except for their own negligence, i.e., that plaintiffs' and not defendants' negligence was the proximate cause of the plaintiffs' loss, are sound conclusions of the court. The case should be followed in future decisions in like circumstances.

LIABILITY OF THE PUBLIC ACCOUNTANT TO HIS CLIENT FOR NEGLIGENT DISCLOSURE OF CONFIDENTIAL COMMUNICATIONS

Weld-Blundell v. *Stephens*,[58] decided by the house of lords in 1920, appears to be the only case in England and America involving a public accountant's liability for negligent disclosure of a confidential communication from his client. The plaintiff, Weld-Blundell, had lent money to the Float Electric Company, Limited, and, on being asked for a further advance, employed the defendant, Stephens, a chartered accountant, to look into the affairs of the company. In a letter of instructions to Stephens, Weld-Blundell reflected upon Lowe, the previous manager of the company, and Comins, the auditor of the company. Stephens, upon receipt of the letter, handed it to his partner, Swift, with instruction to go to the Float Company's offices and make certain inquiries. Swift accidentally dropped and left the letter in the manager's room of the Float Company's offices. The manager, Hurst, read the letter and communicated its contents to Lowe and Comins, who immediately brought actions of libel against Weld-Blundell, and recovered damages against him. Weld-Blundell then sued Stephens for breach of an implied duty to keep secret the letter of instructions. Three of

---

[57] Burdick's *Law of Torts*, pp. 519-527.
[58] 9 B. R. C. 368, (1919) 1 K. B. 520, 88 L. J. K. N. S. 689, 120 L. T. N. S. 494, (1919) W. N. 46, 35 T. L. R. 245, 63 Sol. Jo. 301.

LIABILITY FOR NEGLIGENCE, FRAUD AND LIBEL 61

the five judges held that the chartered accountant's negligence was not the proximate cause of Weld-Blundell's loss from libelous conduct; the other two judges gave dissenting opinions. The majority view of the house of lords, as represented by a portion of Lord Sumner's opinion, follows:

"The crux of the present question was the intervention of Hurst between the accountant and Lowe and Comins. Further, no want of care had to be proven here against the defendant, for he accepted the decision that he broke his contract by his partner's omission to be careful, though not by any deliberate, intentional or wanton breach. That at once made it possible to lay aside large classes of authorities. What a defendant ought to have anticipated as a reasonable man was material, when the question was whether or not he was guilty of negligence, that is, of want of due care according to the circumstances. That, however, went to culpability not to compensation (*Blyth* v. *Birmingham Waterworks*, 11 Ex., 781; *Smith* v. *L. and S. W. Rly.*, L. R., 6 C. P., 14, per Justice Blackburn). Again, what ordinarily happened or might reasonably be expected to happen was material, where a series of physical phenomena had to be investigated and the remoteness of the damage or the reverse was to be decided accordingly. * * *

"In general (apart from special contracts and relations and the maxim: respondeat superior), even though A was in fault he was not responsible for injury to C, which B, a stranger to him, deliberately chose to do. Though A might have given the occasion for B's mischievous activity, B then became a new and independent cause (e.g., *Cobb* v. *G. W. R.*, (1893) 1 Q. B. 459, 63 L. J. Q. B. 629; *Attorney-general* v. *Conduit Colliery*, (1895) 1 Q. B. 301, 64 L. J. Q. B. 207). It was hard to steer clear of metaphors. Perhaps one might be forgiven for saying that B snapped the chain of causation; he was no mere conduit-pipe through which consequences flowed from A to C, no mere moving part in a transmission gear set in motion by A; in a word, that he insulated A from C. It was quite plain that when Swift dropped the letter and found out his loss, the matter would have ended there but for the idle hands of Hurst. He gave the letter a fresh start and on his original impulse it came to be sued on. Precisely the same result would have happened if the person who dropped the letter in Hurst's office had previously got it by picking Swift's pocket. Again, the matter could not be worse for Stephens than if he had shown Hurst the letter himself, that is, had published to him Weld-Blundell's original libel. What then? Would the defendant have been liable if Hurst had re-published it (as indeed he did) without authority from him and not in accordance with any intention or desire on his part actual or imputable? *Ward* v. *Weeks* (supra) said no. The case was ninety years old and he (Lord Sumner) saw no reason to doubt it. The repetition, said Chief Justice Tindal, was 'the voluntary act of a free agent, over whom the defendant had no control, and for whose acts he is not answerable, and this repetition was the immediate cause of the damage.' Yet, taking men as one found them, few things were more certain than the repetition of a calumny confidentially communicated, even on an honorable understanding of secrecy.

"* * * He (Lord Sumner) could not see that there was any evidence in law in either case, because he could not see that the mere probability that actions might be brought for the libels could turn Hurst's act into defendant's act. It might be material if the want of care were in dispute, but it was not. Remoteness of damage was a question of cause and effect—a different question. That a jury could finally make A liable for B's acts merely because they thought it was antecedently probable that B would act as he did, apart from A's authority or intention, seemed to him to be contrary to principle and supported authority.

"Lord Wrenbury (of majority holding) said that the relations between Weld-Blundell and Stephens were such that the latter no doubt owed a duty to the former and in that duty he was negligent. Weld-Blundell's liability to pay money to Lowe and Comins, however, arose, not from that negligence but from his own wrongful act in indulging in malicious libel. It bore no pecuniary relation to Stephens' wrongful act. Stephens' act was not the cause (whether with or without the word 'effective') of his having to pay but was an act without which possibly he would never have been called upon to pay. It was not causa causans, but at most causa sine qua non.

"In discharging his liability to pay damages for malicious libel Weld-Blundell suffered no damage at all. A man was not damnified by being compelled to satisfy his legal obligation. * * *

"Assuming that it could be said that Stephens made publication to Lowe of the libel on Comins and made publication to Comins of the libel to Lowe, nothing resulted from this for: (1) Weld-Blundell was not liable in respect of that publication which he had not authorized, and (2) he was made liable not for that publication but for the publication made by Weld-Blundell to Stephens, and the last-mentioned publication had been made and its consequence incurred before the events happened that Swift dropped the letter and Hurst picked it up and wrongfully read it, and as a result Lowe and Comins were informed. Nothing that Stephens did created the liability under which Weld-Blundell lay. He (Lord Wrenbury) was quite unable to follow the proposition that the damages given in the libel actions were in any way damages resulting from anything which Stephens did in breach of duty."

In the *Weld-Blundell* v. *Stephens* case it was held that where a chartered accountant received from his client a confidential letter which contained matter reflecting upon two other persons, and where he negligently permitted the letter to be published, through the wrongful act of a third person, to the two injured persons, the chartered accountant was not liable to the client because the client's loss resulted wholly from his own wrongful act in writing and sending the libelous letter to the chartered accountant. The client could not be excused from his libelous conduct on the basis of a privileged communication between him and the accountant because the client was guilty of malice in writing and sending the letter. The accountant's negligence could not have been the direct cause of the publication of the libelous letter after it reached the accountant, because the chain of causation extending from the accountant's negligent act was broken by the wrongful conduct of the third person. Moreover, it was held that the accountant would not have been liable to his client had the accountant authorized the wrongful publication by the third person, or had himself given the letter to one of the two injured persons in publication of the wrongful statement of the other, because the client's loss was due to his own wrongful act.

In harmony with the usual English and the minority view in America, the present case makes the continuous and unbroken effect of defendant's negligent conduct, regardless of ability to foresee injury, the test of liability for negligence. According to this type of holding, ability to foresee injury is merely a test to determine the existence of negligence and is not a test to determine whether the negligent act was the direct cause of the alleged injury.[59] It would appear that the court might have arrived at the conclusion that the accountant's negligence was not the direct cause of the publication by Hurst, on the ground that the accountant could not have reasonably foreseen the wrongful conduct of Hurst. At any rate, the conclusions of the case are sound; the accountant was not liable, first, because his negligent act was not the direct cause of the wrongful publication by Hurst, and, second, because the client's loss was due to his wrongful act and not to the instrumentalities resulting in the exposure of his wrongful act.

The *Weld-Blundell* v. *Stephens* case does not involve the liability which an auditor may incur from negligently disclosing his client's trade secrets learned during the course of an audit where the client is guilty of no wrongful conduct. The negligent disclosure of such information would doubtless be interpreted by courts as a breach of duty implied from the audit contract and would subject the auditor to liability to his client if the client's loss were the proximate result of the accountant's act (see page 197, post).

IV

LIABILITY OF THE PUBLIC ACCOUNTANT TO HIS CLIENT FOR LIBEL

"Libel is a false and unprivileged publication, which exposes any person to hatred, contempt, ridicule, or obloquy, or which causes him to be shunned or avoided, or which has a tendency to injure him in his business."[60] The publication may be effected by means of writing, printing, pictures, images or anything that is the object of the sense of sight, communicated to a third person. At common law libel is generally a criminal offense as well as a private wrong against the injured party. Where the defendant has delivered an untrue and injurious writing to the plaintiff, or to a third person at the request of the plaintiff, the defendant can not be held liable for the defamatory writing. It is necessary to prove that the defama-

---

[59] Note: See leading English case, *In re Polemis and Furness, Withy & Company*, 3 K. B. 560, 90 L. J. K. B. 1353 (C. A., 1921).

[60] *Taylor* v. *Hearst*, 40 P. 392, 107 Cal. 262, 269 (1895).

LIABILITY FOR NEGLIGENCE, FRAUD AND LIBEL

tory writing was read by a third person and that publication of the plaintiff was the intended or discernible result of the defendant's acts before an action can be maintained for libel. The defendant may not have intended or foreseen injury to the plaintiff, but he must have either intended or foreseen publication of the defamatory writing to a third person before an action can be maintained for libel. The libelant may or may not have composed the defamatory writing. It is enough that the defendant published defamatory writing of the plaintiff to a third person in circumstances from which it can be reasonably inferred that the defendant intended or foresaw publication. Libel generally involves malice on the part of the wrongdoer; sometimes it involves only negligence; then, again it may involve only accident. The defendant may have published injurious falsehoods with the intent to damage the plaintiff; a newspaper may have negligently published another newspaper's copy which was untrue and injurious to the plaintiff; or, again, by mere accident the newspaper may have published libelous matter, as where an article described a particular person as a "colored" rather than as a "cultured" gentleman.[61]

The occasions inviting libelous conduct on the part of public accountants are extremely rare. Granted that a public accountant does make an audit from which he prepares a false report which is injurious to his client's business, as where the report falsely shows a condition of bankruptcy, his communication of that report to his client would not amount to libel. Furthermore, if the accountant should, at the direction of his client, present to a third person a false business report injurious to the client, no action for libel could be maintained. If the public accountant should prepare a false report injurious to his client's business, and the report, through no fault of the accountant, should be taken from his (accountant's) possession and read by a third person, the accountant would not be held accountable for libel, since the communication of his report would have been effected in circumstances from which it could not be reasonably inferred that he intended or foresaw

---

[61] Burdick's *Law of Torts*, pp. 349-370; Harper on *Torts*, pp. 497-552; Cooley on *Torts*, volume I, pp. 366-463.

publication of the injurious report.[62] Of course, if an auditor should prepare a false report injurious to his client's business, and cause a third person to read the report, the auditor would be held accountable in an action for libel.

V

LIABILITY OF THE PUBLIC ACCOUNTANT TO THIRD PARTIES FOR NEGLIGENCE AND FRAUD

THE PUBLIC ACCOUNTANT NOT LIABLE TO THIRD PARTIES FOR MERE NEGLIGENCE

In 1919 the supreme court of Pennsylvania rendered the decision in *Landell* v. *Lybrand*[63] as follows:

"Appellees, defendants below, are certified public accountants, and, as such, audited the books and accounts of the Employer's Indemnity Company for the year 1911. The appellant, plaintiff below, averred in his statement of claim that he had been induced to buy eleven shares of the capital stock of that company, at the price of $200 per share, on the strength of the report made by the appellees as to its assets and liabilities at the close of the year 1911, the report having been shown to him by someone who suggested that he purchase the stock. A further averment was that the report was false and untrue, that the stock purchased by him on the strength of it is valueless; and for the loss he sustained he averred the defendants were liable. To enforce this liability an action in trespass was brought against them. In their affidavit of defense they averred that the statement of claim disclosed no cause of action and asked that this be disposed of by the court below as a matter of law, under the provisions of section 20 of the practice act of May 14, 1915, P. L. 483. It was so disposed of by the court below in entering judgment for the defendants.

"There were no contractual relations between the plaintiff and defendants, and, if there is any liability from them to him, it must arise out of some breach of duty, for there is no averment that they made the report with intent to deceive him. The averment in the

---

[62] Burdick's *Law of Torts*, p. 352 (note 27).
[63] 107 A. 783, 264 Pa. 406, 8 A. L. R. 461.

statement of claim is that the defendants were careless and negligent in making their report; but the plaintiff was a stranger to them and to it, and, as no duty rested upon them to him, they can not be guilty of any negligence of which he can complain: *Schiffer* v. *Sauer Company et al.*, 238 Pa. 550. This was the correct view of the court below, and the judgment is accordingly affirmed."

The decision of the *Landell* v. *Lybrand* case that an auditor is not liable to an investor in the shares of stock of the client corporation for loss resulting from the accountant's negligent audit is in agreement with well-settled principles of common law. No case has ever extended the ambit of negligence to include liability to third parties in general. However, where two parties make a contract expressly for the benefit of a third person, that is, a donee or creditor beneficiary, the law operates to create a privity between the promisor and the third party.[64] In such circumstances the promisor would be liable to the third party for the negligent breach of the contract. The principle is well illustrated by the case of an abstractor: "Sound reasoning and the weight of modern authority sustain the rule of liability for negligence resulting in injury to the vendee, where the vendor is under duty, or assumes the obligation, to furnish such abstract for the use of the vendee, and the person making the abstract on the vendor's order has knowledge or notice that the abstract is for such use—this on the ground that in such circumstances the engagement of the abstractor by the vendor is a contract made for the benefit of the vendee, and under such engagement the abstractor owes the vendee, who is to use and rely on the abstract, the duty of using care and skill in examining the records affecting the title and making the abstract." [65] It is well-settled law that the promisor in a valid contract owes no duty of care to an incidental beneficiary of the contract. By the great weight of authority an abstractor is not liable to a third-party beneficiary of the abstracting contract for negligent preparation of the abstract, in the absence of a promise by the abstractor to the vendor of the land to make the abstract for the benefit of the

[64] *Meyerson* v. *New Idea Hosiery Co.*, 115 So. 94 (1927); I. P. Hildebrand, *Contracts for the Benefit of Third Parties in Texas*, 9 Tex. L. R. 125 (1931).
[65] *Shine* v. *Nash Abstract & I. Co.*, 217 Ala. 498, 117 So. 47 (1928).

third-party vendee.[66] The holding of the *Landell* v. *Lybrand* case that a public accountant is not liable to an investor or a creditor of the client for mere negligence in the audit of the client's books, in the absence of a provision in the auditing contract that the audit be prepared for the investor or creditor, finds ample support in the more recent case, *Ultramares Corporation* v. *Touche,* below.

THE PUBLIC ACCOUNTANT LIABLE TO THIRD PARTIES FOR FRAUD

The famous *Ultramares* case follows the ruling in *Landell* v. *Lybrand,* supra, which denies liability of the public accountant to third parties for mere negligence and defines the scope of fraud for which the public accountant may be liable to third parties. The opinion was delivered in 1931 by Chief Judge Cardozo of the New York court of appeals. The facts of the case follow: [67]

A corporation, Fred Stern & Co., Inc., was engaged in the importation and sale of rubber. To carry on its extensive operations this corporation borrowed large sums of money from banks and other lenders. To obtain the necessary loans in 1924 the Stern company employed the defendant auditors, Touche, Niven & Co., who had conducted the Stern company's audits for the three years prior to 1923, to audit its books for 1923 and to prepare a balance-sheet of the Stern company as of the close of that year. The auditors performed the audit, prepared a balance-sheet and certified that the balance-sheet corresponded with the Stern company's records and that in their opinion the balance-sheet presented a correct view of the financial condition of the Stern company as of December 31, 1923. In accordance with agreement, the auditors furnished the Stern company with thirty-two copies of the certified balance-sheet; the auditors knew that the copies would be used to obtain loans; but they did not know, and had no reason to believe, that the balance-sheet would be used to obtain a loan from the particular plaintiff, the Ultramares Corporation. However, the Stern company, with the aid of that balance-sheet, was able to get a loan of $165,000, only partly secured, from the Ultramares Cor-

---

[66] *Peterson* v. *Gales,* 191 Wis. 137, 210 N. W. 407 (1926).
[67] *Ultramares Corporation* v. *Touche,* 74 A. L. R. 1139, 255 N. Y. 170, 174 N. E. 441.

Liability for Negligence, Fraud and Libel 69

poration. The balance-sheet having been found false and the Stern company having been declared a bankrupt in 1925, the Ultramares Corporation brought an action in a trial court of New York in 1926 for negligence and fraud against the defendant auditors to recover the losses sustained from the loans to the Stern company. In the trial court the charge of fraud was dismissed before the jury hearing took place. On the charge of negligence the jury rendered a verdict for the plaintiff; but the trial judge dismissed the verdict. The case was appealed to the New York supreme court, where judgment was given the plaintiff on the basis of negligence. The case was then appealed to the New York court of appeals which denied to the plaintiff judgment on the basis of negligence and granted a new trial on the ground of fraud.

A statement of the character of the audit which involved the alleged elements of negligence and fraud is in order. No general ledger posting had been performed on the Stern company's books since April, 1923. The defendant auditors assigned Siess, a junior member of their staff, to the task of posting journal entries to the general ledger. Siess finished his posting on Sunday, February 3, 1924. The balance of the accounts-receivable account at that time was $644,758.17. Later, on that same day, Romberg, an employee of the Stern company, who had general charge of the Stern company's records, debited the accounts-receivable account with a new item of $706,843.07, which represented fictitious sales. Opposite the entry Romberg placed a folio reference to the journal, but there was no journal entry to support this charge to accounts receivable. There were, however, seventeen fictitious sales-invoices designed to support this new charge to accounts receivable. These sales-invoices were different from the other sales-invoices; they had no shipping number and no customer's order number; they "varied in terms of credit and in other respects from those usual in the business." "A mere glance" would have revealed "the difference." Siess, thinking that verification would be made by the staff later, accepted and included in the balance of accounts receivable this new debit of $706,843.07, entered by Romberg. It happened that neither the junior accountant nor any one else of the staff ever investigated this new charge to accounts receivable.

In a statement of facts Chief Judge Cardozo of the court of appeals expressed the opinion that an item of $113,199.60, due from the Baltic Corporation and charged to accounts payable, ought to have encited the suspicions of a reasonably prudent and careful auditor, in view of the unsatisfactory explanations of the item given by Romberg and Stern. Furthermore, the auditors discovered that the inventory of $347,219.08 as stated by the Stern company was overstated to the amount of $303,863.20. Chief Judge Cardozo thought that the extent of this "discrepancy and its causes might have been found to cast discredit upon the business and the books." Finally, the auditors found that the same accounts receivable "had been pledged to two, three and four banks at the same time." Chief Judge Cardozo was of the opinion that these assignments cast doubt upon the solvency of the business; he thought that, although Romberg made an explanation of the assignments, caution and diligence required the auditors to press further their investigation.

The existence of negligence on the part of the auditors was found by all the courts concerned with the case. The chief problems with which the New York court of appeals was concerned had to do with (1) the extension of the defendants' liability for negligence to incidental beneficiaries of the audit contract; (2) the scope and meaning of fraud. The portions of the lengthy opinion directly in point follow:

"The defendants owed to their employer a duty imposed by law to make their certificate without fraud, and a duty growing out of contract to make it with the care and caution proper to their calling. Fraud includes the pretense of knowledge when knowledge there is none. To creditors and investors to whom the employer exhibited the certificate, the defendants owed a like duty to make it without fraud, since there was notice in the circumstances of its making that the employer did not intend to keep it to himself. * * * A different question develops when we ask whether they owed a duty to these to make it without negligence. If liability for negligence exists, a thoughtless slip or blunder, the failure to detect a theft or forgery beneath the cover of deceptive entries may expose accountants to a liability in an indeterminate amount for an indeterminate time to an indeterminate class. The hazards of business conducted on these terms are so extreme as to enkindle doubt whether a flaw may not exist in the implication of a duty that exposes to these consequences. We put aside for the moment any statement in the certificate which involves the representation of a fact as true to the knowledge of the auditors. If such a statement was made, whether believed to be true or not, the defendants are liable for deceit in the event that it was false. The plaintiff does not need the invention of novel doctrine to help it out in such conditions.

"Even an opinion, especially on opinion by an expert, may be found to be fraudulent if the grounds supporting it are so flimsy as to lead to the conclusion that there was no genuine belief back of it. Further than that this court has never gone.

"Liability for negligence if adjudged in this case will extend to many callings other than an auditor's. Lawyers who certify their opinion as to the validity of municipal or corporate bonds, with knowledge that the opinion will be brought to the notice of the public, will become liable to the investors, if they have overlooked a statute or a decision, to the same extent as if the controversy were one between client and advisor. Title companies insuring titles to a tract of land, with knowledge that at an approaching auction the fact that they have insured will be stated to the bidders, will become liable to purchasers who may wish the benefit of a policy without payment of a premium. These illustrations may seem to be extreme, but they go little, if any, farther than we are invited to go now. Negligence, moreover, will have one standard when viewed in relation to the public. Explanations that might seem plausible, omissions that might be reasonable, if the duty is confined to the employer, conducting a business that presumably at least is not a fraud upon his creditors, might wear another aspect if an independent duty to be suspicious even of one's principal is owing to investors. 'Every one making a promise having the quality of a contract will be under a duty to the promisee by virtue of the promise, but under another duty, apart from contract, to an indefinite number of potential beneficiaries when performance has begun. The assumption of one relation will mean the involuntary assumption of a series of new relations, inescapably hooked together.'

"Our holding does not emancipate accountants from the consequences of fraud. It does not relieve them if their audit has been so negligent as to justify a finding that they had no genuine belief in its adequacy, for this again is fraud. It does no more than say that, if less than this is proved, if there has been neither reckless misstatement nor insincere profession of an opinion, but only honest blunder, the ensuing liability for negligence is one that is bounded by the contract and is to be enforced between the parties by whom the contract has been made. We doubt whether the average business man rceiving a certificate without paying for it, and receiving it merely as one among a multitude of possible investors, would look for anything more.

"The defendants certified as a fact, true to their own knowledge, that the balance-sheet was in accordance with the books of account. If their statement was false, they are not to be exonerated because they believed it to be true. *Hadcock* v. *Osmer,* 153 N. Y. 604, 47 N. E. 923; *Lehigh Zinc & Iron Co.* v. *Bamford,* 150 U. S. 665, 673, 14 S. Ct. 219, 37 L. ed. 1215; *Chatham Furnace Co.* v. *Moffatt,* 147 Mass. 403, 18 N. E. 168, 9 Am. St. Rep. 727; *Arnold* v. *Richardson,* 74 App. Div. 581, 77 N. Y. S. 763. We think the triers of the facts might hold it to be false.

"Correspondence between the balance-sheet and the books imports something more, or so the triers of the facts might say, than correspondence between the balance-sheet and the general ledger, unsupported or even contradicted by every other record. The correspondence to be of any moment may not unreasonably be held to signify a correspondence between the statement and the books of original entry, the books taken as a whole. If that is what the certificate means, a jury could find that the correspondence did not exist, and that the defendants signed the certificates without knowing it to exist and even without reasonable grounds for belief in its existence. The item of $706,000, representing fictitious accounts receivable, was entered in the ledger after defendant's employee, Siess, had posted the December sales. He knew of the interpolation and knew that there was need to verify the entry by reference to books other than the ledger before the books could be found to be in agreement with the balance-sheet. The evidence would sustain a finding that this was never done. By concession the interpolated item had no support in the journal, or in any journal voucher, or in the debit memo book, which was a summary of the invoices, or in anything except the invoices themselves. The defendants do not say that they ever looked at the invoices, seventeen in number, representing these accounts. They profess to be unable to recall whether they did so or not. They admit, however, that, if they had looked, they would have found omissions and irregularities so many and unusual as to have called for further investigation. When we couple the refusal to say that they did look with the admission that, if they had looked, they would or could have seen, the situation is revealed as one in which a jury might reasonably find that in truth they did not look but certified the correspondence without testing its existence.

"In this connection we are to bear in mind the principle already stated in the course of this opinion that negligence or blindness, even when not equivalent to fraud, is none the less evidence to sustain an inference of fraud. At least this is so if the negligence is gross. Not a little confusion has at times resulted from an undiscriminating quotation of the statements in *Kountze* v. *Kennedy,* supra, statements proper enough in their setting, but capable of misleading when extracted and considered by themselves. 'Misjudgment, however gross,' it was there observed, 'or want of caution, however marked, is not fraud.' This was said in a case where the trier of the facts had held the defendants guiltless. The judgment in this court amounted merely to a holding that a finding of fraud did not follow as an inference of law. There was no holding that the evidence would have required a reversal of the judgment if the finding as to guilt had been the other way. Even *Derry* v. *Peek,* as we have seen, asserts the probative effect of negligence as an evidentiary fact. We had no thought in *Kountze* v. *Kennedy,* of upholding a doctrine more favorable to wrongdoers, though there was a reservation suggesting the approval of a rule more rigorous. The opinion of this court cites *Derry* v. *Peek,* and states the holding there made that an action would not lie if the defendant believed the representation made by him to be true, although without reasonable cause for such belief. 'It is not necessary,' we said, 'to go to this extent to uphold the present judgment, for the referee, as has been stated, found that the belief of Kennedy * * * was based upon reasonable grounds.' The setting of the occasion justified the inference that the representations did not involve a profession of knowledge as distinguished from belief. 147 N. Y. at page 133, 41 N. E. 414, 29 L. R. A. 360, 49 Am. St. Rep. 651. No such charity of construction exonerates accountants, who by the very nature of their calling profess to speak with knowledge when certifying to an agreement between the audit and the entries.

"The defendants attempt to excuse the omission of an inspection of the invoices proved to be fictitious by invoking a practice known as that of testing and sampling. A random choice of accounts is made from the total number on the books, and these, if found to be regular when inspected and investigated, are taken as a fair indication of the quality of the mass. The defendants say that about 200 invoices were examined in accordance with this practice, but they do not assert that any of the seventeen invoices supporting the fictitious sales were among the number so selected. Verification by test and sample was very likely a sufficient audit as to accounts regularly entered upon the books in the usual course of business. It was plainly insufficient, however, as to accounts not entered upon the books where inspection of the invoices was necessary, not as a check upon accounts fair upon their face, but in order to ascertain whether there were any accounts at all. If the only invoices inspected were invoices unrelated to the interpolated entry, the result was to certify a correspondence between the books and the balance-sheet without any effort by the auditors, as to $706,000 of accounts, to ascertain whether the certified agreement was in accordance with the truth. How far books of account fair upon their face are to be probed by accountants, in an effort to ascertain whether the transactions back of them are in accordance with the entries, involves to some extent the exercise of judgment and discretion. Not so, however, the inquiry whether the entries certified as there are there in very truth, there in the form and in the places where men of business training would expect them to be. The defendants were put on their guard by the circumstances touching the December accounts receivable to scrutinize with special care. A jury might find that, with suspicions thus awakened, they closed their eyes to the obvious and blindly gave assent.

"We conclude, to sum up the situation, that in certifying to the correspondence between balance-sheet and accounts the defendants made a statement as true to their own knowledge, when they had, as a jury might find, no knowledge on the subject. If that is so, they may also be found to have acted without information leading to a sincere or genuine belief when they certified to an opinion that the balance-sheet faithfully reflected the condition of the business.

"Whatever wrong was committed by the defendants was not their personal act or omission, but that of their subordinates. This does not relieve them, however, of liability to answer in damages for the consequences of the wrong, if wrong there shall be found to be. It is not a question of constructive notice, as where facts are brought home to the knowledge of subordinates whose interests are adverse to those of the employer."

Chief Judge Cardozo, after much floundering about, in the *Ultramares* case held:

(1) An auditor is liable on the basis of fraud to third parties to whom the auditor might reasonably have foreseen loss resulting from the auditor's misrepresentation in making a positive statement of facts, even though the auditor believed his statement to be true. This ruling, however, was made in view of a set of circumstances from which Chief Judge Cardozo seemed to think that a trier of facts would be justified in inferring consciousness of misrepresentation on the part of the defendant auditor. In *Kountze v. Kennedy*, which was reviewed in the *Ultramares* case, the New York court of appeals, in circumstances that justified an inference of innocence on the part of the defendant, held that fraud could not exist without consciousness of wrongdoing. In all of the four cases which Chief Judge Cardozo cited to support his proposition in the case that a public accountant would be liable in an action for deceit for making an honest but false representation of a material fact, the defendants had intended that their representation should be acted upon by the particular plaintiffs. But in the *Ultramares* case the defendant did not know that the plaintiff would use his audit report. Except for the fact that there must have been a consciousness of wrongdoing on the part of the defendant auditor, the *Ultramares* opinion goes further than other courts have gone in treating honest misrepresentation as fraud. Courts have uniformly restricted the application of the rule that fraud may include innocent but false representations to cases where the defendant had intended that the representation should be relied upon by the particular plaintiff. While the scope of fraud as thus restricted would not make the public accountant liable to the world in general for an honest blunder, yet it would be more logical and satisfactory to treat innocent but negligent misrepresentations as negligence rather than as fraud. The subject is fully discussed under the title, below, "The extension of the ambit of negligence rather than that of fraud to cover the public accountant's liability to third parties for innocent but negligent misrepresentation."

(2) The public accountant is not liable to third parties for mere negligence in making a statement of opinion. This ruling is sound and should be followed.

(3) The public accountant is liable to third parties on the basis of fraud for conscious misrepresentation in making a statement of opinion. Consciousness of misrepresentation may be inferred if the grounds supporting the opinion are so flimsy as to lead to the conclusion that there was no genuine belief back of the opinion. This ruling is also based upon sound principles. It is in agreement with the conservative interpretation of the meaning of fraud as laid down by the famous English case, *Derry* v. *Peek*.[68] A full discussion of the subject appears under the topic, below, "Meaning of fraud."

Liability of the Public Accountant to Third Parties for Misrepresentation under the United States Securities Act

The United States securities act of 1933, as amended in 1934, has made the public accountant liable to third parties for both negligence and fraud.

Under this act no "person" is allowed to use the mails or interstate transportation facilities to sell a security unless the security is properly registered with the securities and exchange commission, or exempted from registration by the act. In regard to the civil liabilities of the accountant who prepares or certifies the financial statements of the "issuer" for the purposes of registration with the commission, a number of sections of the securities act of 1933, as amended in 1934, are relevant. These sections follow:

"Sec. 2. When used in this title, unless the context otherwise requires—

"(1) The term 'security' means any note, stock, treasury stock, bond, debenture, evidence of indebtedness, certificate of interest or participation in any profit-sharing agreement, collateral-trust certificate, preorganization certificate or subscription, transferable share, investment contract, voting-trust certificate, certificate of deposit for a security, fractional undivided interest in oil, gas or other mineral rights or, in general, any interest or instrument commonly known as a 'security', or any certificate of interest or participation in, temporary

[68] 14 App. Cas. 117 (1889).

or interim certificate for, receipt for, guarantee of or warrant or right to subscribe to or purchase, any of the foregoing.

"(2) The term 'person' means an individual, a corporation, a partnership, an association, a joint-stock company, a trust, any unincorporated organization, or a government or political subdivision thereof. As used in this paragraph the term 'trust' shall include only a trust where the interest or interests of the beneficiary or beneficiaries are evidenced by a security.

"(3) The term 'sale', 'sell', 'offer to sell', or 'offer for sale' shall include every contract of sale or disposition of, attempt or offer to dispose of, or solicitation of an offer to buy a security or interest in a security, for value; except that such terms shall not include preliminary negotiations or agreements between an issuer and any underwriter. * * *

"(4) The term 'issuer' means every person who issues or proposes to issue any security; except that with respect to certificates of deposit, voting-trust certificates or collateral-trust certificates, or with respect to certificates of interest or shares in an unincorporated investment trust not having a board of directors (or persons performing similar functions) or of the fixed, restricted management or unit type; the term 'issuer' means the person or persons performing the acts and assuming the duties of depositor or manager pursuant to the provisions of the trust or other agreement or instrument under which such securities are issued; except that in the case of an unincorporated association which provides by its articles for limited liability of any or all of its members, or in the case of a trust, committee or other legal entity, the trustees or members thereof shall not be individually liable as issuers of any security issued by the association, trust, committee or other legal entity; except that with respect to equipment-trust certificates or like securities, the term 'issuer' means the person by whom the equipment or property is or is to be used; and except that with respect to fractional undivided interests in oil, gas or other mineral rights, the term 'issuer' means the owner of any such right or of any interest in such right (whether whole or fractional) who creates fractional interests therein for the purpose of public offering.

"Sec. 7. * * * If any accountant, engineer, or appraiser, or any person whose profession gives authority to a statement made by him, is named as having prepared or certified any part of the registration statement, the written consent of such person shall be filed with the registration statement. If any such person is named as having prepared or certified a report or valuation (other than a public official document or statement) which is used in connection with the registration statement, but is not named as having prepared or certified such report or valuation for use in connection with the registration statement, the written consent of such person shall be filed with the registration statement unless the commission dispenses with such filing as impracticable or as involving undue hardship on the person filing the registration statement. * * *

"Sec. 8 (a) The effective date of a registration statement shall be the twentieth day after the filing thereof, except as hereinafter provided, and except that in case of securities of any foreign public authority, which has continued the full service of its obligations in the United States, the proceeds of which are to be devoted to the refunding of obligations payable in the United States, the registration statement shall become effective seven days after the filing thereof. If any amendment to any such statement is filed prior to the effective date of such statement, the registration statement shall be deemed to have been filed when such amendment was filed; except that an amendment filed with the consent of the commission, prior to the effective date of the registration statement, or filed pursuant to an order of the commission, shall be treated as a part of the registration statement.

"Sec. 11. (a) In case any part of the registration statement, when such part became effective, contained an untrue statement of a material fact or omitted to state a material fact required to be stated therein or necessary to make the statements therein not misleading, any person acquiring such security (unless it is proved that at the time of such acquisition he knew of such untruth or omission) may, either at law or in equity, in any court of competent jurisdiction, sue—

"(1) every person who signed the registration statement;

"(2) every person who was a director of (or person performing similar functions) or partner in the issuer at the time of the filing of the part of the registration statement with respect to which his liability is asserted;

"(3) every person who, with his consent, is named in the registration statement as being or about to become a director, person performing similar functions or partner;

"(4) every accountant, engineer, or appraiser, or any person whose profession gives authority to a statement made by him, who has with his consent been named as having prepared or certified any part of the registration statement, or as having prepared or certified any report or valuation which is used in connection with the registration statement, with respect to the statement in such registration statement, report or valuation, which purports to have been prepared or certified by him;

"(5) every underwriter with respect to such security. If such person acquired the security after the issuer has made generally available to its security holders an earnings statement covering a period of at least twelve months beginning after the effective date of the registration statement, then the right of recovery under this subsection shall be conditioned on proof that such person acquired the security relying upon such untrue statement in the registration statement or relying upon the registration statement and not knowing of such omission, but such reliance may be established without proof of the reading of the registration statement by such person.

"(b) Notwithstanding the provisions of subsection (a) no person, other than the issuer, shall be liable as provided therein who shall sustain the burden of proof—

"(1) that before the effective date of the part of the registration statement with respect to which his liability is asserted (A) he had resigned from or had taken such steps as are permitted by law to resign from, or ceased or refused to act in every office, capacity or relationship in which he was described in the registration statement as acting or agreeing to act, and (B) he had advised the commission and the issuer in writing that he had taken such action and that he would not be responsible for such part of the registration statement; or

"(2) that if such part of the registration statement became effective without his knowledge, upon becoming aware of such fact he forthwith acted and advised the commission, in accordance with paragraph (1), and, in addition, gave reasonable public notice that such part of the registration statement had become effective without his knowledge; or

"(3) that * * * (B) as regards any part of the registration statement purporting to be made upon his authority as an expert or purporting to be a copy of or extract from a report or valuation of himself as an expert, (i) he had, after reasonable investigation, reasonable ground to believe and did believe, at the time such part of the registration statement became effective, that the statements therein were true and that there was no omission to state a material fact required to be stated therein or necessary to make the statements therein not misleading, or (ii) such part of the registration statement did not fairly represent his statement as an expert or was not a fair copy of or extract from his report or valuation as an expert; and (C) as regards any part of the registration statement purporting to be made on the authority of an expert (other than himself) or purporting to be a copy of or extract from a report or valuation of an expert (other than himself), he had no reasonable ground to believe and did not believe, at the time such part of the registration statement became effective, that the statements therein were untrue or that there was an omission to state a material fact required to be stated therein or necessary to make the statements therein not misleading, or that such part of the registration statement did not fairly represent the statement of the expert or was not a fair copy of or extract from the report or valuation of the expert; * * *

"(c) In determining, for the purpose of paragraph (3) of subsection (b) of this section, what constitutes reasonable investigation and reasonable ground for belief, the standard of reasonableness shall be that required of a prudent man in the management of his own property. * * *

"(e) The suit authorized under subsection (a) may be to recover such damages as shall represent the difference between the amount paid for the security (not exceeding the price at which the security was offered to the public) and (1) the value thereof as of the time such suit was brought, or (2) the price at which such security shall have been disposed of in the market before suit, or (3) the price at which such security shall have been disposed of after suit but before judgment if such damages shall be less than the damages representing the difference between the amount paid for the security (not exceeding the price at which the security was offered to the public) and the value thereof as of the time such suit was brought: provided that, if the defendant proves that any portion or all of such damages represents other than the depreciation in value of such security resulting from such part of the registration statement, with respect to which his liability is asserted, not being true or omitting to state a material fact required to be stated therein or necessary to make the statements therein not misleading, such portion of or all such damages shall not be recoverable. * * *

"(f) All or any one or more of the persons specified in subsection (a) shall be jointly and severally liable, and every person who becomes liable to make any payment under this section may recover contribution as in cases of contract from any person who, if sued separately, would have been liable to make the same payment, unless the person who has become liable was, and the other was not, guilty of fraudulent misrepresentation.

"(g) In no case shall the amount recoverable under this section exceed the price at which the security was offered to the public.

"Sec. 13. No action shall be maintained to enforce any liability created under section 11 * * * unless brought within one year after the discovery of the untrue statement or the omission, or after such discovery should have been made by the exercise of reasonable diligence. * * * In no event shall any such action be brought to enforce a liability created under section 11 * * * more than three years after the security was, bona fide, offered to the public, * * *.

"Sec. 14. Any condition, stipulation or provision binding any person acquiring any security to waive compliance with any provision of this title or of the rules and regulations of the commission shall be void.

"Sec. 16. The rights and remedies provided by this title shall be in addition to any and all other rights and remedies that may exist at law or in equity.

"Sec. 19. (a) * * * No provision of this title imposing any liability shall apply to any act done or omitted in good faith in conformity with any rule or regulation of the commission, notwithstanding that such rule or regulation may, after such act or omission, be amended or rescinded or be determined by judicial or other authority to be invalid for any reason."

Under the securities act every issuer of securities must have filed a registration statement of his business before any "person" can use the mails or interstate commerce facilities to effect the sale of such securities. Among other data the registration statement must contain statements of the financial condition of the issuer. If the registration statement names an accountant as having prepared or certified the financial statements (balance-sheet and profit-and-loss statement) of the issuer for registration purposes, the written consent of the accountant for the issuer or other person so to use the financial statements must be filed with the securities and exchange commission; but if the registration statement does not name the accountant as having prepared or certified the financial statements of the issuer for registration purposes, then the commission may dispense with the filing of the written consent of the accountant so to use the financial statements where such filing would be impracticable or work hardship upon the person filing the registration statement. The rights and obligations arising out of the act do not become effective until the lapse of twenty days after the proper filing of the registration statement.

If an investor purchases a security after the effective date of the registration of such security, he may bring suit against the accountant for misrepresentation of any material fact in the financial statements used in the registration statement. The investor may sue the accountant upon showing a misrepresentation of a material fact in the accountant's financial statements used in registration and evidence of having purchased the security after the effective date of registration. Of course, to recover, the investor must prove loss; but he need not prove that the loss resulted from the misrepresentation, nor need he prove that he relied upon the misrepresentation unless he bought the security after the issuer made generally available to security holders financial statements of the issuer's business as of a year or more subsequent to the effective date of the registration.

The accountant will be liable to the investor provided the investor establishes his cause of action in the manner indicated above unless the accountant sustains the burden of proving one of the following defenses:

(1) Prior to the effective date of registration the accountant gave written notice to the commission that he would not be responsible for financial statements filed with his client's registration statement.

(2) Where the accountant's financial statements became effective with his client's registration statement, without the accountant's knowledge, upon learning the fact the accountant forthwith requested the commission to withdraw his authority for the accuracy of the statements and gave reasonable publication that the financial statements became effective without his knowledge.

(3) The accountant had, after reasonable investigation, reasonable ground to believe and did believe, at the time his accounting

statements became an effective part of the registration statement, that such accounting statements were true, that there was no omission to state a material fact required to be stated therein or necessary to make the statements not misleading.

(4) The financial statements filed with the commission were not fair copies of the financial reports which the accountant prepared or certified for his client.

(5) Where the accountant's false representation, contained in his client's registration statement, purported to have been accepted from an expert other than himself, the accountant had no reasonable ground to believe and did not believe, at the time his representation became an effective part of the issuer's registration statement, that the representation of the expert was untrue.

(6) The investor knew the falsity of the accountant's representation at the time the investor bought the security.

(7) The action to enforce liability under the act was sought more than a year after the investor learned, or could have learned with the exercise of reasonable diligence, that the accountant had misrepresented the financial condition of the issuer's business.

(8) The action to enforce liability under the act was brought more than three years after the security was offered for sale to the public, that is, more than three years after the security was offered for sale to the public in accordance with the provisions of the act.

(9) In making the misrepresentation the accountant acted in good faith in conformity with some rule or regulation of the commission even though such rule or regulation was, after the effective date of the misrepresentation, declared invalid by judicial authority or was amended by congress.

(10) The investor's loss resulted from causes other than the accountant's misrepresentation. If the accountant can prove that the loss complained of was due partly to causes other than the accountant's misrepresentation, then the accountant's liability will be mitigated to the extent of such portion of the investor's loss as was due to causes other than the accountant's misrepresentation.

If the accountant should become liable under the act, he could recover contribution from any other person who might also be liable for the same loss under the act, unless the accountant had been guilty of fraud and such other person had not.

The amount of recovery provided by the act may be the difference between the price paid for the security (in no case greater than the price at which the security was offered to the public) and (1) the value of the security at the time the suit was brought, or (2) the price at which the security was sold before the commencement of the suit, or (3) the price at which the security was sold after suit but before judgment, if such damage is less than the difference between the purchase price (not exceeding the price at which the security was offered to the public) and the value at the time of the bringing of the suit. The recovery that may be obtained under this act is in addition to any and all other recoveries which may be obtained at law or in equity.

To supplement the main provisions of the act relative to the liabilities of accountants, some comments upon these provisions are appropriate:

The requirement that the accountant's statements should present the true financial condition of the business on the effective date, twenty days after such statements have been filed with the commission, clearly should not be enforced literally. The accountant's responsibility should be as of the time he certified to the financial condition of the issuer.

The meaning of a misrepresentation of a material fact as contemplated by the act deserves consideration. The American Law Institute in its *Restatement of the Law of Contracts* has stated that: "where a misrepresentation would be likely to affect the conduct of a reasonable man with reference to a transaction with another person, the misrepresentation is material." [69]

In regard to the defenses that may be established under section II (b) it should be noted that the act casts the burden of proof upon the defendant, contrary to the usual court procedure in tort actions. In tort cases at common law the plaintiff in order to establish his cause of action must, ordinarily, prove that the defendant's tortious conduct was the direct cause of the plaintiff's loss. This

---

[69] Spencer Gordon, "Accountants and the Securities Act," *The Journal of Accountancy*, New York, 1933, volume 56, p. 440.

Liability for Negligence, Fraud and Libel

common-law rule guards against oppression in litigation. It is much more difficult to prove a cause of action than it is to defend alleged charges, the amount of evidence available and the other conditions of proof for the litigants being equal. The act should place upon the plaintiff investor the burden of proving his cause of action against the accountant. In other words, the investor should be required to prove that the negligent or fraudulent conduct of the accountant was the direct cause of the investor's loss before the investor would be permitted to obtain judgment against the accountant.

As to the dependence of the accountant's liability upon the reasonableness of his conduct, it should be noted that the reasonableness of a prudent man in the management of his own property is the standard set by the act. The law would have been more definite in respect to the care and skill required of the accountant had the framers of the act stated that the defendant accountant must have exercised such reasonableness of conduct as a reasonably skillful accountant would have exercised if such accountant had made the financial statements for his own use in purchasing the security.

In providing for the liabilities of accountants and other persons, the act makes no distinction between negligence and fraud, except in the case of one defendant recovering contribution from another person who might have been liable for the same loss under the act. Either negligence or fraud, or both, may be involved in the liabilities provided in the act. There are inherent differences between the two kinds of causes of action, which an act should recognize. Fraud involves consciousness of misrepresentation and renders the defendant liable for injury to any one of that class of persons (investors) whom, the defendant intended, should, and did, rely upon his misrepresentations; while negligence merely involves innocent but unreasonable conduct and makes the defendant liable for injury only to such plaintiffs as those to whom he owed a duty of care. The law should require the accountant to state as a matter of fact whether or not the balance-sheet and profit-and-loss statement show the true and correct financial position of the issuer's business on the date when the accountant gave his written consent to have his financial statements used with the registration statement.

The law should make the accountant liable on the basis of fraud for conscious misrepresentation in the financial statements of the issuer to any investor who, as a result of reliance upon such misrepresentation, sustained losses from the purchase of a security of the issuer. Only where the accountant intended that particular security purchasers should rely upon his statements and where such investors did rely upon his statements to their loss in the purchase of securities of the issuer should the law make the accountant liable to the investors on the basis of negligence for losses resulting from the accountant's innocent but negligent misrepresentation of the financial condition of the issuer's business. If these changes in the statute were made, an honest blunder would not render the accountant liable to that host of investors who, as a result of reliance upon the accountant's misrepresentation, happened to sustain losses from the purchase of securities. For a detailed discussion of the essential differences in fraud and negligence, see: "Extension of the ambit of negligence rather than that of fraud to cover the accountant's liability for innocent but negligent misrepresentation," below.

Liability of the Public Accountant to Third Parties for Misrepresentation under the United States Securities Exchange Act of 1934

Under the United States securities exchange act of 1934, designed to control the organized security exchanges of the country, securities can not be bought and sold in such markets without the proper registration of the issuer with the securities and exchange commission. Among other data required in such registration are balance-sheets and profit-and-loss statements of the issuer. The accountant who prepares or certifies the accuracy of such balance-sheets and profit-and-loss statements may be held liable under the act to investors who sustain losses from fraudulent misrepresentation in such statements. A portion of the act follows:

"Sec. 18. (a) Any person who shall make or cause to be made any statement in any application, report or document filed pursuant to this title or any rule or regulation thereunder, which statement was at the time and in the light of the circumstances under which it was

Liability for Negligence, Fraud and Libel

made false or misleading with respect to any material fact, shall be liable to any person (not knowing that such statement was false or misleading) who, in reliance upon such statement, shall have purchased or sold a security at a price which was affected by such statement, for damages caused by such reliance, unless the person sued shall prove that he acted in good faith and had no knowledge that such statement was false or misleading. A person seeking to enforce such liability may sue at law or in equity in any court of competent jurisdiction. In any such suit the court may, in its discretion, require an undertaking for the payment of the costs of such suit and assess reasonable costs, including reasonable attorneys' fees, against either party litigant.

"(b) Every person who becomes liable to make payment under this section may recover contribution as in cases of contract from any person who, if joined in the original suit, would have been liable to make the same payment.

"(c) No action shall be maintained to enforce any liability created under this section unless brought within one year after the discovery of the facts constituting the cause of action and within three years after such cause of action accrued."

From the context of section 18 of the securities exchange act, it appears that in order for an investor to maintain an action against an accountant for misrepresentation of a material fact in the financial statements of the issuer of securities traded on a national exchange, the investor in the security would have to prove that the accountant's statements were false or misleading at the time and in the light of the circumstances in which they were made and that the investor's loss was the result of such misrepresentation. The accountant may defeat the suit by proving that he acted in good faith and had no knowledge of the falsity of the statement, that is, that he was not guilty of fraud. The accountant might have been negligent, but as long as he was not conscious of misrepresentation he would not be liable under the securities exchange act of 1934. Furthermore, the accountant could set up an effective defense by showing that the action was not brought before the lapse of a year after discovery of the cause of action, or that the action was not brought within three years after the cause of action arose. The accountant's liability for damages may be mitigated through recovery from other persons liable for the same loss under the act—that is, if the accountant has been required to pay the whole damage, he can recover contribution from such other persons as would be liable for the same loss under the act. In respect to the liability of the accountant to investors for conscious misrepresentation the securities exchange act appears to be just.

VI

EXTENSION OF THE AMBIT OF NEGLIGENCE RATHER THAN THAT OF FRAUD TO COVER THE PUBLIC ACCOUNTANT'S LIABILITY TO THIRD PARTIES FOR INNOCENT BUT NEGLIGENT MISREPRESENTATION

Meaning of Fraud

In 1887 the supreme court of the United States gave a definition of fraud, which is in agreement with the usual meaning attached to the word by both eminent legal authority and laymen: "In order to establish a charge of this character the complainant must show, by clear and decisive proof, first, that the defendant has made a representation in regard to a material fact; secondly, that such representation is false; thirdly, that such representation was not actually believed by the defendant, on reasonable grounds, to be true; fourthly, that it was made with intent that it should be acted on; fifthly, that it was acted on by complainant to his damage; and, sixthly, that in so acting on it the complainant was ignorant of its falsity and reasonably believed it to be true." [70] There have been deviations from the conception of fraud as set forth in this decision of the supreme court of the United States. In fact, the majority of American courts do not adhere strictly to this definition of fraud. The deviations in which the public accountant is particularly concerned involve the knowledge or consciousness of wrong on the part of the defendant. The majority opinion in America has taken the view that fraud may exist where there is no

---

[70] *Southern Development Co.* v. *Silva*, 125 U. S. 247, 8 S. C. Rep. 881, 31 L. Ed. 678. For a discussion of the nature of negligence, see page 4, ante.

consciousness of wrong on the part of the defendant, as where the defendant has made an innocent but negligent misrepresentation. A number of decisions have gone so far as to hold that fraud may exist, not only in the absence of knowledge of wrongdoing, but also in the absence of negligence, on the part of the defendant. According to this theory, mere innocent misrepresentation may amount to fraud. It is worth while to devote detailed attention to these three views of fraud which will be considered in reverse order.

A substantial number of cases has adopted the view that an action for deceit for misrepresentation may be upheld where the misrepresentation involved no negligence or dishonesty on the part of the defendant. A few excerpts from some of these opinions will help in forming an understanding of this concept of fraud. The supreme court of Massachusetts in speaking of an action for deceit in representing a horse to be sound held: [71]

"It is not always necessary to prove that the defendant knew that the facts stated by him were false. If he states, as of his own knowledge, material facts susceptible of knowledge, which are false, it is fraud which renders him liable to the party who relies and acts upon the statement as true, and it is no defense that he believed the facts to be true. The falsity and fraud consists in representing that he knows the facts to be true, of his own knowledge, when he has not such knowledge."

Then, again the Massachusetts supreme court held: [72]

"The fraud consists in stating that the party knows the thing to exist when he does not know it to exist; and if he does not know it to exist, he must ordinarily be deemed to know that he does not. Forgetfulness of its existence after a former knowledge, or a mere belief of its existence, will not warrant or excuse a statement of actual knowledge."

The same court, in a later decision, held: [73]

"Due diligence to ascertain the truth in regard to statements made as of matters of fact within one's own knowledge is not enough to

[71] *Litchfield* v. *Hutchinson*, 117 Mass. 195.
[72] *Chatham Furnace Co.* v. *Moffatt*, 147 Mass. 403.
[73] *Huntress* v. *Blodgett*, 206 Mass. 318.

relieve the maker of them of liability if they are false and relied upon as true, and the person to whom they are made suffers loss thereby."

The supreme court of Michigan held: [74]

"That the doctrine is settled here, by a long line of cases, that if there was in fact a misrepresentation, though made innocently, and its deceptive influence was effective, the consequences to the plaintiff being as serious as though it had proceeded from a vicious purpose, he would have a right of action for the damages caused thereby either at law or in equity."

Many other American decisions have gone as far or nearly as far as the above cases in holding a defendant liable, irrespective of good or bad faith, for making a positive false statement as to which he had special means of knowledge.[75] The doctrine set forth in these cases has been limited "to cover only cases where the profit of the misrepresentation inures to the benefit of the defendant, or he is a party to a contract with the plaintiff induced by the misrepresentation." [76] In all of these cases the circumstances were such that it could reasonably be inferred that the defendant, though he did not intend to deceive, must have intended that his representation should be relied upon by the plaintiff. According to Professor Bohlen, those courts which have treated honest and careful statements of fact capable of knowledge as fraud have created a new type of warranty but have erred in calling the cause of action fraud and in allowing action for deceit to give warrantual effect to such statements.[77]

Incidentally, it may be said that public accountants, like other professional men, are not insurers of the accuracy of their work. In the absence of negligence in making the audit and in preparing the audit reports the public accountant would not be liable for making an innocent misrepresentation in regard to the financial

[74] *Holcombe* v. *Noble*, 69 Mich. 396.

[75] Samuel Williston, "Liability for Honest Misrepresentation," 24 *Harvard Law Review*, 1910-1911, p. 429; Harry M. Harrington, "Torts—Liability for Negligent Language," 12 *Texas Law Review*, Dec., 1933, p. 67.

[76] Samuel Williston, "Liability for Honest Misrepresentation," 24 *Harvard Law Review*, 1910-1911, p. 429.

[77] F. H. Bohlen, "Should Negligent Misrepresentation be Treated as Negligence or Fraud?" 18 *Virginia Law Review* 704, 1932.

condition of his client's business, unless, of course, he had expressly stated in the auditing contract that he would guarantee the accuracy of his work.

Some other courts have rejected the idea of treating a breach of warranty as fraud, but have held that negligent, though innocent, misrepresentation constitutes fraud. In 1903 the supreme court of Nebraska held:[78]

> "We think, however, that the authorities are uniform in holding that an action of deceit is an action separate and distinct in its nature from an action for breach of warranty, and that it lies in cases where there is a warranty as well as where there is none.
>
> "We do not think that it is necessary to show actual knowledge of a false representation by the defendant to sustain an action for deceit, if the representations were actually false, and induced the contract, and were relied upon by plaintiff, to his damage, as being true. Under such conditions, defendants can not excuse themselves by simply showing that they did not actually know the representations to be false, for it was their duty to know them to be true before making them."

A decision similar to this was rendered in 1932 by the supreme court of Texas.[79] In that case the defendant was a banker and an expert in verifying signatures. The defendant verified to the plaintiff a signature on a note owned by the banker's customer and thus induced the plaintiff to purchase the note. At the time of the transaction the defendant concealed from the plaintiff the fact that the defendant received from the seller of the note $450 for securing its sale. A portion of the opinion reads:

> "The testimony brings him under another well settled rule, which is more exacting, that an expert's opinion as to a matter susceptible of knowledge is regarded as a statement of fact, upon which reliance may properly be placed and, if it is made scienter, that is, either with knowledge of its falsity or in culpable ignorance of its truth, constitutes remediable fraud. * * * The rule is further well established in this state that, where affirmative representations of fact are made

---

[78] *Hitchcock* v. *Gothenburg Water Power & Irr. Co.*, 4 Nebr. (unoff.) 620, 95 N. W. 638. See also *Palmer* v. *Goldberg*, 128 Wis. 103, 107 N. W. 478 (1906).
[79] *Wilson* v. *Jones*, 45 S. W. (2d) 572.

and designed to be acted upon by another and he does so believing them to be true when they are false, one making the representations is liable, regardless of his knowledge of falsity or intent to deceive."

In these two cases, as in the other cases of this type, the defendant had no knowledge of the falsity of his representations. He was negligent; but he had no intention to deceive; he merely intended that his representations should be trusted. The facts of these two cases are typical of this class of cases. If the public accountant should be held liable on the basis of fraud for innocent but negligent misrepresentation, the holding doubtless would be limited to cases in which the defendant had intended that his statements should be relied upon by the particular plaintiff.

A few decisions in America have followed more closely than do the above cases the English rule which restricts fraud to conscious misrepresentation. New York, New Hampshire and Minnesota courts have rendered a number of decisions in which the inherent differences between fraud and negligence were clearly understood.[80] In 1895 the New York court of appeals in the case of *Kountze* v. *Kennedy* held:[81]

"The principle has been obscured by the use by judges of the phrase 'legal fraud', which has sometimes been interpreted as meaning fraud by construction, and as indicating that something less than actual fraud may sustain an action for deceit. The gravamen of the action is actual fraud, and nothing less will sustain it. The representation upon which it is based must be shown not only to have been false and material, but that the defendant, when he made it, knew that it was false, or, not knowing whether it was true or false, and not caring what the fact might be, made it recklessly, paying no heed to the injury which might ensue. Misjudgment, however gross, or want of caution, however marked, is not fraud. Intentional fraud, as distinguished from a mere breach of duty or the omission to use due care, is an essential factor in an action for deceit. The man who intentionally deceives another to his injury should be legally responsible for the consequences. But if, through inattention, want of judgment, reliance upon information which a wiser man might not credit,

[80] Harry M. Harrington, "Torts—Liability for Negligent Language," 12 *Texas Law Review* 67 (1933).
[81] 147 N. Y. 124, 41 N. E. 414, 29 L. R. A. 360, 49 Am. St. Rep. 651.

misconception of the facts or of his moral obligation to inquire, he makes a representation designed to influence the conduct of another, and upon which the other acts to his prejudice, yet, if the misrepresentation was honestly made, believing it to be true, whatever other liability he may incur he can not be made liable in an action for deceit."

In the *Ultramares* case, supra, Chief Judge Cardozo said in respect to the public accountant's liability for fraud in the accountant's statement of opinion:

"Fraud includes the pretense of knowledge when knowledge there is none. * * * Even an opinion, especially an opinion by an expert, may be found to be fraudulent if the grounds supporting it are so flimsy as to lead to the conclusion that there was no genuine belief back of it. Further than that this court has never gone. * * * Our holding does not emancipate accountants from the consequences of fraud. It does not relieve them if their audit has been so negligent as to justify a finding that they had no genuine belief in its adequacy, for this again is fraud."

Actual fraud is made of sterner stuff than an innocent misrepresentation negligently rendered. Lord Herschell in *Derry* v. *Peek* [82] held that a statement made "recklessly, careless whether it be true or false," is fraudulent. In *Derry* v. *Peek* and many other cases conscious dishonesty is prerequisite to fraud.[83] To the average lawyer as well as to the layman the word fraud connotes consciousness of the falsity of representation or the lack of genuine belief in the truth of a representation. If a person says he knows a statement is true when he merely believes that it is probably true, he has not the sort of belief which would remove his case from the realm of consciousness of false representation.[84]

If the scope of fraud be held to include innocent negligence, the decisions would run counter to logic and the common understanding of the mass of mankind as to the meaning of fraud. It would also follow that an accountant's liability to third parties for negli-

---

[82] 14 App. Cas. 337.

[83] Samuel Williston, "Liability for Honest Misrepresentation," 24 *Harvard Law Review* 430.

[84] F. H. Bohlen, "Should Negligent Misrepresentation Be Treated as Negligence or Fraud?" 18 *Virginia Law Review* 706, 712 (1932).

gence in rendering service which results in gratuitous statements to third parties would be treated like that arising from negligence in the course of service performed for compensation, for, if the defendant be guilty of fraud, it is immaterial whether the service be gratuitous or for compensation. And finally, if the third party's action against the defendant public accountant for mere negligence be treated as fraud, the defense of contributory negligence on the part of the third party plaintiff will not be available to the defendant, for contributory negligence is never allowed as a defense where the defendant is guilty of fraud.

The Negligence Formula as a Mode of Extending the Public Accountant's Liability to Third Parties for Mere Negligence

If the ambit of the liability for mere negligence be extended so as to make the public accountant responsible to third parties, it will be necessary to define the limits of such liability; and unless some limitation be placed upon such liability, an honest blunder on the part of the public accountant might subject him to liability to an indeterminate number of third persons. No such onerous burden should be imposed by the courts so long as the public accountant's fees remain anything like as low as they are today. The public accountant's liability for mere negligence might well be limited to those third persons who, the public accountant knows, will use his statements as a basis for entering upon transactions with his client. Furthermore, it would seem fair for the courts to require on the part of the public accountant a less degree of care in rendering gratuitous service to third parties than that owed to his client who pays for the accountant's service. And finally, the public accountant would have available the defense of contributory negligence.

No case has ever extended the ambit of negligence so as to make the promisor of a contract liable to third parties in general, i. e., to incidental beneficiaries of the contract. The New York court of appeals has rendered two decisions which tend in that direction. *Glanzer* v. *Shepard*,[85] the first of these two cases, was reviewed in the *Ultramares* opinion. In that case the defendant, a public weigher,

[85] 233 N. Y. 236, 135 N. E. 275 (1922).

had agreed with the seller of beans to weigh the beans and render certified copies of weights to both the seller and buyer. The seller paid for the service. The public weigher was negligent in the performance of his undertaking; and as a result of such negligence the buyer sustained losses. In an action brought by the buyer against the public weigher the court held the defendant liable for negligence. There was almost a contractual relation between the defendant and the third-party buyer of beans. Though the services were paid for by the seller, they were for the benefit of both seller and buyer. Furthermore, the defendant intended that his representations should be relied upon by the particular plaintiff. This holding certainly restricts the defendant's liability for an honest blunder in making a positive statement of fact to a determinate lot of third parties. If the public accountant's liability for negligence in making positive statements of fact be limited to third parties who, the accountant intended, should use and did use the false statements, such liability would not exceed that imposed upon the public weigher in the *Glanzer* v. *Shepard* case.

In the other case, the Celotex Company, a manufacturer of insulating material for hot and cold air ducts, negligently made false representations to some engineers that the celotex material was fit for insulating hot and cold air ducts. The engineers bought some of the celotex material from a middleman and used it in the reconstruction of a heating system for the owner of a house. The engineers represented to the house owner that the material was fit for use in the reconstruction. Due to defects in the heating system as reconstructed by the engineers the house burned; and the owner brought suit against the engineers for negligently recommending the use of celotex material in his heating system. The defendant engineers made a motion to bring in as party defendant, and to take judgment over against, the Celotex Company. While the court refused to take judgment over against the Celotex Company, under a New York statute designed to prevent circuity of action, because of the lack of identity of the Celotex Company's representations and those of the engineers, the court did rule that the Celotex Company would be liable to the engineers for the loss resulting from the false representations of the Celotex Company. The most significant portions of the opinion follow: [86]

"* * * In other words, the only representations made by the Celotex Company were that 'celotex' was an insulating material fit for the covering of hot air and cold air ducts and was better than other insulating materials. The defendants (engineers) do not say that 'celotex' was recommended to them as fit for insulating the ducts and pipes designed and planned by these engineers. The complaint says that the engineers claimed that 'celotex' was not inflammable and was an adequate insulator for hot air ducts and pipes as planned and designed by them. * * *

"* * * There is no claim in this complaint that the 'celotex' manufactured by the company was defective or improperly manufactured or inherently dangerous. The cause of action, if any, is rather based upon the recent doctrine of negligence in the spoken word and liability for carelessness in making statements upon which others were expected to rely and upon which they did act to their damage. A negligent statement may be the basis for recovery of damage. * * *

"The recommendations relied upon by the defendants in this case do not amount to warranties, as there was no sale. No purchases were made of the Celotex Company by the defendants or their agents. Therefore, any express or implied warranty is not in the case. The utmost that has been pleaded are recommendations or representations, statements, carelessly and negligently made, upon which recommendations the engineer defendants acted, it is said, to their loss. We think that if the Celotex Company recommended to the engineers 'celotex' as a fit and proper covering for the duct and pipes as used and planned for the plaintiff's house in New Jersey, or for such a like or similar use, and the defendants acted upon the representations and statements, and will suffer damage in consequence, that then the Celotex Company may be liable for its careless and negligent words and representations, if, in fact, they are false and untrue."

In the Nichols case the misrepresentations were spoken directly to the ones injured (the engineers); hence, the court did not determine the manufacturer's liability, if any, to parties to whom such misrepresentations might be repeated by the engineers. There was no contractual relation between the engineers and the Celotex

---

[86] *Nichols v. Clark, MacMullen & Riley*, 261 N. Y. 118, 184 N. E. 729 (1933).

Company; but the Celotex Company intended that the engineers should rely upon its negligent representations, and the Celotex Company expected that it would be benefited, as it was, through increased sales from the representations. It would seem that the Celotex Company's liability would not have been different had it made those same representations in writing and handed the writing to a dealer of the celotex material with the intention that the dealer should give the writing to the particular engineers in order to get the engineers to rely upon the representations and purchase celotex material, as the engineers did. This last situation would be analogous to the case where an accountant sent his negligent audit report to his client with the intention that the client should give the report to a particular third person in order that the third person might use the report. In this case the auditor would not only have intended that the third person should rely upon his report, but would have expected a benefit from the third person's use of the audit report, because such use would have been an inducement to the client to employ the auditor.

The chief value of the *Nichols* case to the public accountant lies in the fact that "the recent doctrine of negligence in the spoken word and liability for carelessness in making statements upon which others were expected to rely and upon which they did act to their damage" was adopted by the New York court of appeals. With such a doctrine courts could keep within the bounds of conservatism and establish a rule making the defendant public accountant liable to third parties for honest but negligent misrepresentations where the statements were intended by the accountant for specific third parties even though not delivered directly to them. Where the public accountant knew that his client would pass a copy of the audit report to a particular third party for that third party's use, and such third party did use the negligent report to his loss, the public accountant should be deemed to have intended that the third party should rely upon his audit report.

Let us turn now from that phase of the negligence formula which limits liability to the particular persons who, the defendant intended, should rely upon his statement, to that limitation of liability arising from the fact that the defendant's service to the plaintiff was gratuitous but coupled with a benefit. No court has decided whether the defendant is liable for misrepresentation of a financial matter given gratuitously but negligently.[87] There is a dictum in *Glanzer* v. *Shepard,* supra, to the effect that there would be no such liability. However, in the *Nichols* case the representations were made not purely as a gratuity. The manufacturer expected an ultimate benefit from the representations concerning the insulating material, in the way of sales through middlemen handling that product. Likewise, the public accountant derives an ultimate benefit from the use of his statements by third parties. Without the use of such statements by third parties clients would have little need of employing auditors to prepare statements of their business enterprises.

Logically, then, what degree of care should be required of the public accountant rendering a gratuitous service coupled with a benefit? In the lending of a chattel as a pure gratuity the owner is bound only to warn of hidden defects of which he knows. If the owner of the chattel is paid for its use by the borrower, the owner must exercise reasonable diligence to discover the condition of the chattel and is liable for injuries caused by defects of which he should have known. It would seem that if the owner should lend a chattel as a gratuity but coupled with a benefit, the owner would owe some duty to the borrower to discover and report to him defects. From this analogy, then, it would appear that the public accountant for a gratuitous service coupled with a benefit should exercise some care to ascertain the truthfulness of his positive statements of fact. The public accountant would not owe to the third party for a gratuitous service coupled with a benefit as high a degree of care and skill as that owed to his client for "paid-for" service; yet, he would owe to such third party a duty to exercise some degree of care and skill to ascertain the truthfulness of his accounting certificate. It would seem that the public accountant's duty to the third party—to exercise some care in rendering a gratuitous service, coupled with a benefit, to determine the accuracy of the statements—should apply merely to the public accountant's

[87] F. H. Bohlen, "Should Negligent Misrepresentation Be Treated as Negligence or Fraud?" 18 *Virginia Law Review* 707 (1932).

positive statements of fact. It would seem that as long as the public accountant merely expressed his opinion in respect to the results of his audit, he should not owe in the way of ascertaining the accuracy of such opinion any duty to third parties for gratuitous service even though coupled with a benefit. Thus, where public accountants were employed to do less than a detailed audit they could free themselves from liability to third parties by merely making their certificates in the form of opinion. Unless the public accountant can in some way restrict his liability to third parties he will be reluctant to undertake any audit less than a detailed audit.

The usual tort defense of contributory negligence would be another antidote to the fear of extending too far the public accountant's liability for negligence, by including a duty owed to third parties to exercise care and skill in the preparation of an audit. There has been no case holding that where a misstatement is merely negligent the plaintiff is barred by his failure to use obvious means to determine its accuracy.[88] The reason is probably due to the failure of many courts to distinguish clearly between deceit and negligence in making a positive statement of fact, for contributory negligence has never been a defense to an intentional injury.[89]

By restricting the public accountant's liability to such third parties as those who, the public accountant intended, should use the statements; by limiting the degree of care owed such third parties when the service was gratuitous but coupled with a benefit, and by making available the defense of contributory negligence, it would seem that there is no basis for the fear of extending too far the public accountant's liability for mere negligence in making positive statements of fact. The public accountant's liability for an honest blunder in certifying merely his opinion as to the results of his audit should not extend to third parties. The expression of opinion should put third parties on notice that they should be cautious in the use of the statements, and at the same time the public accountant would be free to undertake audits involving less than a complete review of all the records.

[88] F. H. Bohlen, "Misrepresentation as Deceit, Negligence, or Warranty," 42 *Harvard Law Review* 733 (1929).

[89] Harry M. Harrington, "Torts—Liability for Negligent Language," 12 *Texas Law Review* 72 (1933).

The recent doctrine of liability for negligence in making statements upon which others were expected to rely and upon which they did act to their damage is sound in principle and will probably produce the most satisfactory results that can be reached. The negligence formula will take the place of the action of deceit in cases based upon honest but negligent misrepresentations. The action of deceit will still be available where there is consciousness of wrongdoing on the part of the defendant. However, it may well be expected that the courts will be slow in adopting the new doctrine of negligence.

VII

CRIMINAL LIABILITY OF THE PUBLIC ACCOUNTANT FOR FRAUD

Case Law on the Public Accountant's Liability for Fraud

An exhaustive search has revealed not a single American case in which a public accountant has been held liable in a criminal suit for fraud. An English case furnishes a precedent.

In 1931 the central criminal court (Old Bailey) of London, England, a court of first instance, tried on criminal charges of fraud [90] the chairman and the official auditor of the Royal Mail Steam Packet Company.[91] Lord Kylsant, the chairman of the company, was sentenced to imprisonment for one year; and his conviction was upheld by the English court of criminal appeal.[92] Morland, the company auditor, was acquitted in the central criminal court.

The *Royal Mail Steam Packet Company* case has attracted worldwide interest. The company was one of the largest and most important in England; it was a holding company of some thirty-five leading shipping companies of the kingdom. The auditor charged was a partner of one of the largest firms of accountants in the

---

[90] The criminal charges of fraud were brought under a statute which made it a criminal offense for an officer of a company to perpetrate fraud upon shareholders or investors of the company.

[91] *Rex* v. *Kylsant and Morland, The Accountant*, London, 1931, volume 85, p. 109.

[92] *Rex* v. *Kylsant*, 48 T. L. R. 62, 23 criminal appeal reports 83.

LIABILITY FOR NEGLIGENCE, FRAUD AND LIBEL 101

world.[93] Some of England's greatest legal talent was involved in the case. As a matter of furnishing a legal precedent for the accounting profession it is unfortunate that the auditor's case did not reach the English court of criminal appeal. However, the case is valuable for the light thrown upon the accountant's legal duties in respect to the form and content of accounting reports and the nature of secret reserves. Only that portion of the trial having to do with Morland, the company auditor, is given here.

It was alleged in the charges against Morland that he was guilty of fraud in certifying false financial statements of the Royal Mail Steam Packet Company for the years 1926 and 1927, whereby the company chairman, Lord Kylsant, was enabled to sell a large issue of the company's debenture stock to stockholders and the general public at a price greatly in excess of their true value.

Quite in harmony with the usual English accountancy practice, the statements in question consisted of a balance-sheet in the form of an account, with the liabilities and proprietorship appearing on the left and the assets on the right side. Just below the balance-sheet columns followed the certificates of Lord Kylsant and Morland respectively. Following these certificates was a brief profit-and-loss account in which the distribution of profits was placed on the left and the incomes on the right side of the account. The alleged fraud resulted from the showing of some surplus reserves on the right side of this profit-and-loss account under such titles as would lead stockholders and the public, it was alleged, into believing such surplus reserves were current income items for the years 1926 and 1927. Thus, it was claimed, the chairman, Lord Kylsant, was able to show prospective purchasers large operating incomes rather than huge losses for the years 1926 and 1927 and to effect the sale of a large issue of the company's debenture stock.

The facts as presented by Sir William Jowitt, attorney-general, were in substance as follows:

The Royal Mail Steam Packet Company experienced a period of unusual prosperity during the world war. It was during this period

[93] Henry Morgan, "The Auditor's Responsibility in Relation to Balance-sheet and Profit-and-loss Accounts," *International Congress on Accounting*, 1933, London, Gee & Co., p. 11.

that many reserves were built up and expanded beyond the needs for which they were set aside. Among these was a large excess-profits reserve which was not needed for taxes after 1921. A war contingency reserve was created to cover possible claims of officers for the differences in the salaries the company had been paying regularly and the salaries such officers were receiving while they were in the British navy. This claim never materialized. It had been the practice of the company during the war to write off excessive depreciation charges. Many of the company's ships were destroyed; and the insurance money received for the losses far exceeded the book value of such ships. This excess provided another earned-surplus reserve account. Another large earned-surplus reserve was that for income taxes, the amount of which continued to be augmented after 1921, when losses were being sustained and no taxes were being paid to the government, by making deductions from dividends and carrying such deductions into the income-tax reserve account. An idea of the magnitude of all these earned-surplus reserves may be obtained from the fact that their amounts ranged from £725,000 to £1,600,000 for 1921.

Said the attorney-general, Sir William Jowitt, "To give the R. M. S. P. Co. a good showing in its profit-and-loss account for 1921, bonus stock was issued by the subsidiary companies over several years. There was nothing improper, but it was utilizing for one year's purpose something which in the very nature of things did not relate only to that year, except that it was paid in that particular period."

An actual operating loss of £135,000 was sustained in 1922; but by including in the profit-and-loss account some non-recurring income items a net profit of £725,000 was shown. These non-recurring income items were made up of a total of £860,000 from the special earned-surplus reserves and profit on the sale of steamers.

In the year 1923 there was transferred from the special surplus-reserve accounts into the profit-and-loss account total credits amounting to £800,000 so as to turn a net loss into a profit of £779,114 for the period. This particular item in 1921 and 1922 had been called "profit for the year"; but in 1923 it was called "balance for the year."

LIABILITY FOR NEGLIGENCE, FRAUD AND LIBEL 103

A similar showing was made for 1924. Reserve credits amounting to £870,000 were transferred to profit-and-loss so as to change an operating loss into a "balance for the year including dividends on share in allied and other companies, less depreciation, etc.," of £772,829.

During 1925, beside the usual reserves which were transferred to profit-and-loss, non-recurring profit resulting from the excess of receipts from the winding-up of one of the subsidiaries over the holding company's book value of its investments in the subsidiary was shown as a part of the profit-and-loss. The profit-and-loss account for 1925 showed "balance for the year, including dividends on shares in allied and other companies, adjustment of taxation reserves, less depreciation of fleet, as £731,103."

In 1926 the profit-and-loss account showed as such a credit of £150,000 taken from the surplus-reserve accounts. But there was one credit entitled, "Balance for the year, including dividends on shares in allied and other companies, adjustment of taxation reserves, less depreciation of fleet, etc." of some £439,212. This item of £439,212 resulted from a current net loss of £272,000 and a transfer of £711,212 from the surplus-reserve accounts. The auditor certified that he had compared the statements with the company books, and that in his opinion the statements were properly drawn and gave a correct view of the state of the company's affairs as shown by the books of the company.

A similar report was prepared by Mr. Morland for 1927.

The prosecution contended that the reports for 1926 and 1927 were misleading to the average investor and that the auditor who approved them was criminally liable for fraud.

Justice Wright's summing-up is reported in part as follows:

"* * * Then there was the question of the auditor. The law required the appointment of an auditor who was the servant of the company, and his duty was to report on the accounts which the directors were going to present to the shareholders. The law did not impose an impossible burden on auditors. It did not make them insurers; it did not require skill and vigilance beyond their power, but it did require from the auditor a careful examination of the accounts and for him to give a certificate saying that the accounts had been properly drawn up so as to exhibit a true and correct view of the state of the company's affairs, according to the best of his knowledge and the information given to him.

"* * * If the accounts on which the dividends were being paid or the expenses were being met were being fed by undisclosed reserves, it seemed very difficult to see how an auditor could discharge his duty of giving a true and accurate view of the state of the company's affairs without drawing attention to that fact, which was vitally important. No doubt an auditor in his delicate duties had to use a certain amount of discretion, but he had to remember that he was under a statutory duty and that he might come under the penalties of the law if he failed in that duty in any specific way.

"* * * In the present case the jury would remember that they were not dealing with a company to which the companies act applied, but with one which was formed as a corporation and had the privilege of limited liability, the corporation being governed by the terms of a royal charter. The Royal Mail Steam Packet Co. was a very old one, having been formed in September, 1839, and there were certain conditions which governed the keeping of accounts; prior to the annual meeting a report had to be prepared and the assets and debts of the corporation set out for the purposes of the meeting. The directors also had to give such other information to put before the shareholders as might seem necessary, and the accounts had to be signed by one of the auditors of the corporation. That was an obligation on the court of directors to prepare and lay before the meeting in each year an account of the debts and assets of the corporation and an account of the profits made every year. In 1904 it was decided to alter certain conditions, because in the old days the auditor was not a professional auditor but perhaps a member of the company. Then professional auditors were appointed, but that did not alter the provision requiring the directors to give an account of the profits which had been earned. The law provided that the auditor had to sign a certificate stating whether his requirements had been complied with and to make a report on the accounts and then to state in that report whether in his opinion the report was properly drawn up.

"The profit-and-loss account contains information for the benefit of the shareholders. We are not concerned with the question of policy, as to whether a dividend is properly or improperly declared, but if there is something in the accounts to which the attention of the shareholders should be drawn, the question at issue is whether that information is correctly given. * * *

"* * * So far as I know, in those charters there is no provision for the maintenance of any secret reserve. There may be, but it has not been pointed out to me, and I have been unable to discover it. The question to be decided here is not whether the two defendants or either of them has committed any breach of his duty to the company, either as chairman or as auditor, but whether he has committed a breach of this section (meaning section 84 of the larceny act of 1861).

"If there has been any breach or negligence of anything for which the directors or auditor may be liable to the company, that is a matter entirely beyond your (the jury's) purview or consideration. You are not here dealing with questions of civil liability, for civil liability can be settled by action for damages. But when a matter comes before this court, it comes as a matter of criminal liability; it comes before this court because something has been done, some breach of the law which goes beyond the purview of civil liability, which may not be answered by damages, but which amounts to a crime against the state and for which there is provided for the party convicted an appropriate sentence by the court. One sometimes hears it said in a criminal case that questions of public policy, questions of public morality, questions, it may be, of financial purity are involved, but these are not questions which you have to decide in arriving at your decision. You have to decide on the facts and on the evidence in this special case, and therefore those considerations to which I have referred are not your considerations.

"The section involves three things, a false written document, knowledge of the falsity—that means the recognition, the understanding, the realization of the falsity by the person who publishes it and puts it forward—and thirdly, the intent to deceive. The intent to deceive is quite a separate thing. You may have a false document, and you may have published it knowingly, and yet there may not be circumstances which justify the finding that there was an intent to deceive. In fact, in one of the sections under the new act—I think it was in one of the earlier companies acts as well—you have a definition of the offence or misdemeanor, of publishing a false document, knowing it to be false, but with no reference to the intent to deceive. It is left out, just as in some other criminal offences, the intention is not a necessary ingredient.

"Here the intention to deceive is a necessary ingredient as regards a man who deceives shareholders, and in regard to a prospectus to deceive a possible investor. * * *

"Here again, in the case of Mr. Morland, the jury must be satisfied that the statement which he signed was false, and false to his knowledge, was published by him with knowledge of its falsity, with an appreciation of its falsity, and with the intention that it should deceive the shareholders.

"There were many differences, of course, on any view of the case, between Mr. Morland's position and that of Lord Kylsant. Mr. Morland was an accountant and the auditor of the company. He had the accounts put before him, but not until they had passed the court of directors. He had nothing to do with the preparation of the accounts and nothing to do with the declaration or decision to declare dividends. He had nothing to do with the general policy of the company. He had no knowledge—except incidentally with regard to the Meat Transport—of the subsidiary companies and their position. All he knew was the dividends which from time to time he had to deal with as representing the profits coming from those companies. He had, so far as could be seen, no motive at all for deceitful intention.

"But, of course, it might be said against Mr. Morland that he did in fact add the sanction of his name as auditor to a document which, taking those two years 1926 and 1927, was false and misleading. As he had pointed out in another connection, however, it was not a question of whether or not Mr. Morland did something less than what could be expected as the full duty of a conscientious, careful auditor. He had to come honestly, according to his skill and understanding, to the conclusion that the accounts of the company presented a true state of the company's accounts. That was what he signed—that it was a true and correct view of the company's affairs. If he was not satisfied that he could give that certificate, his duty was either to qualify that certificate or to ask to have the accounts altered in such a way that he could sign them without qualification. It was obvious enough that in the year 1926, when the accounts for 1925 were being dealt with, he was not satisfied with the position, because he thought that some words ought to be added to intimate to the shareholders that moneys which were being used were being used in order to produce the balance which appeared. That being so, it was admitted that without some qualification in some form or another, he ought not to give a certificate, and the qualifications which he put in were those words which the jury must almost be tired of hearing about—adjustment of taxation reserves. Those were the words which Lord Plender had turned into plain English.[94] Mr. Morland had said that that had satisfied his doubts. He thought then that he had done enough to cure the defective character of the balance-sheet and profit-and-loss account with those words. If he was right in that, if he discharged his duty sufficiently and properly, it seemed that in any view of the matter, there was an end of the case against him, and he was not guilty. If on the other hand he was wrong in this sense, that in a civil action against him for not showing due care and skill, he would be held liable as a defendant because he had broken his duty and had not discharged his office, then again his liability would be a civil liability. That was assuming against him that he ought to have done something else and taken some more drastic, some more effective steps in order to bring to the mind of the shareholder the true position of the company's affairs. It might be that he did not discharge his duty sufficiently and properly. It might well be that an auditor in his position, standing as he did between the directors and the shareholders, to protect the interests of the shareholders against any possibility of their being misled by the directors —it might well be that he took an imperfect view, an inadequate view of the very grave duties which rested upon auditors.

"The profession of accountancy, as you know, is very distinguished and very honourable, and a very essential profession in the commercial affairs of this country. Great trust must be reposed on the skill and the judgment and the honor of accountants. It may well be that on occasion, through error of judgment, one of them may fail to do all that the requirements of his high office demands. But again we are not concerned here with any question of civil liability or breach of duty. What you have to determine is whether, assuming that Lord Kylsant was guilty of the offence, there was any deliberate and conscious act on the part of Mr. Morland in carrying out that design by putting his hand to a certificate which he knew was not justified by the facts and he knew did not correspond with his duty.

[94] Note: Lord Plender, internationally known public accountant, testifying as an expert witness said: "The definition of 'adjustment' is this: The difference between the sum or sums reserved or set aside to meet maturing obligations whose precise ascertainment is not known at the time such provisions are being made, and the amount of the actual liability when it is ascertained and settled."

"The prosecution alleged that the true and accurate view of the state of the company's affairs was not given. Did Mr. Morland know that, and did he give the statement which had been published currency and validity by means of his certificate, and did he do so with criminal and wicked intent?

"Three accountants had said in the witness box that they *would* have signed the certificate in the same form. He supposed that they would say that they would do so, in the same circumstances as Mr. Morland. It might be so, or not, he did not know. He was quite sure that they believed what they had said, but that did not relieve the jury of deciding whether the certificate was one which Mr. Morland ought to have signed if he really appreciated his duty. They would have to say to themselves did he appreciate that he was doing something wrongful, or did he honestly believe that he had discharged his duty by putting into the balance-sheet those mystic words?

"Supposing that Mr. Morland honestly thought that that was enough, the jury on any view of the case would not find him guilty of fraudulent intent. However mistaken a man might be, however unfortunate the consequences of his mistake might be, that did not constitute a criminal offence or criminal intent.

"He had looked through Mr. Morland's evidence very carefully and he did not know that he could help the jury by going through it at any further length. They would recollect that Mr. Morland did not dispute that he was not satisfied with the accounts for 1925 in the form in which they were presented to him."

Mr. Morland was acquitted; Lord Kylsant was sentenced to imprisonment for one year.

In the *Royal Mail Steam Packet Company* case it was held that a company auditor was not guilty of fraud under an English statute providing for criminal punishment of company officers who have committed fraud upon stockholders or investors in the company, where the auditor had merged surplus reserves into the current profit-and-loss account under the caption "Balance for the year, including dividends on shares in allied and other companies, adjustment of taxation reserves, less depreciation of fleet, etc.," and stockholders had sustained losses as a result of relying upon the statement of profit-and-loss. The court applied the orthodox test of one element of fraud, namely, consciousness of wrongdoing and found that the auditor did not have, at the time of the preparation of the audit, knowledge that laymen would be deceived by the sort of report he made.

The court was apparently correct in finding no fraudulent intent on the part of the auditor. The court was also correct in the dicta holding that the auditor was guilty of negligence. It certainly ought to be the duty of an auditor to show plainly on his reports what the figures represent.

THE PUBLIC ACCOUNTANT'S CRIMINAL LIABILITY FOR FRAUD UNDER STATUTES

Nearly half of the states of the union have statutes making public accountants liable criminally for fraud.[95] In Texas the public accountancy statutes limit such liability to certified public accountants.[96]

A public accountancy statute of Arizona is typical of such state laws. The Arizona statute follows: [97]

> "If any person practising in this state under this act as a certified public accountant or a public accountant, or who is in the practice of public accountancy as a certified public accountant, or a public accountant or otherwise, shall wilfully falsify any report or statement bearing on any examination, investigation or audit made by him, or under his direction, he shall be deemed guilty of a misdemeanor, and upon conviction thereof shall be punished by a fine of not less than three hundred dollars, nor more than one thousand dollars, or shall be imprisoned in the county jail for a term of not less than three months nor more than one year, or by both such fine and imprisonment for each time he may so have falsified such report, statement or audit."

The United States securities act of 1933 also provides for the criminal liability of accountants and other persons who have been wilfully guilty of misrepresentation relative to the registration

---

[95] *Certified Public Accountant Laws of the United States,* American Institute Publishing Co., Inc., New York, 1930.
[96] Ibid.
[97] Laws of Arizona, regular session 1933, chapter 45, section 8.

statement of an issuer of securities. Section 24, which was not amended in 1934, reads as follows:

"Any person who willfully violates any of the provisions of this title, or the rules and regulations promulgated by the commission under authority thereof, or any person who willfully, in a registration statement filed under this title, makes any untrue statement of a material fact or omits to state any material fact required to be stated therein or necessary to make the statements therein not misleading, shall upon conviction be fined not more than $5,000 or imprisoned not more than five years, or both."

A public accountant may be criminally liable under the United States securities exchange act of 1934 for having willfully made a false representation of a material fact in the balance-sheets and profit-and-loss statements filed with the securities and exchange commission pursuant to the provisions of the act. Section 32 of the act reads as follows:

"Any person who willfully violates any provision of this title, or any rule or regulation thereunder the violation of which is made unlawful or the observance of which is required under the terms of this title, or any person who willfully and knowingly makes, or causes to be made, any statement in any application, report, or document required to be filed under this title or any rule or regulation thereunder, which statement was false or misleading with respect to any material fact, shall upon conviction be fined not more than $10,000, or imprisoned not more than two years, or both, except that when such person is an exchange, a fine not exceeding $500,000 may be imposed; but no person shall be subject to imprisonment under this section for the violation of any rule or regulation if he proves that he had no knowledge of such rule or regulation."

As long as the public accountant acts with honest intentions he need have no fear of punishment for misrepresentation under the state and federal statutes.

Chapter II

LAW AND THE CERTIFIED PUBLIC ACCOUNTANT'S CERTIFICATE

Issuance of Certified Public Accountant's Certificate

In a broad way the statutes of the District of Columbia and the forty-eight states set forth the requirements for the issuance of the certified public accountant's certificate, namely, the training and experience prerequisite to the examination and the fields covered in the examination. However, in the main the requirements for the certified public accountant's certificate are left to the discretion of the board of public accountancy. In a number of jurisdictions cases have arisen in which the courts have defined the powers of the board of public accountancy. Under appropriate topics those cases are discussed in this chapter.

Among our American decisions only one appeal case deals directly and exclusively with the power of the board of public accountancy to lay down rules for the issuance of the certified public accountant's certificate. That case arose in 1925 in the appellate division of the supreme court of New York.[1] The court upheld the rule of the regents of the University of the State of New York [2] requiring applicants for the certified public accountant's certificate to have had at least two years of accounting practice under the employ of a certified public accountant. A portion of the decision reads:

"'The regents have the right to make and interpret their own rules. The court can not, in construing the regents' rules, in effect, pre-

[1] *Davis* v. *Sexton,* 207 N. Y. S. 377, 211 App. Div. 233.
[2] Note: Chapter 261, article 57 of the laws of New York, 1929, provides for the creation of the board of certified public accountant examiners. This board is appointed by the board of regents of the university of the state of New York. Though it is the function of the board of certified public accountant examiners to carry on the practical conduct of examinations, whatever rules may be established by this board are subject to the approval of the board of regents of the university

scribe a different rule from that duly enacted by the regents. If the conduct of the regents in the application of this rule to the petitioner's case has not been arbitrary and capricious, surely the court can not command the issuance of a certificate. The power to fix the professional requirements has been granted to the regents by the legislature. The rule has been uniformly applied. The rule itself as interpreted by the regents is not arbitrary and capricious. It has a basis in reason. The reason assigned by the regents is that the integrity and high standard of the group of public accountants who are to be certified by the regents as worthy of this honorable rank in their profession, justifies the test of a substantial period of experience as an employee of one who has been certified and who will feel a personal and professional responsibility as the employer of such candidate. A coëmployee has no such direct responsibility for the character and quality of the candidate's work and has no power to select him or discharge him. Proper supervision and training of the candidate are more likely to be secured if the employer is a certified accountant for the reason that 'he is responsible professionally as well as personally for the acts of the candidate and is bound to exercise a much greater degree of supervision than would be exercised by any mere employee. His own self-interest demands it.' These are the reasons for the rule assigned by the regents in their opposing affidavits. We accept them as true and reasonable."

The fact that the candidate for a certified public accountant's certificate had worked two years under the supervision of two coemployees who were certified public accountants, the supreme court of New York held was not sufficient to comply with the regents' rule that the candidate must have had two years of practice in the employ of a certified public accountant. Neither the rule nor the requirement of strict compliance with the rule was unreasonable in the opinion of the court. The court took the position that rules for the issuance of a certificate are technical and should, as long as such rules do not appear to the court to be unreasonable and arbitrary, be left to the discretion of those responsible for the issuance of the certificate. The court, also, required uniformity of application of the rules. Were the rules not uniformly applied, persons discriminated against would in effect be deprived of the right to pursue an honorable profession, and the favored few would be given a virtual monopoly on the practice of public accountancy. The sanction of such a condition would clearly be violative of the due process and equal protection clauses of the federal and state constitutions.[3] The fourteenth amendment to the constitution of the United States provides: "Nor shall any state deprive any person of life, liberty or property without due process of law; nor deny to any person within its jurisdiction the equal protection of the laws." The discrimination could not be upheld under the state's police power since the effect of the discrimination would not be in the interest of the public welfare.

While *Davis* v. *Sexton* is the only American case dealing with the statutory power of a public accountancy board to lay down reasonable rules for the issuance of a certified public accountant's certificate, the opinion is consistent with the reasoning set forth in other cases dealing with the powers of accountancy boards to carry out their duties. The logic of the case is sound; and doubtless the case will be followed in future decisions in similar circumstances.

Recognition of a Certified Public Accountant's Certificate Issued by Another State or a Foreign Country

The District of Columbia and nearly all the states of the union have placed within the discretion of their respective state boards of public accountancy the power to register the certificate of any certified public accountant who is the lawful holder of a certified public accountant's certificate issued under the laws of another state, provided the state that issued the original certificate grants similar privileges to the certified public accountants of the registering state. A few states extend that reciprocal recognition to foreign countries.[4]

Several court decisions have been rendered, defining the public accountancy statutes of some of the states, and laying down the attitude of the courts toward recognition of the certified public accountant's certificate which has been issued by another state or a foreign country.[5]

[3] Willoughby on the *Constitution*, volume II, sec. 759.

[4] *Certified Public Accountant Laws of the United States,* American Institute Publishing Co., Inc., New York, 1930.

[5] Note: For the power of a board of public accountancy to refuse to register certified public accountants' certificates from other states that do not recognize

The supreme court of North Carolina in 1926 rendered such a decision.[6] The plaintiffs in this case, *Respess* v. *Rex Spinning Company*, were certified public accountants of Georgia but not of North Carolina. In Atlanta the plaintiffs entered into an auditing contract with the agents of the defendant corporation of North Carolina. The plaintiffs assigned a senior accountant and several others to the task of preparing the working papers from the records at the defendant's mill in North Carolina. After spending several weeks on this job the senior accountant and his staff returned to Atlanta with the audit "in the rough with pencil." The reports were made up in Atlanta. The plaintiffs later brought an action to recover compensation for their services. The defense was set up that the plaintiffs were unlawfully holding themselves out as certified public accountants in North Carolina and also were doing business in North Carolina without having obtained the legally required licence. (It is a well-settled principle in the law of contracts that an agreement is unenforceable if made in the course of transactions which are prohibited unless the required licence is obtained.) A portion of the opinion reads:

> "* * * C. S., 7008 et seq. section 7023, provides that if any person shall practise in this state as a certified public accountant without having received such certificate he shall be guilty of a misdemeanor; and section 7020 defines a public accountant as one 'actively engaged and practicing accounting as his principal vocation during the business period of the day.' The revenue act, schedule B, imposed on public accountants the sum of five dollars as a licence tax for the privilege of carrying on their business and made it unlawful for any person to carry on any business for which a licence was required without having the licence or a duplicate thereof in his actual possession at the time. Laws 1921, ch. 34, secs. 31, 88; laws 1932, ch. 4, secs. 29, 95. * * * It is no doubt true that as a rule a contract will not be enforced if it rests upon a consideration which contravenes good morals, public policy or the common or statute law. * * *
>
> "To practise a profession or to carry on a business usually signifies the regular pursuit of such profession or business as an occupation—

certificates issued by the board see *Goldsmith* v. *Clabaugh* (1925) 55 App. D. C. 346, 6 F. (2d) 94.

[6] *Respess* v. *Rex Spinning Company*, 133 S. E. 391, 191 N. C. 809.

to make a practice of it or actively to engage in it customarily or habitually. This is not without exceptions. As the legislature may prohibit a general practice until prescribed conditions are complied with, it may attach the same conditions to a single transaction of a kind not likely to occur otherwise than as an instance of general practice. * * *

"In these circumstances we are of the opinion that the plaintiffs did not practise or carry on the business of certified public accountants in this state within the meaning of the statutes. To carry on the business of a public accountant or to practise as a certified public accountant is much more than is implied in the series of detached acts done by the plaintiff's representatives in acquiring information upon which to base their report. We are the more inclined to this view because the statutes are penal and should be construed strictly against the offender and liberally in his favor. * * *"

The question under consideration in *Respess* v *Rex Spinning Company* was whether the preparation of working papers meant the practice of public accounting under the North Carolina statute, which prohibited the practice of public accounting without the required licence, and the practice of public accounting as a certified public accountant without proper registration with the board of public accountancy of North Carolina. The court held that a single instance, a single audit, would constitute practice of accounting, but that preparing merely the working papers in North Carolina did not amount to practice of accounting in that state. Every trained accountant knows full well that the collection of data known as the accountant's working papers does not require as high an order of skill as does the rendition of the audit reports. The working data, though indispensable, are only a part of the practice of public accountancy.

Only one other American case deals with the question of whether the preparation of working papers constitutes practice of public accounting, *Haskins & Sells* v. *Kelly,* 93 P. 605, 77 Kan. 155. The *Haskins & Sells* v. *Kelly* case held that merely preparing working papers in Kansas was not doing business in that state. Doubtless the courts in similar circumstances will follow these precedents in the future.

The public accountancy statutes of the remaining states and the District of Columbia are similar to those of North Carolina in requiring a certified public accountant of another state to register as such with the public accountancy board of the state into which the accountant comes to practise as a certified public accountant. It follows from the decision that the preparation of working papers only does not constitute the practice of public accounting, that under the present statutes of the states and the District of Columbia a certified public accountant of one state may, without obtaining recognition of his certificate from the board of public accountancy of another state, be permitted as a certified public accountant to prepare working papers, and nothing more, for clients in such other state. This privilege would not be altered by the fact that after the certified public accountant returned to his office in the state where his certificate was registered he made up the audit reports and certified them in the capacity of a certified public accountant.

The matter of recognition and registration of a certified public accountant's certificate was set forth in 1927 for the state of Louisiana in the case of *Thoman* v. *State Board of Certified Public Accountants* as follows: [7]

"(Quoting from the Louisiana statutes) 'The state board of certified public accountants may, in its discretion, register the certificate of any certified public accountant who is the lawful holder of a certified public accountant's certificate issued under the law of another state, * * * provided that the state issuing the original certificate grants similar privileges to the certified public accountants of this state. * * *'

"All that we mean is that the board must treat alike all applicants similarly situated and may not arbitrarily discriminate between them.

"Relator alleges that he is the lawful holder of a certificate as certified public accountant issued to him by the state of Mississippi; that the state of Mississippi recognizes and registers similar certificates issued by the state of Louisiana; that he presented his said certificate to the defendant board and made application to it to recognize and register the same; that the board denied his said application without giving any reason for its said refusal; wherefore he prays that a

[7] 113 So. 757.

mandamus issue commanding said board to recognize and register his said certificate.

"* * * Moreover, defendant * * * stands squarely on the proposition that relator has no right of action because the board may 'in its discretion' refuse to register any such certificate for any reason or for no reason at all. And that proposition, as we have said, is unsound."

In 1931 the supreme court of Louisiana in reviewing the retrial of *Thoman v. State Board of Certified Public Accountants* further defined the powers of the state board of public accountants:[8]

"* * * On the other hand, we have no right to substitute our judgment for that of the board of certified public accountants, as to whether the relator is worthy of a C.P.A. certificate. All that we have to decide in such cases is whether the board discriminated arbitrarily against the applicant for a certificate, or exercised its discretion fairly and impartially. Whether the board's judgment was exercised wisely or unwisely is not for us to decide. * * *"

Thoman v. State Board of Certified Public Accountants holds that a statute which gives power to the board of certified public accountants to register, in its discretion, certified public accountants of other states is limited to reasonableness. The statute, in itself, was held valid; but the board was not allowed, in the application of the statute, to refuse to register a certificate on purely arbitrary and whimsical grounds under the cloak of acting within its discretion.

In reviewing acts of administrative boards, courts inquire into the reasonableness, and not the wisdom, of such acts. Under the police powers of a state statutes may expressly or impliedly grant authority to the public accountancy board to refuse to recognize all certified public accountants' certificates issued in another state. Such a policy on the part of the board might be unwise because of retaliations; yet, because of the reasonableness, and the uniformity of the application of the rule, courts would not interfere.

The *Thoman* case is in accord with the weight of authority on the rule that under the due process and equal protection clauses of

[8] 172 La. 262, 134 So. 85.

our constitutions an administrative board can not perform its duties in an arbitrary and discriminative manner.[9]

Another Louisiana case, *Eberle v. State Board of Certified Public Accountants*,[10] decided in 1930, deals with the powers of a public accountancy board to refuse to register a certified public accountant's certificate issued by another state. In this case the plaintiff, a resident of New Orleans, held a certified public accountant's certificate from the state of Mississippi, and made application for the registration of his certificate with the defendant board of Louisiana. The defendant board refused to register the certificate on the ground of moral unfitness of the applicant. Mandamus proceedings were instituted to compel the defendant board to register the certificate. The supreme court held:

"* * * The legislature has seen proper to create the board and to vest it with the power to determine to its satisfaction whether the applicant for a certificate as a certified public accountant, or simply as a public accountant, possesses the required qualifications, including the qualifications of good moral character. When the qualification of the applicant as to good moral character is regularly determined, and in determining it he is not deprived of his legal rights or of the law of the land, the ruling of the board is final, and its finding of fact must be considered correct, for it is not the courts that are vested with the power to determine whether in truth the applicant's character is good, but it is the board that is vested with that power, and it is only upon legal questions involved that the appeal lies to the courts. Under the clear wording of subsection 1 of section 2 of the act, unless the applicant satisfies the board of his good moral character, he is not entitled to the certificate."

Quite in agreement with the *Thoman* case, *Eberle v. State Board of Certified Public Accountants* held that moral unfitness of the applicant was a sufficient reason for refusing to register a certificate issued in another state. The power to determine facts, such as the moral fitness or the skill of the applicant, is a prerogative of the board rather than of the court. The courts will not interfere with actions of the board as long as the ruling of the board does not

[9] Willoughby on the *Constitution*, volume II, sec. 759.
[10] 171 La. 318.

deprive the applicant of his constitutional rights. The holding of the *Eberle* case is consistent with the other cases in point.

An important case, *James v. State Board of Examiners of Public Accountants*,[11] relating to the registration of a certified public accountant's certificate came before the supreme court of South Carolina. In this case the plaintiff, a non-resident of South Carolina, was a certified public accountant of Georgia, Tennessee and North Carolina. The plaintiff made application to have his certificate registered with the state board of examiners of public accountants of South Carolina. His application was rejected mainly because the plaintiff did not maintain an office in South Carolina. In regard to the plaintiff's petition to compel the state board of examiners of public accountants to issue plaintiff a certificate the court held:

> "Our examination of the statutes fails to disclose any requirement contained therein that a non-resident certified public accountant, properly qualified in all other respects to practise the profession, must maintain an office in this state. It appears, therefore, that the respondents have placed an additional requirement upon non-residents which is not in harmony with statutory provisions. We do not regard this additional requirement as a reasonable one. A certified public accountant may do his work without the necessity of maintaining an office of his own in South Carolina. In fact, his work is most usually done at places of business of his clients.
>
> "The purposes of the statutes under consideration, as we view them, were to protect real certified public accountants from the competition of persons engaged in accounting business who were not certified public accountants, and to protect the people generally from having audits made by persons who were not certified public accountants when it was desired to have such audits by only that class of accountants. We find nothing in the law which would justify us in holding that a non-resident certified public accountant, duly qualified in all respects to practise his profession in our state, must actually maintain an office in South Carolina. If the statute had a requirement of that kind therein, it might result in a holding that the enactment contravened the provisions of the constitution of the United States for the reason that it discriminated against citizens of the United States who happened not to be residents of this state. * * *"

[11] 155 S. E. 830.

James v. State Board of Examiners of Public Accountants held that the requirement that a non-resident certified public accountant must maintain an office in South Carolina in order to qualify for registration as a certified public accountant in South Carolina was unreasonable, arbitrary and discriminative. This decision is unquestionably fair. If public accountants doing interstate business could not gain recognition of their certificates in other states without maintaining offices in such other states, interstate practitioners would have an unreasonable burden placed upon them. The requirement laid down by the board was certainly unreasonable and arbitrary, and hence violative of the due process and equal protection clauses of our constitutions.[12] The opinion is in harmony with the well-recognized rulings on the point.

Had the requirement that non-resident accountants maintain offices in South Carolina in order to obtain recognition of their certificates been statutory rather than a rule of the public accountancy board, doubtless the statute would have been held invalid for the same reasons that the administrative rule was not upheld.

ILLEGAL ISSUE AND ILLEGAL ASSUMPTION OF THE CERTIFIED PUBLIC ACCOUNTANT'S CERTIFICATE OR MEMBERSHIP IN AN ESTABLISHED ACCOUNTING FRATERNITY

In both England and the United States the law is well established that a person can not falsely hold himself out as being a certified public accountant or a member of a professional accounting organization.

In the English case, *Society of Accountants and Auditors* v. *Goodway and London Association of Accountants, Ltd.*,[13] the chancery division held:

"So far as I am aware, there is no case, and no case has been cited to me, in which the question has been decided whether an incorporated body, such as the society here, can be regarded as suffering a legal injury by reason of a person who is not a member of that body representing himself to be a member of it; but a case of that nature did come before the court of session in Scotland in *Society of Ac-*

[12] Willoughby on the *Constitution*, volume II, sec. 759.
[13] (1907) W. N. 45, (1907) 1 Ch. 489.

countants in Edinburgh v. *Corporation of Accountants, Ltd.,* 20 R. 750. * * * The plaintiffs were three chartered societies of accountants in Scotland, one in Edinburgh, one in Glasgow and one in Aberdeen. Their members were accustomed to use as their professional designation the letters 'C. A.' after their names, indicating 'chartered accountants.' It was established that those letters, when used after a person's name, denoted that the person so using them was a member of one or other of those three societies. The defendants were a limited company called the Corporation of Accountants, and (and this was the point) used the letters 'C. A.' as an abbreviation of 'corporate accountant.' The lord ordinary and the lords in the inner house unanimously came to the conclusion that the chartered societies were entitled to prevent the defendants from using the letters 'C. A.' or any similar designation which would lead people to believe that they were members of one or other of those chartered societies.

"* * * In the case before me there seems to be little difficulty in coming to that conclusion, for the reason that it is established by evidence that membership of the society confers a status, a valuable privilege, on its members. It is, therefore, a matter of pecuniary interest to the society that it should have as many members as possible. Obviously the possession of this definite status arising from the fact of membership is an inducement to persons to become members, and anything which would reduce the value of that status would tend to remove some of the inducements which would actuate persons in becoming members of the society. Looked at in that way, it seems to me that the society has a pecuniary interest in preventing persons who are not its members, and are not entitled to the status which its membership confers, from representing that they are its members and are entitled to that status. It seems to me, therefore, both on the authority of the case to which I have referred and on principle, that the unauthorized use of the designation 'incorporated accountant' representing, as on the facts I think it does, that the person using it is a member of the society, does inflict a legal injury on the society, in respect of which it is entitled to relief."

In the *Society of Accountants and Auditors* v. *Goodway and London Association of Accountants, Ltd.,* case the chancery division of England upheld an injunction to restrain an accountant from using a title which would lead the public to believe that he was a member of the Society of Accountants and Auditors when, in fact, he was not. The reason given for the court's decision was purely on the grounds of protecting the financial interests of the Society of Accountants and Auditors. The chief income of this society was derived from membership fees. Hence, practice such as the false assumption of membership in the society would make less desirable membership in that honorable body and in that way reduce the volume of membership fees. It was impossible to make an accurate measure of damages in the continuous false assumption of membership in the Society of Accountants and Auditors, hence equity proceedings became available.

In 1918 the chancery division of England in the case of the *Institute of Chartered Accountants in England and Wales v. Hardwick* [14] upheld an injunction to prevent an accountant who had been expelled from the Institute of Chartered Accountants in England and Wales from representing himself through the use of letter-paper headed "Honors, final, Institute of Chartered Accountants" to be a member of that professional accountants' organization. The injunction in this case was sustained in order to protect the Institute of Chartered Accountants from damage resulting from the expelled member's representing to the public that he was still a chartered accountant.

While the injunctive process against persons falsely assuming the certified public accountant's degree or membership in a professional accountants' organization has never been sought in the American appeal courts, the controlling principles in the two English cases are sound; and it is most probable that the injunction may be granted in similar circumstances in our American courts, wherever it can be shown that the criminal statutes on the point do not afford an adequate remedy.

The statutes of the forty-eight states and the District of Columbia make it a criminal offense for a person who has not received a certified public accountant's certificate from the state board of public accountancy or who has had his certified public accountant's certificate revoked to hold himself out to the public as a certified public accountant by the use of the letters, "C. P. A.," "C. A.," or

[14] 34 T. L. R. 584, 62 S. J. 702.

similar letters, or by any other device.[15] The penalty is generally a fine, not exceeding two hundred dollars, or imprisonment for one year, or both.

The passage of these statutes forbidding the unfair assumption of the certified public accountant's designation was not accidental. The illegal issuance of the certified public accountant's degree was flagrantly practised by the National Association of Certified Public Accountants, Incorporated, Washington, D. C. In 1923 the story of the debacle was graphically revealed by Chief Justice Smyth of the District of Columbia court of appeals in the case of the *National Association of Certified Public Accountants* v. *United States* [16] as follows:

> "In its brief the corporation admits it was formed under section 599 of the code of the district. This section authorizes citizens of the United States, a majority of whom being also citizens of the district, who desire to associate themselves for benevolent, charitable, educational, literary, musical, scientific, religious or missionary purposes, and societies formed for mutual improvement or for the promotion of the arts to form a corporation by filing in the office of the recorder of deeds a certificate in writing, which shall state the name adopted, the term for which the corporation is organized, its particular business and objects, and the number of its managers for the first year of its existence. There is nothing in the section which says that the corporation thus formed shall have the power to confer degrees, or admit its members to degrees, or to issue to its members a certificate pertaining to degrees. No mention whatever of the degrees is made in it. The certificate, however, which was filed by the organizers of the corporation, provides that when the members of the corporation shall present 'satisfactory evidence of knowledge in the theory and practice of accounting, and shall have satisfactorily passed the prescribed qualifying examination of the association', the corporation shall have power 'to admit said members to the degree of certified public accountant, and to issue to such members the association's formal certificate to that degree pertaining.' The corporation claims the right to do these things, and admits that it has done them in many instances.

---

[15] *Certified Public Accountant Laws of the United States,* American Institute Publishing Co., Inc., New York, 1930.
[16] 292 F. 668, 53 App. D. C. 391.

"According to the bill the corporation admitted one of its members to the degree of certified public accountant (usually indicated by the letters 'C.P.A.') on his own unsupported statement as to his qualifications, without any instruction or examination by the corporation or any of its representatives. Persons residing in California, desiring to test the methods employed by the corporation, presented to it an application for a certificate as a certified public accountant in the name of one Duarfy. The certificate was issued on the recommendation alone of persons wholly unknown to the corporation. Later it developed that Duarfy existed only in the minds of those who had arranged the test. In other words, he was a fictitious person. Other instances are given in which the corporation granted degrees without any examination or test of the applicant. All these allegations are admitted by the answer. In no place does the answer assert that any other or different test of an applicant's fitness for a degree was employed by the corporation. * * *

"It is urged that, because the corporation provided, in the certificate which it filed with the recorder of deeds, that one of its purposes was to admit members to the degree of certified public accountant and to issue certificates to that effect, the corporation has the power to do these things. But this can not be admitted. By making the statement in the certificate it did not acquire a right not granted by the section. It might have taken less than the section gave, but not more. The section measures the maximum power which a corporation organized under it can exercise. * * *"

The injunction against the issuance of certified-public-accountant certificates by the National Association of Certified Public Accountants was upheld for two reasons:

(1) In America a corporation has no powers but those expressly conferred on it, and such incidental powers as may be reasonably necessary to carry those expressly granted into effect.[17] Even a power granted in a charter, not expressly provided in a statute, will not be upheld, unless such power is reasonably necessary to carry out the powers expressly conferred by statute. In this case the power to grant degrees was not expressly conferred by the statutes under which the defendant was incorporated. Furthermore, it was not reasonably necessary for the defendant to confer degrees in order

---

[17] *Thomas* v. *Railroad Co.*, 101 U. S. 71, 82, 25 L. Ed. 950.

to carry out the powers expressly authorized by the statutes under which the defendant corporation was created.

(2) Even where a corporation has a power expressly granted by statute the corporation will not be permitted to abuse such power. Selling degrees for ten dollars each, as was done in this case, would certainly be an abuse of the power to confer educational degrees.

The two controlling principles upon which the case was decided have been evolved to protect the public from corporate abuses. These principles are supported by the great weight of American authority.[18]

A short time before the District of Columbia court of appeals granted a permanent injunction prohibiting the National Association of Certified Public Accountants from conferring degrees, the supreme court of New York permanently enjoined the National Association of Certified Public Accountants from conferring certified public accountants' or similar degrees in the state of New York, and laid down the following rule in the case, *People* v. *National Association of Certified Public Accountants:* [19]

> "It is entirely clear from sections 80 and 81 of the general business law above quoted, that no person may hold himself out as a certified public accountant, or use the abbreviation 'C.P.A.' or any similar words, letters or figures to indicate that the person using the same is a certified public accountant, except upon the authorization of the regents of the university of the state of New York.

While at common law an injunction may not be granted in the interest of the public welfare where a criminal statute prohibits the wrongful act, in the present case the National Association of Certified Public Accountants was enjoined from conferring degrees under a New York statute which provides for the use of the injunctive process to restrain an unlawful act. The court definitely established that it is a misdemeanor under the statutes of New York not only for anyone except the regents of the University to confer the certified public accountant's certificate, but also for anyone to hold himself out as a certified public accountant in New York except upon the authorization of the regents of the university

[18] *Independent Medical College* v. *People*, 55 N. E. 345, 346, 182 Ill. 274.
[19] 197 N. Y. S. 775, 204 App. Div. 288.

(board of certified public accountant examiners under authority of the regents of New York university). It was stated by the court that the activities of the National Association of Certified Public Accountants were in opposition to the educational policy of New York. It is apparent that to permit a foreign corporation or anyone else to practise the abuses exemplified in the operations of the National Association of Certified Public Accountants would foster the perpetration of deceit upon the uninformed public. The holding of this case is based upon reason and justice and is supported by a number of cases involving similar facts.

In 1923 a member of the National Association of Certified Public Accountants advertised himself in the city of New York as a "Certified public accountant, (N. A.)." In a criminal prosecution of this member, the court of special sessions of the city of New York held that such an act renders the wrongdoer punishable for misdemeanor.[20]

During the year 1924 two cases came before the Texas court of criminal appeals, in which the defendants were charged with unlawfully advertising themselves as certified public accountants.[21] The defense in each case was that the defendant was a member of the National Association of Certified Public Accountants, Incorporated, Washington, D. C. The convictions were upheld.

In view of the fact that over twenty-five hundred persons obtained their certified public accountant's degree from the National Association of Certified Public Accountants chiefly through the payment of a ten dollar fee, it is surprising that not more cases arose for litigation.[22]

Another case involving the false issue of the certified public accountant's certificate came before the supreme court of North Carolina. The North Carolina state board of accountancy shortly after the world war adopted the practice of holding its regular certified public accountants' examination in Raleigh and two weeks later holding a duplicate examination in Washington, D. C. for the convenience of North Carolinian applicants who were in Wash-

[20] *People v. Marlowe*, 203 N. Y. S. 474, 40 N. Y. Cr. R. 448.
[21] *Henry v. State*, 260 S. W. 190, 97 Tex. Cr. R. 67. *Crow v. State*, 260 S. W. 573, 97 Tex. Cr. R. 98.
[22] *Nat. Ass'n. of C. P. A.s v. U. S.*, 292 F. 668, 53 App. D. C. 391.

ington. As a matter of fact, North Carolinians traveled from Raleigh to Washington to take the duplicate examination. The supreme court of North Carolina in this case, *McCullough* v. *Scott*,[23] enjoined the state board of accountancy from holding its certified public accountants' examination outside the state of North Carolina. A portion of the opinion reads:

> "The state in the lawful exercise of its police power has created the state board of accountancy and required examinations of applicants to safeguard the public against incompetent accountants. Every citizen of the state is in a certain sense injured when the duties of the board are performed in such a manner as to let down the bars and lower the standards of the profession. There is an especial injury to properly accredited members of the profession who have met the conditions imposed by law, in the manner prescribed by law. Poor Richard says, 'He who hath a trade hath an estate.' A man's profession is his capital. The state has set standards for entrance into this profession, and those who have entered in the manner prescribed by law are entitled to the protection of the state to the extent, at least, that they shall not be unjustly discriminated against by admission of others into the profession in any other way than that prescribed by law."

In *McCullough* v. *Scott* the court based its judgment largely on three principles:

(1) That the state board of accountancy was a quasi-public corporation and was prevented from holding its examinations in Washington under a state statute which makes ultra-vires acts of corporations illegal.

(2) That the giving of examinations was not a mere incidental or ministerial duty such as might be delegated by the state board of accountancy to others, but was a judicial or quasi-judicial duty required to be performed by the members themselves. Hence, the board was not permitted to hold its examinations outside North Carolina for the reason that by well-settled law the place of sitting of a court must be limited to the territory of its jurisdiction.

(3) That the act of the board in letting down the bars to the issuance of certificates was detrimental to the interests of the public and the certified public accountants who had met the legal require-

[23] 109 S. E. 789, 182 N. C. 865 (1921).

ments for their certificates. It is well-settled law that an abuse of discretionary power of a public officer, resulting in favoritism to a few and discrimination against others is contrary to the due process and equal protection clauses of our constitutions.

The principles set forth in the present case are supported by the great weight of authority.[24]

Another case, *State* v. *De Verges*,[25] involving the false assumption of the certified public accountant's certificate, arose in Louisiana. The supreme court of that state in 1923 held:

"It is important to note that the law does not purport to prevent or punish the practising of accountancy without a licence or certificate from the board, but only the holding of one's self out to the public as possessing the certificate which it is authorized to issue under the provisions of the act, the practising as a certified public accountant, and the using of the abbreviation 'C.P.A.', or similar letters or designation, to deceive the public into believing that the person so acting is a certified public accountant under the law, without first undergoing the examination by the state board of accountants as required by said statute and otherwise complying therewith. In other words, any one is at liberty to practise as an accountant, notwithstanding this law, so long as he does not represent himself to be a certified public accountant, as defined thereby, or use the abbreviation 'C.P.A.' or similar letters or device to indicate that he is a certified public accountant.

"It is true that neither morals, health nor safety of any one is jeopardized by the practising of this profession, public accounting, however incompetent a person may be, but the power of the state in matters of this sort is not confined to professions involving such consequences. It may also act whenever the general welfare requires to protect the public in the skilled trades and professions against ignorance, incompetence and fraud."

State v. *De Verges* held that the state was in the lawful exercise of its police power in prohibiting the false assumption of the certified public accountant's designation. In the interest of public welfare a state is empowered to protect the public from ignorance, incompetence and fraud resulting from the false assumption of the certified public accountant's title.

[24] Willoughby on the *Constitution*, volume II, sec. 759.
[25] 95 So. 805, 153 La. 349, 27 A. L. R. 1526.

Liability of a Publisher Who Falsely Advertises One as a Certified Public Accountant

Only one American case, *Goldsmith* v. *Jewish Press Publishing Company*,[26] deals with the publisher's responsibility for falsely advertising a person as a certified public accountant. This case, decided by the New York supreme court in 1922, set forth dicta to the effect that under the New York penal law relating to untrue and misleading advertisements a publisher is an accessory to a misdemeanor if he publishes, after notice, an advertisement which falsely represents one as a certified public accountant.

This New York case was not a criminal action. Had it been, the publisher, who printed the advertisement falsely representing the accountant as being certified, doubtless would have been held criminally liable.

The public accountancy statutes of the District of Columbia and all of the states of the union are silent on the liability of a publisher who prints a false advertisement of a public accountant. It is probable, however, that the general statutes covering false advertisements would in most of the other jurisdictions of our union, as in the state of New York, make it a misdemeanor for a publisher to advertise falsely for any one the certified public accountant's title.

In the present case a public accountant certified in New York sought to enjoin the defendant publisher from publishing the false advertisement. The court refused to uphold the injunction because the plaintiff had not showed any financial loss as a result of the false advertisement. It is a fundamental rule in equity that an injunction restraining a criminal act will never be given merely because the act would be a crime.[27] Protection of the public from crimes by punishment under the criminal law is the normal and usual means by which organized society guards against the antisocial conduct of its members. But where the criminal law will not afford an adequate relief a court of equity will enforce the injunction.

Though the legal principles upon which the case is founded are sound, it seems that the judge underestimated the financial loss that

[26] 195 N. Y. S. 37, 118 Misc. Rep. 789.
[27] Walsh on *Equity*, sec. 39.

may come to bona-fide certified public accountants as a result of competitors' falsely holding themselves out as certified public accountants. Proof of substantial competition between the plaintiff and the accountants whose false advertisements were printed should be sufficient grounds for restraining the publisher from continuing the false advertisements. It is quite conceivable that a fine assessed upon the publisher may not be sufficient to cause him to discontinue the printing of the false advertisements.

The court's interpretation of the New York penal law making it a misdemeanor to publish untrue and misleading advertisements is correct. But courts in the future should allow the injunction to prevent the publication of advertisements falsely representing persons as certified public accountants where the only evidence of financial loss sustained by the plaintiff is proof of substantial competition between the plaintiff and the accountants falsely advertising themselves as certified in the area of competition.[28]

CANCELLATION OF A CERTIFIED PUBLIC ACCOUNTANT'S CERTIFICATE

All the states and the District of Columbia provide in their statutes for the cancellation of the certified public accountant's certificate by a governmental body of properly constituted authority. Most of the states vest that power in the board of public accountancy, a few in the state university, some in the courts of competent jurisdiction and others in the governor.[29] The usual provision is for the revocation to be effected upon proof of bad moral character, dishonesty, conviction of crime, incompetency or unprofessional conduct.

Court decisions have upheld the statutes empowering the state board of public accountancy to revoke certified public accountants' certificates. In 1922 the supreme court of Alabama was asked to grant an injunction in the case of *Lehmann* v. *State Board of Public Accountancy*[30] to prevent the Alabama state board of public

---

[28] Note: For a treatment of the ethics of professional advertising by the public accountant, see, on pages 226 and 227, sections 11 and 12 of the "rules of professional conduct of the American Institute of Accountants."

[29] *Certified Public Accountant Laws of the United States*, American Institute Publishing Co., Inc., New York, 1930.

[30] 94 So. 94, 208 Ala. 185. (Affirmed by United States supreme court, 44 S. Ct. 128, 263 U. S. 394, 68 L. Ed. 354.)

accountancy from hearing charges preferred by other public accountants against one Lehmann, a certified public accountant. The injunction also sought to prevent the board of public accountancy from cancelling Lehmann's certificate. The court held:

> "* * * Hence there is no equity in the bill, for the reason that a court of equity will not enjoin a board or commission vested with quasi-judicial and administrative authority from acting as to matters within their jurisdiction and power merely because it is apprehended that they may decide erroneously. This is not a bill to restore to complainant his right to a certificate or licence of which he has been unlawfully deprived, nor to compel the issuance to him of a licence or certificate to which he is entitled, but it is, essentially, a bill to prevent the hearing of charges preferred against complainant."

In *Lehmann* v. *State Board of Public Accountancy* the court held that by the same authority—police power—under which the state made provision by statute for the issuance of the certified public accountant's certificate the state was justified in making provision by statute for the cancellation of certificates so issued. The court held that the complainant accountant could not accept the benefits of the public accountancy statute without bearing the burdens or inconveniences imposed by it. The court further held that the board of public accountancy is a quasi-judicial body whose function it is to pass judgment upon the revocation as well as upon the issuance of a certified public accountant's certificate. It should be remembered that in a case such as *Lehmann* v. *State Board of Public Accountancy* the decision of the board is subject to review by the courts of the particular jurisdiction, and if the board is found to have acted arbitrarily and unreasonably, the courts will overrule the board's judgment.

That a state may enact and enforce statutes for the cancellation of certified public accountants' certificates and that a public accountancy board may sit as a judicial or quasi-judicial body are well-established laws.

The supreme court of Alabama in the case of *Miller* v. *Alabama State Board of Public Accountancy* [31] laid down the law that in a trial to revoke a certified public accountant's certificate members

[31] 98 So. 893, 212 Ala. 619 (1925).

of the state board of public accountancy can not act both as prosecutors and as judges. A portion of the opinion follows:

"For the sake of brevity, we summarize the grounds of disqualification as follows: That appellees as individuals and also as members of the social organization known as the Alabama Society of Certified Public Accountants, of which they are members, contributed money to the prosecution of the charges against appellant, then pending before the board; that they had been active, personally and professionally, against appellant and were biased and prejudiced against him; that they had theretofore taken an active part in procuring his expulsion from said Alabama Society of Public Accountants, and which expulsion appellees, sitting as members of the board, without notice to appellant, had determined was sufficient cause for revocation of the certificate; that 'one or more' members of the board had stated that, in the hearing of this proceeding against appellant, the board would revoke his certificate, irrespective of any proof or defense, and that, so far as the board was concerned, 'such certificate now stood as revoked.'

"That the rule of disqualification applicable to judges extends also to every tribunal exercising judicial or quasi-judicial functions is established by the decided weight of authority. * * *

"* * * Under the averments appellees are charged with a direct interest in the proceedings against him and are both prosecutors and judges in the same cause. The averments, for the present purposes, being considered as admitted, we think, very clearly place appellees within the influence of the rule of disqualification."

It is a well-established principle of common and constitutional law that a person who is personally interested in the outcome of a trial is incapacitated to sit as a judge in the trial.[32] Even the layman's sense of justice would be averse, it would seem, to permitting the members of a quasi-judicial board of public accountancy to sit as judges in a case which the members had been actively prosecuting.

In the *Miller* v. *Alabama State Board of Public Accountancy* case it was argued by the defendant board that the doctrine of necessity should cause the court to refuse the mandamus petition to compel the board members to recuse themselves from sitting as

[32] 15 R. C. L. 526.

judges in the trial. It is an established rule of law that the disqualification of judges must yield to the demands of necessity, as, for example, in cases where, if applied, it would destroy the only tribunal in which relief could be had. But in the *Miller* case no great necessity for a speedy settlement of the controversy existed, since the public was not primarily concerned and the appellant (accountant) could continue the practice of his profession until the legislature made provision for the appointment of new members of the board to sit in the trial.[33]

For the reasons given above, the court was justified in overruling the lower court's order sustaining the demurrer to the petition for a writ of mandamus. In other words, the court rightly held that the board members in the admitted circumstances would be disqualified to sit in the trial.

The Reissuance of a Certified Public Accountant's Certificate Which Has Been Cancelled

The states differ in their laws relative to the reissuance of the certified public accountant's certificate after the certificate has been lawfully cancelled. The statutes of Florida, Mississippi, New York and Rhode Island specifically empower the boards of public accountancy [34] of those states to issue a new certified public accountant's certificate to a person whose certificate has been lawfully revoked.[35] The requirements of reissuance are left largely to the discretion of the board of public accountancy. No cases testing these statutes have arisen.

The statutes of the great majority of the states and the District of Columbia do not specify directly the powers of the board of public accountancy to reissue a certified public accountant's certificate which has once been lawfully cancelled. One court decision, *Wright v Alabama Board of Public Accountancy*, arising under such a statute denied such power to the board.[36]

[33] 15 R. C. L. 541.
[34] The board of certified public accountant examiners through power vested in the board of regents of New York university, in the case of the state of New York.
[35] *Certified Public Accountant Laws of the United States*, American Institute Publishing Co., Inc., New York, 1930.
[36] 123 So. 33, 219 Ala. 632 (supreme court of Alabama, 1929).

"The statute clearly confers no authority on the board, either expressly or by necessary implication, to reinstate one whose certificate has been cancelled for unprofessional conduct, or to revive and restore to life a certificate so revoked and cancelled; and, if such certificate was restored to the petitioner, it would confer no authority on him to practise as a certified public accountant."

In *Wright* v. *Alabama Board of Public Accountancy* the only reason given by the court for refusing to compel the board to reissue the cancelled certificate was that the power to reissue a certificate cancelled for unprofessional conduct was not either expressly or impliedly conferred by statute. The court implied in its opinion that, if the legislature had conferred the power of reissue of a cancelled certificate upon the board, the court would have upheld the statute.

Doubtless occasions may arise in which it would be just for an accountant to have reissued to him his certificate which was cancelled for a cause that no longer exists. It is probable that the courts in states where statutes provide for the reissuance of certificates cancelled for unprofessional conduct will uphold such statutes.

RESTRICTION OF THE PRACTICE OF PUBLIC ACCOUNTING TO PERSONS WHO HOLD THE CERTIFIED PUBLIC ACCOUNTANT'S CERTIFICATE

Oklahoma,[37] Illinois[38] and Tennessee[39] have enacted public accountancy laws restricting the practice of public accounting to certified public accountants; and the supreme court of each of those states has declared such restrictive laws to be contrary to the fourteenth amendment to the constitution of the United States. The Illinois case, *Frazer* v. *Shelton,* reads in part as follows:

"* * * Throughout the history of the law in relation to accountancy in this and other states there runs a distinction between a public accountant and a certified public accountant. * * * The act under consideration here not only does not destroy that distinction, but, on the other hand, accentuates it. In the states of Louisiana, Maryland, Michigan, North Carolina and Tennessee acts have been passed pro-

---

[37] *State* v. *Riedell*, 233 P. 684, 109 Okla. 35, 42 A. L. R. 765 (1924).
[38] *Frazer* v. *Shelton*, 150 N. E. 696, 320 Ill. 253, 43 A. L. R. 1086 (1926).
[39] *Campbell* v. *McIntyre*, 52 S. W. (2d) 162, 165 Tenn. 47 (1932).

viding for the registration of accountants, both as certified public accountants and as public accountants. In none of these states, except Tennessee, is one prohibited from practising accountancy, but the certificate as certified public accountant is by the act taken as evidence of investigation and certification of certain qualifications which are not so signified by the certificate as public accountant. No one in the four states mentioned is denied the right to do accounting for as many persons as will employ him. Numerous states have likewise provided that certain audits and investigations shall be made by certified public accountants. In Massachusetts the legislature in 1921 passed an act authorizing certified public accountants, approved by the state commissioner of banks, to make audits of savings banks. Mass. gen. laws 1921, chap. 168, section 17. In Pennsylvania it is provided that certain school districts may employ certified public accountants to audit their books. Pa. laws 1925, p. 382, sections 2603, 2623. In Michigan, finance companies operating under declarations of trust are required to be examined by the state banking commissoner, who in turn is authorized to accept the report and audit of a certified public accountant in place of such examination. Mich. pub. acts 1925, p. 461.

"* * * In 1924 congress created the United States board of tax appeals * * *, authorized to adopt rules pertaining to the conduct of its business. An examination of those rules discloses that the only accountants authorized to appear and practice before those boards are certified public accountants. * * *

"The right to follow any of the common occupations of life is an inalienable right. That right is one of the blessings of liberty and is accorded as a privilege to the citizens of the United States by the preamble to the federal constitution and by the declaration of independence, under the language 'pursuit of happiness.' The right of a citizen to pursue ordinary trades or callings upon equal terms with all other persons similarly situated is a part of his right to liberty and property. * * * 'Liberty', as used in the constitution, embraces the free use by all citizens of their powers and faculties subject only to the restraints necessary to secure the common welfare. The right to contract is both a liberty and a property right. * * *

"It is, of course, well established that the right to liberty, property and the pursuit of happiness is subject to the reasonable exercise of the police power of the states. The end to be secured by the exercise of the police power is the furtherance of the public health, comfort, safety or welfare, and, unless an act restricting the ordinary occupations of the citizen can be shown to fall within the police power such act is void, as violating the right of the citizen to liberty and the pursuit of happiness. Whether or not the regulation of an occupation has in it the elements of protection to the public health, comfort, safety or welfare is a matter not always easy to determine. The question is here presented: Does the business of accounting affect the public health, comfort, safety or welfare? Unless it does, its restriction is not permitted under the constitution. It is readily seen that the profession of law, by reason of its influence on the safety of the rights of property and liberty, does affect the public welfare; that the science of medicine, surgery and other treatment of human ills or the prevention of disease directly affects the public health; and that the manner of construction of buildings may well be said to affect the public safety. What is there in the business of accounting upon which the exercise of the police power may be based? Any act of accounting, as distinguished from bookkeeping, when for more than one employer, is deemed by this act to be public accounting and may not be engaged in without the prescribed certificate. The statute in this case is not limited to those who would do an accounting business with municipalities or other public agencies; therefore the necessity for police regulation must appear, if at all, by reason of the relationship of an accountant to private business concerns by which he is employed, and thereby to the public welfare. An 'accountant,' as that term is defined by standard lexicographers, is one who is skilled in, keeps or adjusts accounts. 'Accounting' is defined as the act or system of making up or stating accounts. It is readily seen that an incompetent accountant may render an inaccurate report and cause his employer to make a business error. This creates no effect upon the public, however, unless the relationship existing between the public welfare and the private business so affected is so close as to establish that influence. Assuming that an audit shows a business failure, such failure, while by no means desirable, does not ordinarily affect the public welfare, and, if it did, it is not the work of the accountant, but the condition of the business, that bears such influence. In order to say that private business must, in the interest of public welfare, employ one certified by the state, it must appear that the effect of an audit of that business is a matter of public welfare and not of private concern. If it is the latter, the audit has no element of public welfare in it, and a law prohibiting or licensing the business of one who makes such audit is but an unwarranted regulation of private business and the right to contract. To say that private business must submit to an audit on stated occasions goes no further, in principle, than to say that private business may not employ whom it chooses to make such audit. While restrictions of such a character are imposed upon public-utility corporations by reason of the interest of the public therein, no law, so far as we are advised, has gone to the extent of attempting to so regulate purely private business. The business of accounting for private employers has in it none of the elements of a public utility. Laws passed by various states on this subject have authorized the conferring of degrees upon accountants who pass an examination or have provided for the issuance of certificates of qualification. These laws have been passed in the interest of those engaged in the business and for their protection and advantage rather than in the interest of the public welfare."

The holdings of the three cases on state statutes restricting the practice of public accounting to accountants who are certified were fundamentally the same. The conclusions of the opinions were to the effect that restrictive legislation, (1) deprived the uncertified public accountants of the liberty to choose and practise a common occupation; (2) infringed upon the right of private business interests to choose accountants to perform their auditing service; (3) was not justified by police power in that the public welfare was not promoted by such legislation.

(1) Let us consider the first of the three controlling principles of these cases. It is unquestionable that the courts were correct in their statement of our constitutional guaranties of liberty and property. In 1872 the minority of the United States supreme court in the famous slaughter-house cases [40] defined property to mean not merely physical things one might own, but one's trade, calling or the occupation which he pursues. The minority opinion also held that liberty includes one's right of choice, his right to choose a calling, occupation, trade, or the direction in which he would exercise his labor. The principles laid down in the minority holding

[40] 16 Wall. 36.

of the slaughter-house cases were later made laws in the Minnesota rate case [41] and in *Allgeyer* v. *Louisiana*.[42]

No one would argue that restriction of the practice of public accounting to those who are certified is not depriving uncertified public accountants of liberty and property without due process of law unless such restriction is justified as being in the interest of the public welfare.

(2) In regard to the courts' consideration of the right of a business to choose its auditors, it should be said that their statements of the law relative to one's right to enter into legitimate contracts are correct. The *Allgeyer* case also held that the liberty mentioned in the fourteenth amendment to the United States constitution includes the right of a person to enter into all contracts which may be proper, necessary and essential in the pursuit of his livelihood or vocation.

It can not be doubted that, under the well-settled constitutional law of the United States, the denial to private business interests of the right to choose the public accountants with whom they would contract is a deprivation of the liberty of such business operators.

(3) The statutes restricting the practice of public accounting to certified public accountants are invalid in that they deprive persons of liberty and property without due process of law, unless such statutes are justified by a lawful exercise of the police power reserved to the states.

The police power of the state is the indefinite power reserved to the state under the federal constitution to control men and things so as to protect the public peace, safety, morals, health and welfare. The interpretations of the police power change as each tomorrow offers different social, political and economic conditions.[43]

During the first seventy-five years of our national history the individualism of Adam Smith dominated political and legal thinking. The police power of the state was greatly over-shadowed by the prevailing public opinion to let every man find his own life,

[41] 134 U. S. 418 (1890).
[42] 165 U. S. 578 (1897).
[43] F. Harold Essert, *What is Meant by Police Power?* 12 Neb. L. B. 208-221.

liberty and property, and seek protection for them as best he could, with the least possible interference by the state.[43] In an effort to preserve this individualism the fourteenth amendment was made a part of the constitution. However, following the civil war the growth of population, the rise of urban life, and the industrialization of business made a greater degree of social control imperative. The changed social and economic conditions were reflected in the United States supreme court's allowing in the slaughter-house [44] and the granger [45] cases a greater exercise of the police power of the state. Until the present moment the police power of the state has continued to be broadened in its application to meet the changed political, social and economic conditions.

In a recent case, *Home Building and Loan Association* v. *Blaisdell*,[46] Chief Justice Hughes of the United States supreme court wrote the opinion which upheld the right, under the police power, of Minnesota to delay the foreclosure of real-estate mortgages. Holding that while emergency does not create power, emergency may furnish the occasion for the exercise of power, Chief Justice Hughes said, "It is manifest from this review of our decisions that there has been a growing appreciation of public needs and of the necessity of finding ground for a rational compromise between individual rights and public welfare. The settlement and consequent contraction of the public domain, the pressure of a constantly increasing density of population, the interrelation of the activities of our people and the complexity of our economic interests have inevitably led to an increased use of the organization of society in order to protect the very bases of individual opportunity. Where, in earlier days, it was thought that only the concerns of individual or of classes were involved, and that those of the state itself were touched only remotely, it has later been found that the fundamental interests of the state are directly affected; and that the question is no longer merely that of one party to a contract as against another, but of the use of reasonable means to safeguard the economic structure upon which the good of all depends."

[44] 16 Wall. 36.
[45] *Munn* v. *Illinois*, 94 U. S. 113.
[46] 54 S. Ct. 231 (1934).

In view of the business events that have transpired during the depression, in view of the widespread losses sustained by the investing public due in no small measure to inadequate and incompetent accounting reports, used as the bases for the sale of securities to hundreds of thousands of investors in every part of the nation, some means of securing more efficient public accounting services is vital to the safeguard of "the economic structure upon which the good of all depends."

The federal government has realized the great importance of the public accounting profession to the general public welfare in placing upon public accountants, in the securities act of 1933 [47] and the securities exchange act of 1934,[48] heavy penalties for preparing or certifying financial statements known by such accountants to be false. In fact, the United States government extends to certified, and denies to uncertified, public accountants the privilege of practice before the board of tax appeals.[49]

[47] See page 76 of this treatise.
[48] See page 86 of this treatise.
[49] Note: *Rules of Practice before the United States Board of Tax Appeals*, revised to Feb. 1, 1931, rule 2, admission to practice: "A register will be maintained by the board in which will be entered the names of all persons entitled to practise before the board. Corporations and firms will not be admitted or recognized.

"The following classes of persons whom the board finds, upon consideration of their applications, to be citizens of the United States, of good moral character and to possess the requisite qualifications to represent others may be admitted to practice before the board:

"(a) Attorneys-at-law ***

"(b) Certified accountants duly qualified under the law of any state or territory or the District of Columbia.

"An application under oath for admission to practice shall be addressed to the United States board of tax appeals, Washington, D. C., and must state the name, residence address and office address of the applicant, the applicant's connection as a member or an associate of any firm of attorneys or accountants, the name of any professional societies of which applicant is a member, and the time and place of his admission to the bar, or qualification as a certified public accountant. The application of an attorney-at-law shall also state whether the applicant has ever been suspended or disbarred from practice as an attorney in any court or before any department or agency of the United States. The application of a certified public accountant shall also state whether applicant has been suspended or expelled from any professional society or society of certified public accountants, whether his right to practise as a certified public accountant has ever been suspended or revoked in any jurisdiction and whether applicant has ever been suspended or disbarred from practice before any department or agency of the United States. Such application shall be accompanied by a certificate of the clerk of the court in which the applicant is admitted to practice to the effect that he has been so admitted and is in good standing; or a certificate by the proper state, terri-

The requirements for the issuance of the certified public accountant's certificate and the responsibilities attached to a continuous holding of the certified public accountant's certificate constitute a great step in the direction of securing for private businesses and the investing public alike honest and skillfully prepared accounting reports.

The cases, *Lehmann* v. *State Board of Public Accountancy*, 208 Ala. 185, 94 So. 94, *State* v. *De Verges*, 153 La. 349, 95 So. 805, *People* v. *Marlowe*, 203 N. Y. S. 474, and *Henry* v. *State*, 97 Tex. crim. rep. 67, 260 S. W. 190, cited as authority for holding invalid the restrictive statute merely stated that the statutes with which those cases were concerned dealt only with the false assumption of the certified public accountant's certificate and not with the restriction of the practice of public accounting to those certified. It can not be correctly said that these cases cited went further than to imply dicta to the effect that restrictive legislation for public accountants is invalid.

In view of the present political, social and economic conditions demanding greater control of private business, it is probable that the United States supreme court would uphold a statute restricting the practice of public accounting to those certified.

torial or district authority to the effect that the applicant is a certified public accountant in good standing, duly qualified and entitled to practise in such state or territory or the District of Columbia. Each applicant shall take an oath in the form prescribed by the board.

"The board may, in its discretion, deny admission, suspend or disbar any person who, it finds, does not possess the requisite qualifications to represent others or is lacking in character, integrity or proper professional conduct. An attorney or a certified public accountant who has been admitted to practice may be disbarred only after he is afforded an opportunity to be heard.

"The board shall have the right at any time to require a statement, under oath, of the terms and circumstances of any contract of employment of an attorney or a certified public accountant with the taxpayer he represents."

Chapter III

THE ADMISSIBILITY OF THE PUBLIC ACCOUNTANT'S EXPERT TESTIMONY IN COURT

General Nature of Expert Testimony

Before entering upon consideration of the law relating specifically to the expert testimony of public accountants, some attention may well be devoted to the general nature of expert testimony.

Whether or not one is an expert witness is a matter of degree.[1] Expertness is a result of experience. Between the extremes of a baby with practically no experience and a highly trained technician there are a great many degrees of expertness. Every one who takes a witness stand has acquired many experiences in life; he has formed concepts which make it possible for him to reach decisions as to the matter that reacted upon his senses, about which he is testifying. If the experience is one common to mankind, the witness is presumed to be able to understand the meaning of what he saw, heard, smelled, tasted or felt and can give to the court his shorthand interpretation of his sensations, that is, his mental reaction to the happening at the moment of the experience. Though the witness can not express his judgment on the main issue before the trier of facts, he, in common with all mankind, must interpret his sensations in the light of his past experience. If his experience has been that common to mankind, then the witness is presumed to be qualified to testify on an inferential fact which came into his experience. In a sense, he is an expert; but he is not the sort of expert who is required to have preliminary evidence of a knowledge, skill and technique not common to mankind.

An expert witness, in the sense the term is generally used, means one who possesses peculiar knowledge, wisdom, skill or information

---

[1] Wigmore on *Evidence*, volume I, section 555. McKelvey on *Evidence*, pp. 230-271.

in respect to a subject-matter under consideration. The knowledge and technique of the expert witness must be such as is acquired only by study, investigation, observation, practice or experience, which does not fall to the lot of mankind in general. The witness is said to be expert because he can present and interpret inferential facts involving a science or an art not known to the average juror. The expert witness is used in order to make the material under review intelligible to the jurors who are presumed to have had only the experience of men moving in the ordinary walks of life. The jurors utilize the expert's knowledge of facts and interpretations for the same reason that the business man or layman seeks the advice and aid of persons who possess special skill and technical knowledge.[2]

The qualifications of the witness to produce expert testimony should be shown by the witness's statements in response to the questioning of the proponent's counsel. The right of cross-examination of the witness to determine his qualifications to testify as an expert may be claimed by the opponent. The determination of the competency of the witness to testify as an expert is always left to the discretion of the trial judge. Appeal courts will not overrule the trial court's discretion in such matters except in extreme cases of abuse, as where it is shown that the trial judge was prejudiced.[3]

ENGLISH LAW RELATIVE TO THE ADMISSIBILITY OF AN ACCOUNTANT'S EXPERT TESTIMONY

A careful search through the issues of the English professional accountants' organ, *The Accountant*, published in London, for the years 1893 to 1933, inclusive, revealed several strong articles on the technique of rendering service as an expert witness in accountancy but not a single reference to any English statute or court decision on the subject. Likewise, an exhaustive search through the English digests of law revealed not a single case or statute on the scope of the admissibility of an accountant's expert testimony. A request

[2] Wigmore on *Evidence*, 1923, volume I, sections 555 and 556. McKelvey on *Evidence*, pp. 230-271.
[3] 22 *Corpus Juris*, p. 526, sec. 610.

was sent to the editor of *The Accountant* for a statement of the English law with respect to the admissibility of the expert testimony of an accountant. The editor of *The Accountant* graciously set forth the English law on the subject in a letter, dated November 24, 1933. A portion of the letter reads as follows:

> "In reply to your letter of November 6th, your question is a little difficult to answer as, so far as we are aware, the scope of the evidence which an accountant is permitted to give has never been legally defined, nor has there been any case on this point. As a matter of practice, however, an accountant's evidence is always admissible on any question of practice relating to the audit or presentation of accounts or on such matters as professional charges."

AMERICAN LAW RELATIVE TO THE ADMISSIBILITY OF AN ACCOUNTANT'S EXPERT TESTIMONY

No law in American jurisprudence relating peculiarly to accountants is so well defined and settled as that concerning the admissibility of the testimony of an expert accountant. More than three score of cases have included rulings on the admissibility of an expert accountant's testimony. One case dates as far back as 1854; other cases were spread sparingly from that date to 1920; then from 1921 until 1934 a great many decisions arose clarifying the law on the accountant as a witness.

The case rulings on admissibility of the accountant's testimony have grown out of both criminal and civil actions; and in these rulings no distinction is made between civil and criminal actions.

THE ADMISSIBILITY OF ACCOUNTING RECORDS AS EVIDENCE

The admissibility of an accountant's statements and schedules and also his expert testimony must necessarily be predicated upon the admissibility of the accounting records themselves as evidence in court. The law relative to the admissibility of accounting records has evolved through a steady process of growth; and to obtain a proper understanding of its present status it is necessary to follow this growth.

As early as 1600 in England traders and handicraftsmen established the custom of recording in their books (parties' account-books) evidence of sales made on account. Quite often the trader or handicraftsman failed to give customers credit for their payments and used their bookkeeping records to prove in court the claims against the customers who in fact had already settled their debts. These records were regularly admitted as evidence in court, whether the entries were made by the owner or by one or more of his clerks and whether the entrant were living or dead. To correct this abuse a series of statutes was passed in the reign of Charles I. The statutes virtually prohibited the admission of parties' account-books, i.e., books prepared by the litigant himself, as evidence.[4] The statutes were based on the theory that a man should not be permitted to make evidence for himself. It was not until the nineteenth century that parties' account-books, that is, books prepared by the litigant himself, were, by statute, made admissible evidence in England.[5]

However, in the eighteenth century the English courts held that records prepared by servants or clerks who swore under oath that they prepared the records in the usual course of business for their master were admissible evidence. The decisions also provided that, in case the clerk or servant had died, proof that the records were prepared by such clerk or servant in the usual course of the business rendered the records admissible evidence. A little later, in the nineteenth century, the general scope of the rule was enlarged so as to cover all entries made "by a person, since deceased, in the ordinary course of business," whether a person wholly unassociated with the owner or the clerk of the owner or the owner himself. This rule is universally recognized in England today.[6]

In the American colonies laws were passed making parties' account-books inadmissible evidence where the entries were made by the party himself, unless such party swore to the accuracy of the entries under oath. Such statutes made it possible for small traders to produce evidence in court, even though such traders were themselves incompetent to take the stand, by merely swearing to the genuineness of the records. The parties' account books subject to a

---

[4] Wigmore on *Evidence*, volume III, sec. 1518.
[5] Ibid.
[6] Ibid.

great many limitations are still admitted in American courts under the parties'-account-books doctrine.

The practice of admitting as evidence a litigant's accounting records prepared by third persons, such as clerks, servants or strangers since deceased was established by the American courts in the early part of the nineteenth century, following the English decisions on the point. This rule for the admissibility of a litigant's records prepared by a third person in the regular course of the litigant's business as evidence in court, rather than the rule of the parties' account-books, is generally applied today in American cases wherever the question of the admissibility of accounting records arises.

It is worth while to consider the nature of the doctrines of the parties' account-books and the third person's entries in the regular course of the litigant's business.

While in the early English law the admission of account-books as evidence was objected to on the ground that a man should not be allowed to make evidence for himself, in more recent times the usual objection to such evidence is that accounting records are past, extrajudicial, hearsay data. However, modern courts generally hold that accounting records constitute an exception to the hearsay rule of evidence. The reasons for making this exception to the hearsay rule are given below separately for the doctrine of regular entries in general and the doctrine of parties' account-books.

The regular entries in general are accepted as admissible evidence because of necessity and the circumstantial guaranty of trustworthiness.[7] Where the entrant is unavailable the records themselves may be admissible because the records are the only testimony available from the entrant.

The entrant is deemed unavailable to testify in case of: (a) death; (b) insanity; (c) illness effectively preventing attendance; (d) absence from the jurisdiction. It is held by some courts that, on the ground of inconvenience, it is not necessary in a large business to have all the employees who had anything to do with the transactions under consideration testify, but that, instead, the records verified by one employee may be admitted as evidence.

[7] Wigmore on *Evidence*, vol. III, secs. 1521-1535.

Admissibility of Accountant's Testimony 147

Practical inconvenience as an excuse, subject to the judge's discretion to require the entrant's production for cross-examination where the nature of the dispute renders it desirable, should be the guiding principle for courts to follow. In fact, statutes provide for the admission of corporation books, banker's books, hospital books, and common carrier's books as evidence without the verification of those who had to do with the records.

Beside necessity there is the circumstantial guaranty of trustworthiness which justifies the admission of regular entries in general, which, of course, are not subject to cross examination. The courts agree that: (a) the habit of making entries with regularity insures, in some degree, accuracy and honesty—it is easier to enter transactions correctly than to falsify them; (b) the entrant generally realizes that his errors or misstatements will eventually be disputed by customers or others with whom his employer deals; hence, the entrant will be inclined to make his entries correct; (c) the probability of censure from his employer is a strong deterrent to the entrant against his making erroneous records.

The circumstantial guaranties of trustworthiness may be overcome by proof of a motive to prepare false records.

The entries offered as evidence must relate to the business and must have been made in the regular course of the business—they must be a part of the system of entries. A single, isolated entry made after the books have been closed is not admissible. Whether or not an entry has been made in the regular course of the business is a matter for the trial judge to determine. An entry to be admissible must have been made at or near the time of the occurrence of the transaction. In the usual course of a business the entries are prepared contemporaneously with the transaction. In making the entries there is no limitation as to the mode of written expression. A mark or sign that is interpretable as having a definite meaning will suffice. The absence of an entry where an entry ordinarily would have been made had there been a transaction should be interpreted to mean that no transaction occurred. While in some jurisdictions the original memoranda of the transactions have been required as evidence, generally the original records, the journals, are all of the records that courts require as evidence. Some courts have allowed the ledger to which were posted the journal entries as evidence where the journals could not be produced.

The parties' account-books were made admissible evidence in exception to the hearsay rule because of necessity and the circumstantial guaranty of trustworthiness.[8] Though, under modern rules of evidence, the justification of the admission of the parties' account-books as evidence on the ground of necessity is not plausible, the rule admitting such books as evidence persists in exception to the hearsay rule. The parties' account-books were made admissible in the colonial and state courts of America to meet the needs of the early small traders who kept their own accounts and were not competent to give evidence under a rule of evidence then existing, which prevented an interested party from testifying in a trial.

The great limitations upon the use of the parties' account-books (often called parties' shop-books in legal discussion) as evidence may be recognized after a presentation of a few of the restrictive rules. The trader's own entries of cash payments or loans were not admissible because the trader could have notes or other memoranda of such transactions. A few courts have admitted such evidence under the parties'-account-books doctrine, while many other courts have admitted this sort of evidence, that is, entries of cash payments and loans recorded by the owner himself, under the doctrine of entries made in the regular course of the business, as explained above. Under the latter doctrine the regularity of the entries during the usual course of the business is the basis of the trustworthiness of the entries and is the justification of their admission. Under the parties'-account-books rule entries of a guaranty for the performance of a third person have been held inadmissible where the third person's evidence was available. Under the parties'-account-books rule an entry of a special contract was not admissible evidence where the special written contract itself was available. Also, in certain occupations the parties' account-books were not admissible evidence where better evidence could be obtained. For instance, it was deemed that pupils afforded better evidence than the schoolmaster's records. Finally, the admission of the parties'

[8] Wigmore on *Evidence*, vol. III, secs. 1536-1561.

account-books was limited to small transactions and transactions not in violation of good morals.

The rules involved in the parties' account-books doctrine were and are extremely rigid.[9] Under such rules the parties' account-books may be admissible even though witnesses of the transactions are available, and they may not be admissible even though witnesses of the transactions are not available. The admissibility of the records is not dependent upon the actual necessity of the particular case, but upon the question whether or not the case falls within the requirements of the doctrine of the parties' account-books.

In addition to the description of the parties'-account-books doctrine already presented, a consideration of some other characteristics of the doctrine is desirable. The circumstantial guaranties of trustworthiness of the party's entries in his own books are based upon the belief that regularity of habit, difficulty of falsification and fair certainty of detection will balance or outweigh his tendency to falsify his records for self-interest. Under this doctrine it is required that the entries be contemporaneous with the transactions—that the books present an honest appearance. In some states the suppletory oath that the books were correctly kept is still required by statute; while in other jurisdictions cross-examination of the litigant who prepared the books is allowed to take the place of his suppletory oath. Finally, under the parties'-account-books doctrine courts interpret an omission of an entry to mean that no transaction occurred.

Under modern legislation removing the disqualification of witnesses on account of interest in the issue, a party to a suit has been made competent to testify in his own behalf;[10] hence, there no longer exists the necessity of introducing the party's account-books prepared by himself. The party produces infra-judicial evidence himself; he is subject to cross-examination and uses his records merely to refresh his memory. In taking the witness stand the party is not now subject to all the delimitations surrounding his account books as was the case when he had to offer his own account-books

---

[9] Wigmore on *Evidence*, vol. III, secs. 1536-1561.
[10] Wigmore on *Evidence*, vol. III, secs. 1559, 1560.

as evidence because of the fact that he was not permitted to testify in his own interest.

Though it remains possible under American law, as a result of tradition, to admit as evidence parties' account-books, it is generally not wise to do so because of the many rigid limitations placed upon such evidence. The usual course of practice is to use the parties' account-books merely to refresh the memory of the party witness and thus avoid the inconveniences concomitant with the account-books doctrine. Records prepared by persons unavailable are admissible under the doctrine for entries prepared in the regular course of business, which has already been described.[11]

In the preceding pages the discussion has been concerned with the admission of the party's records as evidence to support his own case. The extent to which a party's records may be used as evidence against him or to support the cause of the opponent in the suit deserves consideration. Let us now in this consideration shift the point of view, the owner of the records becoming the party-opponent and the one seeking such records as evidence becoming the party.

During the eighteenth century the chancery of England regularly enforced what was known as a bill for discovery to require a party-opponent to produce to the court for inspection any documents containing evidence which bore on the party's case. The party was not permitted to inspect any portion of the documents not directly supporting the party's case. In other words, the party was not allowed to inspect such portions of the documents as bore solely upon the party-opponent's case. It is apparent that it was impossible in many cases to separate the information into the two classes of data. But such was the theory of the rule; and the rule was applied regularly in equity trials.

The common-law courts would not enforce the discovery of the party-opponent's records. However, a litigant in a common-law court could obtain either production or access for inspection of his opponent's records by filing with the chancery a bill for discovery. This process was long, tedious and expensive. At present statutes in England and America have extended to the litigant in a

[11] Wigmore on *Evidence*, volume III, sections 1517-1561.

civil action the same privilege of discovering the genuineness and contents of his opponent's records as may be obtained in an equitable proceeding. This privilege is allowed after the issues are joined either before or during the trial. Under authority granted by the statutes the court compels either the production or access for inspection of the party-opponent's records usually through a subpoena or the traditional order for discovery utilized by the chancery. Before the records are submitted to the party for inspection, the court determines what information may be sought by the party in establishing his own case.[12]

The party-opponent is exempt from disclosure of his records where his records contain self-incriminating evidence or certain trade secrets. The matter of privilege for an accountant's working papers would follow the principles governing the admissibility of confidential communications between accountant and client. (See page 175.)

As a result of centuries of legal conflict the principle that a witness is entitled to immunity from the production of self-incriminating evidence has become well established in the common and constitutional law of England and America. This privilege merely protects one from the disclosure of his privately owned records by means of a legal process against him as a witness. If through a subpoena or any other order of the court in a process treating one as a witness it is sought to compel an ordinary witness or a party-witness to produce his privately owned accounting records the tendency of which is self-incriminatory, the witness may have full protection in refusing to give up custody of the records. By virtue of the testimonial process the witness would at any time be liable to take oath to the identity or authenticity or origin of the accounting records. The oath in such circumstances would violate the privilege of immunity from self-incriminating testimony. Hence, the courts deny such evidence produced through any testimonial compulsion. But, on the other hand, if the accounting records are obtained, not through a testimonial process, but through any means, legal or not legal, the records may be used to incriminate the ordinary witness or the party-witness, provided the proof

[12] Wigmore on *Evidence*, volume III, secs. 1857-1861, and volume IV, sec. 2219.

of their identity, authenticity or other circumstance affecting them is made by other persons, without any employment of the accused's oath or testimonial responsibility.[13]

Records of the government and accounting records of corporations and banks are not deemed privately owned records of the officers of such institutions and can be produced in court, where removal from the institution is not prohibited by statute, even by testimonial process to afford evidence against accused officers. Even where removal is prohibited by statute, courts will enforce the testimonial process to gain access to the records of such institutions. It has been held that where it can be shown that records nominally belong to a corporation but in reality belong to an officer of the corporation such records may be withheld by an accused corporate officer against a testimonial process.[14]

Courts in England and America generally allow to a limited degree freedom from disclosure of private trade secrets. The private secrets which are protected by the privilege of non-disclosure in court may be the chemical and physical composition of substances, the mechanical structure of tools and machines, names of customers and the subjects and amounts of expense. In order that the freedom from disclosure of trade secrets may be obtained the exigency of secrecy must be made particularly plain to the court. Generally, the privilege is allowed only when the disclosure of the secret facts is merely a subordinate means of proof as compared to the other available evidence in the case. Often the disclosure is restricted to the judge or his delegate; and in this way a fair degree of protection is obtained. Where full disclosure of trade secrets appears to the judge as being indispensable to the ascertainment of truth, revelation is generally required. The principles governing the privilege of trade secrets apply to the production or access to accounting records as well as to other documents and testimonial evidence.[15]

[13] Note: A much criticized minority holding has broken away from the long-settled fundamentals, and has held that the party whose documents were obtained by illegal search has a right to obtain their return by motion before the trial, *Weeks* v. *U. S.*, 232 U. S. 383, 34 Sup. Ct. 341 (1914), *Flagg* v. *U. S.*, 233 Fed. 481 (1916). The *Flagg* case applies specifically to books and papers.
[14] Wigmore on *Evidence*, vol. IV, secs. 2250-2265.
[15] Wigmore on *Evidence*, vol. IV, sec. 2212.

Admissibility of an Expert Accountant's Statements and Schedules of Voluminous and Multifarious Books

In 1854 the supreme judicial court of Massachusetts held, as admissible, evidence consisting of summary statements of accounting records in the case of *Boston & Worcester Railroad Corporation* v. *Dana* [16] in the following language:

> "The defendant further objects that schedules, made from the original papers and documents previously proved in the case, showing certain data and results obtained therefrom, and verified by the witness by whom they were prepared, were improperly admitted. But it appears to us that questions of this sort must necessarily be left very much to the discretion of the judge who presides at the trial. It would doubtless be inexpedient in most cases to permit ex-parte statement of facts or figures to be prepared and submitted to the jury. It should only be done where books and documents are multifarious and voluminous, and of a character to render it difficult for the jury to comprehend material facts without the aid of such statements, and even in such cases they should not be admitted, unless verified by persons who have prepared them from the originals in proof, and who testify to their accuracy, and after ample time has been given to the adverse party to examine them and test their correctness. Such was the course pursued in the present case, and there can be no doubt that, in a trial embracing so many details and occupying so great a length of time as the case at bar, during which a great mass of books and documents were put in evidence, it was the only mode of attaining to an intelligible view of the cause before the jury."

In the *Boston & Worcester Railroad Corporation* v. *Dana* case the court held that, because of the need of presenting to the jury an intelligible view of multifarious and voluminous accounting records, summary statements and schedules of such records were admissible as evidence provided the persons who prepared the statements and schedules verified their accuracy and provided the adverse party had ample time and opportunity to examine and test the accuracy of the summaries. Apparently there is no American authority in conflict with the principle of this case. Much of the language of the case has been appropriated in more than a

[16] 67 Mass. (1 Gray) 83.

score of the cases cited in the succeeding pages of this chapter. A holding almost identical was rendered in 1930 by the Ohio court of appeals.[17] Without question the principle of the above case may be accepted as established law.

Admissibility of Expert Testimony of an Accountant

In 1899 the rule in *Boston & Worcester Railroad Corporation* v. *Dana,* supra, was broadened by the supreme court of California in the case of *Crusoe* v. *Clark* [18] so as to make admissible the testimony of an accountant who has summarized the records in question.

The American courts are uniform in holding that an accountant's expert testimony is admissible. A clear justification of the rule was set forth in 1932 by the supreme court of Mississippi in the case of *Crawford* v. *State* [19] as follows:

> "An elemental requirement in the production of evidence is that it shall be intelligible to the triers of the facts and to the person being tried; and the further requirement is that it shall be definite and that the right of cross-examination shall be preserved. Moreover, the production must be in such a state of preparation as to expedite the trial and prevent trespasses upon the time of courts and juries. It follows, therefore, that, when intricate accounts and voluminous business records are to be inquired into and the facts upon particular issues said to be disclosed by said records are to be adduced in proof, it must be done by way of the previous preparation, by a competent person, of definite and pertinent schedules, tabulations, or other suitable and practical compilations, and the person who has made the compilations must be introduced as a witness, so that the records in evidence may be explained and the pertinent parts thereof definitely and cogently pointed out, and so that cross-examination may be permitted to search into the soundness of the compilations or schedules and of a reasonable compliance with the foregoing requirements, a pile of books of account will prove no more in law than, as a practical matter, they have disclosed in a concrete and definite form to the minds of those who are to determine the issue or issues, and

---

[17] *McNaughton* v. *Presbyterian Church,* 172 N. E. 561, 35 Ohio App. 443.
[18] 59 P. 700, 127 Cal. 341.
[19] 138 So. 589.

this, save in rare cases, could reasonably be, in actual and dependable substance, but little more than nothing."

In *Crawford* v. *State* the court gave as a reason for making admissible the expert accountant's testimony as to the content and meaning of intricate and voluminous accounting records the need for the jury to obtain an understanding of the accounting material. It is apparent to the layman that accounting records are unintelligible to the average juror, and that without an explanation of such records the average jury would be left without a proper understanding of the inferential facts of the case. Necessity is the justification of the rule. The rule is uniformly accepted in American courts.

The Parol-evidence Rule and the Expert Accountant's Testimony

The parol-evidence rule renders inadmissible any evidence the effect of which is to vary the terms of a written instrument or to change, cut down or alter the effect of the instrument.[20] The rule applies to written instruments which give evidence of voluntary relations between two or more parties—relations which may be created, defined, transferred or extinguished by expressed will of the parties. Among examples of such voluntary relations are sales, contracts, negotiable instruments, wills, releases and deeds.

Generally, contracts are expressed in writing to avoid the indefiniteness and misunderstanding which often accompany oral agreements. In the writing of a contract there is generally a greater amount of deliberation and consideration than is found in the making of oral contracts. Hence, the courts are disinclined to disturb the condition of matters embodied in a written contract. The courts generally refuse to admit evidence tending to show that the parties had intentions different from those revealed by the writing itself. This rule, however, is so narrowly circumscribed by exceptions that it has well nigh ceased to be a rule of law. The rule is little more than a convenient way of saying that the party to a valid contract should live up to his agreement.

[20] McKelvey on *Evidence*, fourth edition, pp. 475-491.

Oral evidence may be introduced to show that a contract is not what it appears from the writing to be. Since, after all, the binding effect of an agreement is dependent upon circumstances external to the writing itself, oral evidence may be used to invalidate the agreement on account of fraud in the execution of the agreement, failure of consideration, duress, undue influence or a mistake as to the identity of the subject matter involved. Where the full tenor of an agreement does not appear from the writing, collateral oral testimony may be offered to show fully the parties' intentions. Such incompleteness of the instrument must appear from either the writing itself or the surrounding circumstances. Any collateral oral agreement modifying or rescinding a written agreement, if made subsequent to the written agreement, may be proved in court. Where a business custom enters into and becomes a part of a contract, such custom may be proved by oral testimony if the writing is silent as to the custom. It has been repeatedly held that where technical language, signs or abbreviations have been employed in a written contract expert witnesses may give explanations and interpretations of the instrument so that the jury may acquire an understanding of the intentions of the parties to the agreement.[21]

The American courts are uniform in holding that the testimony of an expert accountant does not come within the parol-evidence rule. The supreme court of North Carolina in 1928 definitely stated the position of the American courts in the case of *State* v. *Maslin* [22] as follows:

"Several exceptions relate to expert testimony which was admitted to elucidate certain entries in the books of the bank. The objection is that the entries were free from ambiguity and that parol evidence was not admissible in explanation. The principle that as a rule parol evidence can not be received to contradict, alter or modify the terms of a written instrument which speaks for itself has no application here. The evidence was offered for the purpose of tracing sundry entries on the books through a series of transactions which tended to show that funds had been taken from the trust account and elsewhere applied. It is hard to see how the jury could have understood

[21] McKelvey on *Evidence,* fourth edition, pp. 475-491.
[22] 143 S. E. 3, 195 N. C. 537.

the significance of these entries without the aid of expert testimony, or how they could have taken the books and satisfactorily have traced any of the funds while making up their verdict. The entries were not changed; their meaning was explained. There was no invasion of the province of the jury by the expression of an opinion upon a fact in issue. * * *"

California has provided by statute that the expert testimony of an accountant is an exception to the rule that the only evidence of the contents of a writing is the writing itself. That statute was quoted in part by the supreme court of California in 1930 in the case of *Johnstone* v. *Morris* [23] as follows:

"* * * Section 1855 of the code of civil procedure provides in part: 'There can be no evidence of the contents of a writing, other than the writing itself, except in the following cases: * * * 5. When the original consists of numerous accounts or other documents, which can not be examined in court without great loss of time, and the evidence sought from them is only the general result of the whole.'

"Although it is true that Mr. Dolge did not do all of the actual checking required, we do not deem that essential to permit the summary to be introduced. He testified very clearly that his report was made from the original tags, cheques, and books of account, and that he had personal knowledge of the same. The tags, cheques and books were all made available to appellant, and could all have been introduced into evidence, but it was to prevent such a time-wasting and lengthy procedure that section 1855, subdivision 5, of the code of civil procedure was passed. * * *"

In each of the two cases, *State* v. *Maslin* and *Johnstone* v. *Morris,* supra, the court admitted as evidence the expert accountant's explanations of the accounting records under consideration. This is in harmony with the well-settled law which permits oral testimony to explain technical matters included in written agreements.[24] The rule is enforced to give to the jury a proper understanding of the written data in the shortest and easiest way possible.

---

[23] 292 P. 970.
[24] McKelvey on *Evidence,* 4th ed., pp. 487-490. *Quigley* v. *De Haas,* 98 Pa. 299.

The Accountant's Expert Testimony Not Barred by the Rules of Hearsay or Primary Evidence

If A, while on the witness stand, testifies as to what he heard B, who is not a witness or a party to the suit, say in regard to fact X, which is the subject of proof, A's assertion is hearsay evidence. Hearsay evidence is testimony of something that has been said or written by a person who is not a witness or a party to the suit. The general rule followed by courts in respect to hearsay evidence is to reject such evidence because it has not been tested by cross-examination. A fundamental rule of law in England and America is the requirement that all evidence be purified by the process of cross-examination. The cross-examination allowed to the opposing party is designed to reveal the errors, inconsistencies and falsehoods of the testimony of the witness. The right of cross-examination is thought by some eminent jurists to be the greatest legal engine ever invented to test the trustworthiness of evidence and to discover the truth.[25]

However, the test of cross-examination may be dispensed with where the necessities of the case require evidence from witnesses who are unavailable and where the circumstances are such as to make it sufficiently clear that the evidence is free from inaccuracy and untrustworthiness. If a witness is unavailable by reason of death, absence from the jurisdiction or any other cause acceptable to the court, the court is presented with the alternative of receiving the statements of the witness without the test of cross-examination or failing to utilize the knowledge of the witness. In a situation of this sort the court is always confronted with the problem of determining whether in the interest of truth it would be better to reject or to receive such information untested by cross-examination. If in addition to the necessity of receiving statements from an unavailable witness there is some degree of trustworthiness more than the ordinary to be expected of the statements, the statements may be admitted as evidence. Courts have not attempted to obtain uniformity in the degree of trustworthiness which various circumstances presuppose. The courts take the view that common sense

[25] Wigmore on *Evidence*, volume III, sec. 1367.

and experience have from time to time pointed out certain circumstances as practically adequate substitutes for the test of cross-examination wherever there exists a necessity of the information in the case.

In permitting exceptions to the hearsay rule, courts have not applied the principles of necessity and trustworthiness of the information with equal strictness [26]—sometimes one, sometimes the other, has carried the greater importance in the decision. Any attempt to give a thorough survey of the exceptions to the hearsay rule of evidence would involve a whole volume. For present purposes it will not be necessary to do more than merely to enumerate some of the exceptions and to apply the two principles, necessity and trustworthiness, to the cases in which it was held that a public accountant's expert testimony is an exception to the hearsay rule of evidence.

Matters of family pedigree may be proved by written or oral statements handed down from father to son. Statements made by witnesses in other trials where the parties and the issues in dispute were the same as those in the case in which it is sought to introduce the statements form an exception to the hearsay rule. Hearsay statements have uniformly been admitted to prove matters of public interest, such as the location of territorial boundaries and the incorporation of a governmental subdivision. Where any act such as a crime or tort has occurred and declarations relevant to the act were made spontaneously at the time when the act occurred, the declarations are admissible evidence. The term, res gestæ, applied to this last situation means that the acts speak for themselves. Books and documents of a public nature, in which are recorded facts to be preserved for public reference, are admissible evidence by common and statutory law. Since the 18th century courts have held that private accounting records form an exception to the hearsay rule of evidence. The necessity for the use of such evidence arose from the unavailability of a witness because of death, absence from the jurisdiction, incompetency or inconvenience. The fact that the entries were made in the regular course of the business, it was thought, justified the belief that the entries were trustworthy as a

[26] Wigmore on *Evidence*, volume III, secs. 1420-1427.

result of the circumstances in which they were normally recorded. The habit of doing accurate work, the fact that it is easier to record the truth than to falsify, the consciousness of the entrant, while recording, that his erroneous or false entries will eventually come to light have been held to be circumstances which will afford sufficient assurance of the trustworthiness of the records and be an effective substitute for the test of cross-examination.[27]

Let us now pass to a consideration of the accountant's expert testimony in its relation to the hearsay rule. The supreme court of Louisiana in 1921 held in the case of *State* v. *Perry* [28] as follows:

> "The fourth bill was taken to a witness being allowed to testify that on the date when the deposit in question was received the bank was insolvent. The objection was that the books of the bank were the best evidence.
>
> "The witness was testifying as an expert accountant, giving the result of his examination of the books of the bank. This kind of evidence is an exception to the rules of hearsay and primary evidence. * * *"

While courts require that the best evidence available, and not secondary or hearsay evidence which may be substituted for the best or primary evidence, be used in a trial, yet, in the case of *State* v. *Perry*, the court was in agreement with sound principles of law in holding that the admission of the expert accountant's testimony was an exception to the rules of hearsay and primary evidence. Granted that the accounting records themselves in a given case are admissible evidence, the expert accountant's testimony as to the content and meaning of the records may be admissible evidence as a result of necessity for the use of such testimony and as a result of the circumstantial guaranty of trustworthiness. It is necessary to accept the testimony of an expert accountant in order to convey to the lay jury an understanding of the records constituting inferential facts which bear upon the main issue of the case. A sufficient assurance of trustworthiness of the accountant's expert testimony is obtained from the fact that an accountant is normally in the habit of doing his work accurately, the fact that it is easier to make

[27] Wigmore on *Evidence*, volume III, sections 1360-1810.
[28] 90 So. 406, 149 La. 1065. See also *Hankins* v. *State*, 213 N.W. 344.

Admissibility of Accountant's Testimony

an honest review than a false one, the consciousness on the part of the accountant that the accuracy and honesty of his report will be tested by cross-examination of him personally and probably by a review of the records by the opposing party. Hence, the public accountant's expert testimony can not be precluded by the hearsay rule of evidence.

Custody of Records

In respect to the custody of records about which the accountant's expert testimony is offered there are three distinct classes of decisions. The universally accepted rule is that the records must be in custody of the court so as to afford the opposing party an opportunity to cross-examine the accountant witness by means of a comparison of his testimonial statements with the records themselves. This requirement is dispensed with where the trial judge is satisfied that the records should not be removed to the court-room because of the great public and private inconvenience that would ensue therefrom and also where the books have been lost before the trial takes place. While many cases have required that the court have custody of records as a prerequisite to the admission of expert testimony concerning the books, only two cases are quoted here. The decision in the first case, *Ruth v. State*,[29] rendered by the supreme court of Wisconsin in 1909, reads in part as follows:

"It is urged by the accused that the court committed prejudicial error in admitting the evidence of the experts respecting the state of the account between the Arcadia and Winona banks, and the condition of the accounts of the Arcadia bank. The claim is that these experts were permitted to testify that items of book entries were shown to be incorrect by means of summary statements and tables which they had taken and made from the book accounts of the books

[29] 140 Wis. 373, 122 N. W. 733. Similar decisions are as follows: *Brown v. First National Bank*, 113 P. 483, 49 Colo. 393; *Young v. State*, 103 S. E. 804, 25 Ga. App. 562; *Herberg v. State*, 222 S. W. 559, 87 Tex. Cr. R. 439; *State v. Williams*, 111 A. 701, 94 Vt. 423; *Camp v. State*, 122 S. E. 249, 31 Ga. 737; *Newton v. State*, 127 A. 123, 147 Md. 71; *People v. Hatfield*, 208 N. W. 682, 234 Mich. 574; *Pierce Pet. Co. v. Osage Coal Co.*, 271 P. 675 (Okla.); *McNaughton v. Presbyterian Church*, 172 N. E. 561, 35 Ohio App. 443; *State v. Olson*, 287 P. 181 (Utah); *Bush v. Board of Education of Clark County*, 37 S. W. (2d) 849, 238 Ky. 297; *Aetna Casualty & Surety Co. v. Mayor and Council of Wilmington et al.*, 157 A. 208 (Delaware).

of both banks, without introducing in evidence all of these books and the entries on which such statements were based, and without producing any evidence tending to show that the book entries and accounts of the Winona bank were correct and true. The practice of permitting expert accountants to examine long book accounts and to give in summary form the results thereof for the information of the court and jury is approved as practical and proper in the trial of causes involving the examination of long book accounts. A proper administration, of course, requires that the opposing party shall be afforded the time and opportunity to test the correctness of the evidence, and for this purpose to have access to the books and the use of them for the purposes of cross-examination. In so far as this practice was adopted in the case, we find nothing in the record showing that the evidence of the experts on this subject was improper. The claim that the failure to offer in evidence all of the account books of the Arcadia bank which was covered by this evidence operated to defendant's prejudice is not shown, for it appears that all such books were brought into court, were identified and were accessible to the defendant and his attorney."

A slight variation from this decision may be noted in the second case, *Stephen* v. *United States*,[30] decided in 1930 by the circuit court of appeals, ninth circuit, which held that the expert accountant's testimony relative to accounting books was admissible where the records were kept in the prosecution's possession in the building, but not in the court room, where the trial was conducted. A portion of the opinion reads:

"* * * The prosecution had in some manner acquired possession of these books of account and records, approximately 250 volumes, and for convenience kept them in two rooms in the building where the trial was had. * * * Ordinarily the party offering such testimony should be required to produce in court or to make available for his opponent's use the documents and books used by the witness, but even that rule is not universally followed and where recognized it is subject to exceptions. * * *"

The reason for requiring production of documents [31] before the tribunal rather than permitting merely oral testimony as to

[30] 41 F. (2d) 440.
[31] Note: Accounting records come within the definition of documents. 2 *Words and Phrases* (2nd series) 167; Wigmore on *Evidence*, volume II, section 1223.

their contents, under the so-called best or primary evidence rule, has been based upon the experience of courts that generally witnesses do not carry accurate recollections of documents.[32] It has been found that the human memory serves as a rather poor medium through which to portray the contents, nature of paper and handwriting, and the signatures of written documents. Hence, the courts have been rigid in their requirements that the documents themselves be produced in court. While accounting records must necessarily be explained to the court by an expert, it is vital to a correct showing of the truth of the case that the opponents be allowed to test the trustworthiness of the accountant's expert testimony through an examination of the records. It is apparent that the most immediate check upon the witness' testimonial statements is made possible where the books are in the court room. Furthermore, it may easily be possible that an exhibition of the records before the jury will reveal the character of the handwriting and the books themselves so as materially to aid the cause of truth-finding. Where the books are stored under the custody of the court in a room adjoining the court room or in the building in which the trial is conducted, the opportunity to test the accountant's testimony may easily be afforded to the opposing party.

This sort of situation would seem to suffice as a means of testing the trustworthiness of the expert testimony. It has uniformly been conceded by courts that the opportunity of cross-examination by the opposing party, even though the opportunity be not availed of, will answer sufficiently the requirement that evidence be tested by cross-examination.[33] Moreover, the records under the court's custody in a room adjoining the court room or in the building in which the trial is conducted could be conveniently made available for an inspection by the jury itself.

The second type of cases which deal with the custody of records, about which the expert accountant's testimony is offered, has dispensed with the requirement of the custody of the records by the court as a prerequisite to the admission of the accountant's testimony concerning the books, where the removal of the books to the

---

[32] Wigmore on *Evidence*, volume II, sec. 1179.
[33] Wigmore on *Evidence*, volume III, sec. 1371.

court-room would work great public and private inconvenience. Two cases of this type are included herein, the first of which, *Pioneer Lumber Co.* v. *Van Cleave*[34] decided in 1925 by the St. Louis court of appeals, Missouri, reads in part as follows:

"* * * We recognize the rule that, where the results of an examination of many books, papers or records are to be proved, and the necessary examination of such documentary evidence can not be conveniently or satisfactorily made in court, it may be made by an expert accountant or other competent person, and the results thereof be proved by him, provided the books, papers, or records themselves are properly in evidence or their absence satisfactorily explained. * * *"

The other case dispensing with the requirement of custody of the books by the court because of the public and private inconvenience of their removal is *State* v. *Matkins*,[35] which was decided in 1930 by the supreme court of Missouri. A portion of the opinion follows:

"* * * In *Citizens' Trust Co.* v. *Ward*, 195 Mo. App. 223, 190 S. W. 364, a witness was permitted to testify to the condition of bank books and records which were not introduced in evidence and so far as the opinion discloses were not even in the courtroom, and it was held that no error was committed."

The determination of the sufficiency of preliminary facts offered as explanation of the absence of the books about which expert testimony is presented is within the discretion of the trial judge.

Where production of the records would work great public inconvenience, as in the case of accounting records kept by banks, railroads, express companies, telephone and telegraph companies, insurance companies and hospitals, courts have accepted expert testimony concerning the records without requiring the presence of the records before the tribunal. In a few jurisdictions statutes excuse the production of corporation books where an accountant's expert testimony relative to the books is offered in court.[36] The statutes are doubtless intended to excuse production of accounting records because of inconvenience; but the statutes are fallacious in

---

[34] 279 S. W. 241.
[35] 34 S. W. (2d) 1.
[36] Wigmore on *Evidence*, volume II, sections 1177-1230.

that they discriminate in favor of incorporated enterprises. Actual inconvenience of production, and not the form of legal organization, should be the basis of excusing absence of the records. Though the cases have extended the privilege of non-production of records on account of inconvenience only to public officers in some instances and to business enterprises affected with a public interest, it would seem that the exigencies of modern private businesses also would justify in many cases the non-production of accounting records on the ground of inconvenience. It is not infrequently true that a private business has a vast network of branches or subordinate units at which records reflecting the financial and operating conditions of each unit are kept. At the head office summary control records of the entire organization are usually kept. To require production of all the original records of such a concern would be highly impracticable. It is questionable, too, whether the opposing party would be able during the course of a trial to check a witness's statements against such records even though the records were in the courtroom. Even an expert accountant employed by the opposing party probably would not find time during the course of the trial adequately to test the expert testimony of the proponent against the records where many books were involved. A better plan would be to require that the opposing party be given ample opportunity to examine the records prior to the trial. The data obtained in such examination might well serve the purposes of cross-examination. Such a mode of cross-examination would prove far more effective than the exhibition of a maze of records before a lay jury in an attempt to invalidate the testimony of an expert accountant who had based his statements upon a great amount of auditing experience.

In the past few years a public realization of the importance of private business enterprises to the general public welfare has developed. Drastic means of social control have been set up for the purpose of promoting the public welfare through the medium of private business. The closing down, stopping or even hampering the operations of a private business by requiring the removal of the accounting records to a court-room may easily cause considerable public and private inconvenience. Hence, trial judges should allow the introduction of expert testimony concerning the absent records of a private business where, in the particular circumstances, the removal of the books from the business would work an unreasonable amount of inconvenience to the business and to the public.

The third class of cases (dealing with the court's custody of records about which expert testimony is offered) dispenses with the requirement of the court's custody of the records as a prerequisite to the admission of such evidence where it is shown that the records have been lost. Two cases setting forth this opinion are presented here. The supreme court of Oregon in 1929 in the case of *Hubble* v. *Hubble* [37] held that where the expert bookkeeper and auditor examined an automobile dealer's books and the books were subsequently destroyed, the accountant was permitted to testify as to the content of the records. In 1932 the circuit court of appeals, third circuit, in the case of *Kay* v. *Federal Rubber Company* [38] admitted testimony of an accountant who had examined an automobile-tire dealer's books which were destroyed before the time of the trial. The decision reads:

"Error is assigned to the admission, under objection, of the testimony of an accountant, who had examined the books of the bankrupt. The ground alleged is that, since some of the books were not produced or could not be found, his testimony was based upon incomplete records. The court rightly held that that fact went to the value, and not to the admissibility, of the accountant's deductions. While an adverse party is entitled to have the best evidence produced against him, there is nothing in the record in this case to show that the books produced were not the best evidence available."

Failure to produce accounting records on account of loss has been held to be not a bar to the admission of an accountant's expert testimony relative to the accounting records. The question of proof of loss of the records deserves consideration. The sufficiency of the proof of loss of documents [39] has been concerned in court decisions not only with loss in the narrow sense of the word but with loss through destruction. Strictly speaking, destruc-

---
[37] 279 P. 550.
[38] 60 F. (2d) 454.
[39] Note: The principles governing the production of documents apply to accounting records. Accounting records constitute one kind of documents.

tion means termination of existence, while loss means merely the inability of discovery. The moment destruction becomes questionable at all, as when not proved by eye-witnesses of a burning, the inquiry is raised whether the search for the documents has been sufficient. The proof of a loss usually carries the implication that the thing not found has ceased to exist and thus resembles the case of destruction. Thus, naturally the sufficiencies of proofs of destruction and loss are inextricably woven together; and courts have sought to determine the amount of search necessary to show loss in the broad sense of the word. While there are conflicting opinions, the doctrine expounded by many classical cases, thought to be correctly decided by most eminent authority, holds that there is not and can not be any universal or fixed rule to test the sufficiency of the search for documents alleged to be lost.[40] The sufficiency of the search to prove loss depends upon the circumstances of each case. The search must have been made with such diligence as was reasonable in the circumstances. The party proving the documents must have used all reasonable means to obtain them. It necessarily follows that the determination of the sufficiency of the search and the sufficiency of the proof of loss of the documents should be left entirely to the discretion of the trial court. This principle is supported by the weight of authority.

The deliberate loss or destruction of documents brought about by the proponent in order to destroy the best evidence will operate as a bar to the admission of testimony as to the content of the documents. However, if the documents were destroyed in the ordinary course of business and without any intent to conceal evidence, courts generally, after explaining to the jury the circumstances of destruction, have allowed testimony relative to those documents. The circumstances of destruction, though apparently innocent, may affect the value of the evidence.

Where documents are detained by the opponent, the proponent is excused from production as a prerequisite to the offering of testimony concerning them. It is apparent that the reason for excusing non-production is the inability of the proponent to obtain the documents. In order that the proponent may be excused from the

[40] Wigmore on *Evidence*, volume II, secs. 1193, 1194.

production of documents, on the ground that they are being withheld by the opponent, he must offer proof of control of the documents by the opponent, demand or notice to opponent for the documents for use in the trial and failure of opponent to produce such documents. An admission by the opponent that the records have been lost or destroyed will make any further proof of loss unnecessary.

Briefly, accounting records must generally be produced in court in order to serve as a test of the trustworthiness of the accountant's expert testimony; but the production of the accounting records may be excused where production is not feasible, as in cases of great inconvenience resulting from the removal of the records from the place of business, loss of the records or detention of the records by the opposing party.[41]

AUTHENTICITY OF RECORDS

That accounting records must be properly authenticated as a prerequisite to the admission of an expert accountant's testimony concerning them is a well-settled rule of law. The principle is presented in the case of *Le Roy State Bank* v. *Keenan's Bank* [42] which was decided by the appellate court of Illinois in 1928. A portion of the opinion follows:

"* * * While the results of the examination of voluminous documents, writings, records and books may be proved by expert accountant or other competent person who has made the examination, the documents, records or books upon which the examination is based must be of such a character as to be themselves admissible in evidence. The oral evidence is admissible because the voluminous character of the instruments of evidence precludes their examination in court, and the testimony to results reached by their examination is merely a statement of what those instruments show. It was, therefore, necessary that the books and papers which the expert accountants examined should themselves have been competent evidence. In order to render an account-book admissible in evidence, it is essential that proof as satisfactory as the transactions are under the circumstances

[41] Wigmore on *Evidence*, volume II, sections 1177-1230.
[42] 169 N. E. 1, 337 Ill. 173. In accord: *Hubble* v. *Hubble*, 279 P. 550; *Brookfield Co.* v. *Mart*, 4 P. (2d) 311; *Stephens* v. *United States*, 41 F. (2d) 440.

reasonably susceptible of, shall be given that the entries made are correctly recorded. * * * Where the testimony of a witness who made the entries is not available, it is competent to establish the authenticity of the book by other evidence. The only evidence produced of the authenticity of the books which the accountants examined is the testimony of the cashier of the Le Roy bank. He did not become cashier until three months after the making of the contract and the transfer of the assets to that bank. He did not make all the entries in the books. He did not testify, and could not testify, to the correctness of all those entries. Entries were made by the assistant cashier and other persons whose names were mentioned in the cashier's testimony, but they were not called to show that the entries were correctly made, and there was no testimony that they were not available. Exhibit A-20, which was used in reaching the results arrived at by the accountants, was in large part not a book of original entry, but was, so far as more than half of the period which it purported to cover was concerned, copied from other books to whose authenticity and correctness no one testified. For these reasons the books were not admitted in evidence. The conclusions of the accountants, however, based on these books, which were not so verified as to make them competent evidence, were received and were made the basis of the judgment which was rendered (in the lower court). * * * Since the books were not shown to be competent evidence, the statement of the conclusions reached by a consideration of them was not competent evidence and should not have been admitted."

The holding of the *Le Roy State Bank* v. *Keenan's Bank* case that the admissibility of an accountant's expert testimony concerning accounting records is dependent upon the authenticity of the records themselves is well-established law. The court in this case also enunciated the rule that the authenticity of the book entries may be established by testimony of a witness who made the entries, or, if the entrant be not available, by other evidence. The dispute involved largely only those records which were prepared prior to the time the cashier became associated with the records. Hence, doubtless the court was correct in holding that the cashier was disqualified to verify the genuineness of the bank books, especially in view of the fact that the persons making the entries could have been offered to testify concerning the entries on the books.

The philosophy upon which the decision is based is in agreement with the well-recognized principles of law on the point.

Because of the great variety of situations that arise in regard to the inferential facts tending to prove to the satisfaction of the trial judge the admissibility of evidence, quite often no general or universal rules governing the proof of admissibility can be established. Hence, in many situations the determination of the proof necessary to justify the admission of evidence is left entirely to the discretion of the trial judge. However, in the case of the authentication of documents, situations have had enough in common to justify some general rules applicable to the establishment of the validity of instruments, i.e., the proving of the genuineness or authorship of the documents.

Some of the general rules applicable to the authentication of documents (including accounting records) are presented here.[43] A writing, of itself, is evidence of nothing and therefore is not, unless accompanied by proof of some sort, admissible as evidence. There must be some evidence of the genuineness of the writing before the writing can be used as a basis for testimonial evidence. Only a reasonable certainty in the proof of the genuineness of the accounting records should be required; it is not necessary that the proof should be conclusive; prima-facie evidence that the records are genuine is sufficient to warrant their reception. Certain modes of indicating the genuineness of documents, including accounting records, are uniformly accepted as sufficient to determine their admission as evidence. Each of the following methods of proof of admissibility of evidence has been held sufficient in itself to justify the placing of evidence before the jury: (1) Testimony of witnesses who had personal knowledge of the entries and the transactions upon which the entries were based; (2) circumstantial evidence, that is, handwriting of the entrant, or age of records under certain conditions.

There have been some variations from the rule that a witness in order to verify accounting records must have personal knowledge of both the transactions and the entries. It has been held repeatedly that the cashier of a bank who oversees all transactions and tests

[43] Wigmore on *Evidence,* volume III, sec. 1530.

the accuracy of the books is competent to testify as to the authenticity of the bank books. It has also been held that a supervising officer who has general knowledge of the transactions and entries is competent to verify the records. It has also been held that the authenticity of accounting records can be proved by testimony of the bookkeepers who had not personal knowledge of the transactions. In such rulings the courts take the position that the production on the witness stand of a numerous host of salesmen, shipping clerks, teamsters, foremen or other subordinate employees would generally be improper. While it can not be said that the testimony of one who has only general knowledge of the transactions and the books or of one who has knowledge of the entries but not of the transactions, may prove sufficiently the authenticity of accounting records is the generally accepted rule, it is to be hoped that courts in the future will uniformly follow this practical rule.[44]

Where the keeper of the records is deceased, authentication of the bookkeeping records can be effected by proving the keeper's handwriting in the records.[45] It is probable that a verification of the genuineness of accounting records through proof of handwriting would be permissible where the bookkeeper has become insane subsequent to the making of the entries or where he is absent from the jurisdiction.

Proof of the genuineness of account books is made conclusive by a judicial admission of the opponent. A judicial admission by the opponent is an agreement before the trial judge after the issues are joined, either before or during the trial, that the opponent will not dispute the authenticity of the records. While in American courts the use of the judicial admission of the opponent is rarely available to the proponent of the records, the practice of dispensing with trouble and expense of producing evidence of the genuineness of accounting records where the opponent has no reasonable grounds to object to their authenticity is to be commended to trial judges and litigants alike.

---

[44] Wigmore on *Evidence*, volume III, section 1530.
[45] Wigmore on *Evidence*, volume III, section 1530; *Delaney* v. *Framingham Gas, Fuel and Water Co.*, 202 Mass. 359, 88 N. E. 776 (1909).

The fact that the opponent has destroyed or suppressed the accounting records is uniformly treated as sufficient evidence of execution to go to the jury.

In many jurisdictions of the United States it is provided by statutes that if the documents are named in the pleading as the foundation of the claim or defense, proof of genuineness is not required unless the opponent denies authenticity of the records on oath either in the formal plea or in a separate affidavit.[46]

While the cases are rare, wherever the courts have ruled on the point they have uniformly held that account books, in common with other documents, may be authenticated by age. However, the ruling of authentication by age requires that the records be at least thirty years old, that there must have been a natural custody of the books, and that the books must be unsuspicious in appearance. Courts have presumed that witnesses who had personal knowledge of the records and transactions have ceased to exist after the lapse of thirty years from the time of the making of the entries. Even where there are living witnesses who had personal knowledge of the transactions and records and are available, courts have not required the testimony of such witnesses.[47] The custody of the ancient books must have been natural. The fact that books have come from a place where it normally would be expected that the books should be kept tends to remove presumptions of fraud and strengthens the belief in their genuineness. Custody by the party offering account books for a period of more than thirty years has been held to have been a proper custody.[48] Again, books kept in custody for more than thirty years by a manorial steward were held to have been in such custody as was necessary to enter the account books as evidence under the ancient documents rule in an action brought by the feudal lord of the estate.[49] While no clear marks of suspicion of improper execution of account books have been accepted, courts ruling upon the point have required that the records must show no appearance of fraud. It should be clearly

---

[46] Wigmore on *Evidence*, volume V, section 2596.
[47] 22 *Corpus Juris*, p. 946, Sec. 1165.
[48] *Bertie* v. *Beaumont*, 146 English reports 105 (1816).
[49] *Wynne* v. *Tyrwhitt*, 106 English reports 975 (1821).

understood that the authenticity of account books can not be established by the ancient-documents rule unless the books have been in existence thirty years or more, have been kept in proper custody and present an honest appearance.[50]

A Certified Public Accountant's Certificate Not a Prerequisite to Qualification as an Expert Witness in Matters of Accounting

The supreme court of Oklahoma in 1928 in the case of *Bell* v. *Tackett*[51] relative to the accountant's qualifications to testify as an expert held, in part, as follows:

> "Counsel objected to this evidence in the trial court, after showing that the witness was not a certified accountant, under sections 10922 to 10928, article 10, chapter 87, C. O. S. 1921 (restricting the practice of public accounting to certified public accountants). We decline to hold that such evidence of a person, otherwise qualified, would be incompetent by such failure to comply with said statutory provisions, inasmuch as said sections have heretofore been held unconstitutional by this court in the case of *State* v. *Riedell,* 109 Okla. 35, 233 P. 684, 42 A. L. R. 765."

The court held in *Bell* v. *Tackett* that a public accountant is not required to have a certified public accountant's certificate in order to give testimony as an expert accountant. This ruling is in harmony with the general practice of trial judges in permitting an expert to testify even though the expert does not belong to a particular class or profession. Though a trial judge may take into account the fact that an expert has a particular degree or diploma, the judge is not bound to permit the expert to testify because the witness holds a degree or diploma. It is equally true that a trial judge may permit an expert to testify as such even though the expert does not possess a particular degree or diploma. Whether or not the witness has acquired special skill relating to the particular subject-matter under review is the controlling fact trial judges consider in the exercise of their discretion in determining the quali-

[50] Wigmore on *Evidence,* volume IV, sections 2128-2160; 22 *Corpus Juris,* sections 1138-1178.
[51] 272 P. 461, 134 Okla. 164.

fications of the witness to testify as an expert. The matter of determining the qualifications of the witness to testify as an expert is nearly always left to the discretion of the trial judge.[52]

CREDIBILITY OF WITNESS

In 1931 the Kentucky court of appeals held, in the case of *Bush v. Board of Education of Clark County* [53] as follows:

"* * * It is argued by counsel for appellants that the evidence was not competent on another ground, that is, that Gustetter was an interested party, and that he had been in possession of the tax books for several months before he completed his audit, and that their verity was thereby destroyed. It is also testified to that he made contradictory statements, and that he offered to settle with Bush without making any report. He denied all of these statements except that he was interested, but none of these things rendered him incompetent as a witness. They only went to his credibility."

The *Bush v. Board of Education of Clark County* case ruled that the fact that the accountant witness was contradictory in his testimony or that he was interested in the ultimate issue of the controversy did not preclude the admission of his testimony but affected merely the trustworthiness of his testimony. This case, while apparently the only American one of its kind affecting the testimony of an accountant, is in accord with the well-settled principles of law involved.

The credibility of a witness is concerned with the probative effect which may be attached to his testimony. In seeking to show contradictions by cross-examination or by other proof, testimonial or circumstantial, the ultimate aim is to persuade the tribunal that the witness has completely erred in regard to the particular facts which the witness has sought to establish. It is the truth of the contradicting evidence as opposed to the truth of the witness' assertions that constitutes the probative end. It is the function of the tribunal, not to dismiss consideration of relevant assertions that have been contradicted, but rather to ascertain the relative

---

[52] 22 *Corpus Juris*, p. 536, section 624; Wigmore on *Evidence*, volume I, sections 555-561.
[53] 37 S. W. (2d) 849, 238 Ky. 297.

trustworthiness of the conflicting assertions of the opposing parties.[54]

The disqualification of a witness to testify on account of his being an interested party became a universal rule of law in England by the seventeenth century, and later it was adopted in America. A century after its adoption a very definite decline in the application of the rule appeared in the English and American law. Today the disqualification has everywhere disappeared except in the case of testimony of the survivor of a transaction with a decedent, when offered against the deceased's estate. The theory of the rule of disqualification on account of interest was based originally on the belief that the interested party would be apt to falsify in behalf of his own interest, and that the jurors, inclined to base their verdict on the number of witnesses testifying under oath rather than on the quality of evidence, would render a false verdict. The reason for the rule no longer exists. The modern courts take the position that interested witnesses often testify honestly, and that, even if the witness attempts to falsify, through the medium of cross-examination the trustworthiness of the testimony of the interested witness is effectively established before the jury. The jury should not be denied the benefit of valuable information which tends to prove or disprove either directly or inferentially the main fact in issue merely because the information offered comes from a witness who is an interested party in the suit.[55]

CONFIDENTIAL COMMUNICATIONS BETWEEN PUBLIC ACCOUNTANT AND CLIENT

Only one case in England and America is concerned directly in establishing the common law governing the confidential communications between public accountant and client. The opinion in that case, *In re Fisher*[56] decided in 1931 by the federal district court, S. D. New York, follows:

"It appears that the witness William Bernstein acted as bankrupt's accountant for a number of years, and, after his admission to the bar, also acted as bankrupt's attorney. Upon the basis of the privilege

[54] Wigmore on *Evidence*, volume II, sections 1000-1004.
[55] Wigmore on *Evidence*, volume I, sections 575-578.
[56] 51 F. (2d) 424.

arising from the attorney-client relationship, he has refused to answer questions relating to bankrupt's books and to produce in evidence monthly account sheets made by accountants in his employ in course of auditing bankrupt's books.

"There is no privilege with regard to communications made to accountants. The information given to the witness and to the accountants in his employ for the purpose of making financial statements and doing other work characteristically performed by accountants is not privileged, despite the fact that the witness may also have rendered legal advice on the basis of such data. * * *

"Furthermore, the privilege accorded to an attorney is the privilege of the client and not the attorney. * * * For this reason the attorney can not claim privilege where the client has already disclosed the substance of the communication. * * * Nor can he claim privilege where the communication was made with the understanding that it was to be imparted to third parties.

"In the case at bar it appears that the bankrupt has already testified with respect to the matters contained in his books and records. And the income-tax returns and financial statements drawn up from the communications made by bankrupt to the witness were obviously intended to be communicated to others.

"For these reasons, the witness should be directed to testify with regard to the bankrupt's books and to produce in evidence the monthly work sheets made by the accountants."

This case, *In re Fisher,* was in accord with well-settled law in holding that the privilege of non-disclosure of confidential communications between the attorney and client was for the benefit of the client and not the attorney. The privilege of confidential communications can be granted an attorney only on motion of his client. However, the accountant's chief concern with *In re Fisher* is the fact that the court refused to allow the privilege of confidential communications in the accountant-client relation. This refusal to allow to the accountant immunity from disclosure of his client's confidential communications is contrary to sound common-law principles and should not be followed in future decisions.

It is well to review the common-law principles involved in the privilege of confidential communications.[57] From the early six-

[57] Wigmore on *Evidence,* volume V, secs. 2285-2329.

teenth to the later eighteenth century in England the privilege of refraining from producing confidential information on the witness stand was universally allowed in the common-law courts in the trial of civil cases. The practice was justified on the ground that the court ought to respect the word or pledge of a man of honor. The decline of the extension of the privilege to refuse to give confidential testimony naturally followed from its obstructive effects upon the cause of justice. By 1800 the privilege to keep secret confidential matters was confined to attorneys, jurors, public officers and husband and wife. Courts no longer concerned themselves with the preservation of the honor of the witness but rather sought to preserve the life, liberty and property of the person who confided the secret to the witness. In the attorney-client relation it was the interest of the client, not the honor of the attorney, for which the courts made confidential information privileged. Hence, the courts allowed, and still do allow, the privilege, not on the attorney's motion, but only on the request of the client. Certain broad principles were laid down by the common law for the purpose of determining the type of relationship which ought to be blessed with privileged information. By common law four conditions were, and are, required to make a relation eligible for the privilege of keeping secret confidential information. (1) The communications must have been made in the belief that they would not be disclosed. (2) The element of confidentiality must be essential to the promotion and continuation of the relation between the parties. (3) The relation must be one which society wishes to encourage. (4) The injury that would result from the disclosure of the confidential communications must be greater than the benefit which would accrue from the correct disposal of litigation.

The attorney-client relation meets all four requirements of the privilege of confidential communications. Practically all the communications between client and attorney are made in confidence. Were it not for the belief that his communications would be kept secret, the client would not give his attorney full information. Though an attorney often does enable a guilty person to escape punishment, for the sake of the innocent the secret relation of the attorney and client should be encouraged. The injury resulting from the attorney's failure to get from his client incriminating information may easily outweigh the benefit which would be obtained from a revelation of the secret information coming from the accused. If the attorney's confidential information were available to the prosecution, the prosecutors would fall into the practice of producing the secret communications of the accused rather than substantiating his convictions with other proof.

It is not necessary to show in detail the application of the four principles to both petit and grand jurors.[58] It is apparent to the reader that the communications between jurors are confidential and must be confidential for a full and satisfactory relationship. The community fosters the relationship. Certainly disclosures of jury proceedings would intimidate jurors from exercising freedom of judgment, resulting in an injury to justice much greater than the benefit that might be derived from disclosures of the communications in other trials.

The relation of public officers with persons in matters of state secrets meets all the tests for the allowance of privileged information required by common law.[59] The subject is almost as broad as the governmental activities. For the purpose of illustrating the application of the common-law principles of privileged communications, let us consider the case of an informer who conveys secret information to a detective. Were the detective not permitted to keep inviolate such information, it might easily be dangerous to the informer. The relation between detective and informer would cease to exist. To be sure, the community is interested in fostering the relation of detective and secret informer so as to discover crime. And, lastly, the injury growing out of the loss of the information would exceed the benefit to be derived from the disclosure of the informer's identity. The rule is well-established law, but is limited to the identity of the informer. Furthermore, a trial judge may compel the disclosure of the identity of the detective's informer where the trial judge deems that such information is necessary to prevent the failure of justice.

[58] Wigmore on *Evidence*, volume V, secs. 2346-2364.
[59] Ibid., secs. 2367-2379.

Admissibility of Accountant's Testimony

It must be apparent that as between husband and wife many communications are confidential, and that the confidentiality of such communications is a vital element entering into the perpetuation of the marital relationship.[60] As a matter of public policy society fosters the institution of marriage. It is generally agreed that the detriment that would follow disclosure of marital secrets would outweigh the benefits that would result from such disclosure.

The physician-patient relationship has been held by common law not to meet the four tests.[61] Failure to meet any one test removes the relationship from the scope of privileged communications. Courts have taken the position that most of the patient's communications are not made in the belief that they will be kept secret. In the second place, the patient would come to a physician even if he knew the nature of his communications and ailments would be disclosed to others—so the courts have ruled. In the third place, society is certainly interested in promoting the relation of physician and patient. Lastly, the injury that would result from disclosure would be insignificant as compared to the benefit that may be obtained from medical testimony. Judges have thought that the patient would not be concerned about disclosures except in cases of abortion and venereal diseases; and in those cases generally the patient does not deserve secrecy. Though the privilege of secret communications has been denied to the relation of physician to patient by common law, the privilege has been extended by legislation in many states.

The public accountant-client relation meets all four requirements of the common law for privileged communications. In practically every audit there are communications of a confidential nature made by the client to the public accountant; and in some instances the public accountant gives confidential information to his client. Without the belief that the secrets of his business—his lists of customers, present and potential, his plan of organization, his costs of operations, his secret processes—would be held in confidence, the client would cease to employ the services of public accountants, for the very existence of his business may be dependent upon these secrets.

---

[60] Wigmore on *Evidence*, volume V, secs. 2332-2341.
[61] Ibid., secs. 2380-2391.

In the third place, the community unquestionably is interested in fostering the relation of accountant and client. If not, why has the community enacted laws promoting the standards of accounting practice? And in the fourth place, the detriment resulting from the disclosure of the client's secrets might easily be far reaching. In many instances the very existence of a business is dependent upon its superior organization, its peculiar knowledge of its market, its low cost of production or other characteristics not known to competitors. The revelation of these secrets might easily destroy the business itself. The knowledge that such secrets might be revealed would deter entrepreneurs from originating promotions. The stifling effect of disclosures would be enormous and doubtless would exceed the benefit that might accrue to the administration of justice through the public accountant's revelation of secrets peculiar and vital to the business.

In the case *In re Fisher,* supra, the court did not take the trouble to analyze the accountant-client relation to determine whether that relation fulfills the requirements of common law for privileged communications. It is true that accounting statements are designed for exhibition to others generally and would not, therefore, constitute a communication in confidence. The working papers of the accountant are not designed for presentation to others. The working papers generally contain confidential matters never revealed in the financial statements. The working papers, as well as other communications made in confidence, meet all the requirements for privileged information.

Until the courts have overruled *In re Fisher* and have held that the common-law doctrine of privileged communications applies to the public accountant-client relation, it is necessary to resort to legislation. Nine states have enacted statutes making confidential communications in the accountant-client relation privileged. Those statutes logically fall into three classes. In the first type are included the public accountancy laws of Arizona, Iowa,[62] Louisiana,[62] Michigan,[62] and Tennessee.[62] The Arizona statute follows.[63]

[62] *Certified Public Accountant Laws of the United States,* American Institute Publishing Co., Inc.
[63] Laws of Arizona, regular session of 1933, chapter 45, section 9.

"Certified public accountants and public accountants practising in this state shall not be required to divulge, nor shall they voluntarily divulge, any information which they may have received by reason of the confidential nature of their employment. Information derived from or as a result of such professional source shall be deemed confidential, provided, however, that nothing in this section shall be taken or construed as modifying, changing or affecting the criminal or bankruptcy laws of this state or of the United States."

This type of statute means, then, that in criminal and bankruptcy trials the confidential communications between public accountant and client are not privileged. The statute helps a little, in that the privilege is extended to all trials except criminal and bankruptcy cases.

In the second class are statutes of Florida and Illinois.[63] The Florida statute enacted in 1931 reads as follows: [64]

"All communications between certified public accountants and public accountants and the person, firm or corporation for whom such certified public accountant or public accountant shall have made any audit or other investigation in a professional capacity, and all information obtained by certified public accountants and public accountants in their professional capacity concerning the business and affairs of clients shall be deemed privileged communications in all courts of this state, and no such certified public accountant or public accountant shall be permitted to testify with respect to any of said matters, except with the consent in writing of such client or his legal representative."

The type of statute exemplified by the Florida law, supra, requires complete immunity from disclosure of confidential communications between public accountant and client in all courts within the jurisdictions of such state laws.

The third type of law granting immunity to secret communications made in the accountant-client relation is found in Colorado. The Colorado statute reads as follows: [65]

"A certified public accountant shall not, without the consent of his client, be examined as to any communication made by the client

---

[64] H. B. Skillman, *1934 Cumulative Supplement to the Compiled General Laws of Florida,* chapter 50, section 3935 (13).

[65] Session Laws of Colorado, 1929, chap. 185, sec. 1(6), p. 644.

to him in person or through the media of books of account and financial records, or his advice, reports or working papers given or made thereon in the course of professional employment, nor shall a secretary, stenographer, clerk or assistant of a certified public accountant be examined without the consent of the client concerned concerning any fact, the knowledge of which he has acquired in such capacity."

The chief distinguishing characteristic of this Colorado statute is the fact that it applies to certified public accountants and not to public accountants in general. In 1931 the supreme court of Colorado in the case of *Hopkins* v. *People* [66] held that where a county or a county court employs a certified public accountant to audit the books of a third party there does not exist that accountant-client relation between the certified public accountant and the third party necessary to make the certified public accountant's information from the audit confidential under the Colorado statute. While the supreme court of Colorado did not find it necessary to determine the validity of the statute in order to decide the case, the court impliedly approved the statute in holding that the case did not come within the statute. This type of statute should meet with the hearty approval of certified practitioners. It should be an inducement to clients to select certified public accountants to do their audits.[67]

PREPARATION OF A PART OF AUDIT BY ASSISTANTS NOT A BAR TO ADMISSION OF EXPERT ACCOUNTANT'S TESTIMONY

That a public accountant's testimony is not rendered inadmissible by the fact that a part of the examination of the records was performed by assistants of the public accountant provided the public accountant has personal knowledge of the accuracy of the audit was set forth in 1930 by the supreme court of Missouri in the case of *State* v. *Matkins* [68] as follows:

"Craig's testimony shows that he was assisted in making the audit by his employee Gibson, that he was personally present about two

[66] 1 P. (2d) 937.
[67] Note: For the public accountant's liability to his client for damages sustained from the negligent disclosure of confidential communications, see page 60.
[68] 34 S. W. (2d) 1. In accord: *Johnstone* v. *Morris*, 292 P. 970 (1930); *Ætna Casualty & Surety Co.* v. *Wilmington*, 157 A. 208 (1931).

weeks of the time the work was in progress, and that it was all done under his direction, and in substance that he had familiarized himself with the records and the results shown by the audit and knew the audit to be correct. We think he was competent to testify to the result of the examination. * * *"

The cases enabling a public accountant to give expert testimony from audits made by assistants where the accountant has supervised the audit and personally knows the audit to be correct represent the weight of authority. In fact, an exhaustive search has revealed no adverse ruling with respect to the matter.

The cases allowing an expert accountant's testimony based upon an audit performed by his assistants are founded upon reason. It would in many audits be impossible for the accountant to perform all the work of the review. If the jury is to have the benefit of summaries, the work of assistants must be accepted as the foundation of the accountant's testimony. The circumstances of the assistant's performance of an audit tend strongly to establish the accuracy of their work. The accountant knows full well that his success as a practitioner is dependent in no small degree upon the quality of service obtained from his employees. He, therefore, selects his assistants so as to obtain only those helpers who will render honest and efficient service. On the other hand, the members of the accountant's staff are aware of the fact that the individual success of each in a large measure will be in proportion to the excellence of the service he gives to his employer. The fact that the accountant directed and supervised the audit is further assurance that the audit correctly shows the condition of the records. Hence, the accountant's testimony based upon the audit prepared in such circumstances should be a trustworthy showing of the condition and contents of the accounting records under consideration.

An Expert Bookkeeper's Testimony Advisory, Not Binding

In 1915 the court of appeals of Georgia held in the case of *Citizens Bank of Tifton* v. *Timmons* [69] that:

"Where a witness duly qualified as an expert general bookkeeper and as a bank bookkeeper, it was not error to admit his testimony,

[69] 84 S. E. 232, 15 Ga. App. 815. In accord: *United States* v. *Porter,* 9 F. (2d) 153.

based upon an inspection and examination of the books of a bank, as to the meaning, interpretation or construction of an account in evidence appearing on such books then under examination, measured by the rules, methods and usages generally prevailing among commercial bookkeepers and bank bookkeepers. Such testimony is advisory merely, and is not binding upon a jury, though they can not arbitrarily disregard it; but the weight and value to be attributed to it is for determination by them."

This decision needs little comment. If the jury were bound by the opinion of the expert witness, the jury would in effect be deprived of its function of fact finding. Under the safeguards surrounding the selection of jurors it is presumed that the jurors are free from bias and partisanship. The expert witness, usually called by a party to the suit, is subject to influences tending toward bias. His pecuniary subservience to a party in the suit could certainly disqualify him as a juror.[70] For this reason, courts will not compel the jury to render its verdict in accordance with an expert's opinion.

Conclusions of an Expert Accountant

The principles evolved by the courts with respect to the admissibility of an expert accountant's conclusions drawn from his audit fall naturally into two groups: (1) The expert accountant's testimony must be confined to a statement of the facts shown by the books. (2) The expert accountant may state to the court his opinion as to value.

Let us first consider the fundamental common-law rule which requires that the expert accountant confine his testimony to a statement of the bare facts shown by the books.[71] An adequate concept of this principle must be based upon a proper understanding of its development. Prior to the eighteenth century there had been little thought on the opinion of a witness in England and America. It was during that century that the word "opinion" came to mean to the legal mind a conclusion of a lay-witness who had no facts to contribute, no knowledge, no personal acquaintance with the

[70] 35 *Corpus Juris*, p. 321, Section 337.
[71] Wigmore on *Evidence*, volume IV, secs. 1917-1929.

man or the land or the loan or the affray about which he was speaking. This sort of evidence was neither objected to nor excluded. The court and jury merely ignored it in forming the verdict. However, during the nineteenth century the conclusions of a lay-witness who had not observed the facts of the case were formally rejected by the courts on the ground that the conclusions were merely superfluous. In the opinion of the courts, jurors as laymen were quite as capable of forming opinions as to facts in issue as were the lay-witnesses who had not personally observed the happenings in dispute. The courts took the position that the jurors should not be confused by diverse opinions of lay-witnesses who had not personal knowledge of the facts. To admit such opinion evidence was thought to infringe upon the time of the jury. This rule is still followed uniformly in England and America with respect to the opinion of a lay-witness who was not a personal observer of the facts of the case. On the other hand, if the witness had personal knowledge of the facts in the case as a result of the exercise of his own senses, he was allowed to state such facts and then express his opinion based upon his observations. However, in stating the facts the witness was required to know the truth of his testimony. He was not permitted to say that he thought, believed or was of the opinion that certain alleged facts of the case were true or untrue. Such is the law in England today; but in the United States a witness is generally required to present before the jurors only the bare facts which he observed. In America the lay-witness is permitted to state to the jury his impressions and opinions of his observations only where the facts were such as could not be described to the jury.

An expert witness may testify in both England and the United States on matters under the consideration of the court even without having had personal observation of the facts of the case. In response to hypothetical questions, he can offer expert opinions on matters that can not ordinarily be interpreted by the jury. The expert witness through study and experience knows facts not available to the lay-jurors, and, using his observations of scientific facts as a basis, he can interpret and draw conclusions such as are indispensable to a proper understanding of the case on the part of the jurors. In the United States if the expert witness need only present the bare facts obtained from his investigation in order that the jury may grasp an understanding of the case, the court will not allow the expert witness to offer his opinion. If the jury can not interpret the bare facts of the investigation, then the court will permit the expert witness to state his conclusions. The purpose of the rules is to afford the jury a proper understanding of the truth of the case.[72]

The admissibility of opinionative testimony of public accountants has come before the courts of the United States in at least a dozen instances. Several opinions giving different effect to the rule that the expert accountant's testimony is limited to a statement of the bare facts shown by the records are presented in the following excerpts. The general principle that the expert accountant's testimony must be confined to a statement of the facts shown by the books was set forth in a syllabus by the supreme court of Georgia in 1923 in the case of *Payne* v. *Franklin County*,[73] as follows:

> "Error is assigned because the court, over objection, permitted a witness, who was an auditor for Franklin county, and who had made an audit of the books and accounts of the treasurer, to testify, in answer to the question, 'From having made an audit of all the books, papers, and documents in evidence, I will ask whether or not you did find any shortage as a result of your examination,' as follows: 'As a result of the first examination we found a deficit of $20,368.21.' The objection was that the question called for a conclusion of the witness, and that the answer was a mere conclusion, and that as an expert accountant he was not authorized to give his conclusion or general opinion. Such evidence was admissible to aid the jury in their investigation, the question as to what are the proper deductions to be made from the entries in the books and papers being at last solely for the jury."

In harmony with the Georgia case, supra, the supreme court of Michigan in 1931, in the case of *Thompson* v. *Walker*,[74] con-

---

[72] Wigmore on *Evidence*, volume IV, sections 1917-1929.
[73] 116 S. E. 627, 155 Ga. 219. In accord: *People* v. *Hatfield*, 208 N. W. 682, 234 Mich. 574.
[74] 234 N. W. 144, 253 Mich. 126. In accord: *Diamond Alkali Co.* v. *Henderson Coal Co.*, 134 A. 386, 287 Pa. 232. See also: *Kersh* v. *State*. 153 So. 284 (1933).

fined the province of the expert accountant's testimony to a statement of facts shown by the books. A portion of the opinion reads:

> "The auditor could not testify from his examination, in advance, of the books, what they would show, if introduced in evidence. It is the books, the contents of which may be summarized, which must be present in court, and introduced in evidence, and the witness may testify to what the books show. He could not invade the province of the jury, who were to pass upon and determine the facts. The auditor could not testify to anything beyond what was shown from an examination of the books themselves, but he could testify as to his compilations, computations and conclusions therefrom or the aggregate amount of any specific items shown thereby. The process of binding component facts into a more concise and general statement is a mere mechanical process."

In 1925 the St. Louis court of appeals in the case of *Pioneer Lumber Co. v. Van Cleave* [75] presented clearly a little different aspect of the controlling principle of the preceding cases, in requiring that the accountant-witness do not express his opinion as to the ultimate issue of the case. The opinion reads in part:

> "* * * but we have found no authority, nor have we been cited any, which has extended the rule to the extent of permitting such accountant witness, after having testified to the results of his examination, to express his opinion as to the ultimate issue in the case. In receiving the opinion of a witness the danger is ever present that the jury may substitute such opinion for their own, and the courts will not require parties to encounter this danger unless some necessity therefor appears. Accordingly, where all the relevant facts be introduced in evidence, and the jury are competent to draw a reasonable inference therefrom, opinion evidence should not be received.
>
> "Courts, as far as practicable, exclude the inference, conclusion, or judgment of a witness as to the ultimate fact in issue to provide against the mischief of invasion of the province of the jury. 22 *Corpus Juris*, 499. The instant case clearly falls within that class in which all of the books and documentary files were in court, and the relevant facts contained in them introduced in evidence, and consequently permitting the opinion of the accountant with reference to the sole question in issue in the case, was obviously an invasion

---

[75] 279 S. W. 241.

of the province of the jury. Therefore, in considering the demurrers at the close of the case, we exclude from consideration the opinion evidence of the said accountant witness as to his opinion of the ultimate issue in the case."

In 1927 the supreme court of Alabama in the case of *Edwards v. State*[76] followed the general principle of the preceding cases and the great weight of authority on the subject and helped to define precisely the scope of the accountant's expert testimony. In this case it was held that the accountant-witness could not explain transactions under dispute, because he had not personal knowledge of the transactions. The accountant was permitted to explain only the books' showing of the transactions. A portion of the opinion follows:

"* * * It was, of course, competent for the auditor to give evidence of what he found upon the books and of the cheques themselves, but, it not being contended that he had any personal knowledge of the transactions, he could not properly explain them and state what they represented, it being manifest that such evidence was predicated solely upon the conclusion or opinion of the witness."

The excerpts given above represent the well-established authority on the admissibility of the accountant's expert testimony. The general rule running through all the cases confines the province of the expert accountant's testimony to a statement of what the books show. The accountant can not express his opinion as to the ultimate issue in the case. Where the auditor does not have personal knowledge of the transactions under consideration—and he generally does not—he can not explain the transactions nor state what they represent; he can merely state what the vouchers and journals show such transactions to be. The auditor can not testify: "I think, I believe, I am of the opinion that, or I conclude that certain transactions took place, or that certain facts in issue are true or untrue." On the other hand, the auditor is permitted to state to the court: "The books show certain transactions to have taken place. The records show a shortage in inventory. The books show that cash is missing to the amount of ———." In other words, the accountant

[76] 111 So. 765.

in producing testimony is limited to a statement of the character and content of the accounting records. The revelation of the facts as found in the books is the scope of the accountant's testimony. The making of inferences from the facts revealed by a statement of the showing of the books is purely within the province of the jury. If the expert accountant's testimony concerns any accounting fact which might properly be understood by the lay-jurors, the accountant testifying is limited to a bare statement of the fact; the jurors alone make deductions from the fact. However, if the accounting fact is one that is not intelligible to the lay-jurors, the accountant-witness is permitted to explain the fact to the jurors. Then, finally, if the fact is such that it can not be explained so that the jury may obtain a proper understanding of the fact, the expert accountant may present to the jury his conclusions as to the fact shown by the books.[77]

The cases defining the scope of the accountant's testimony make his rôle before the jury too narrow, too restricted to accomplish the greatest good in the cause of truth. In theory the courts seek to bring to the jury practically the same degree of understanding of facts as is possessed by the witness. Except in the case of a very simple set of books it is impossible for the accountant to convey an adequate picture of the character and content of accounting records. The jury can not be made to comprehend the meaning of the records in the way the accountant understands it. The accountant through many years of study, training, and practice has acquired an apperceptive background which enables him to place interpretations and meanings upon the accounting data, which are not possible to the lay-jurors. The ability of the jury to discover the truth would be facilitated if the accountant-witness were permitted not

[77] Note: (1885) *Railroad Co. v. Schultz,* 43 Oh. St. 270, 283, 1 N. E. 324: "It must not be supposed that there is any rule of evidence concerning the opinions of witnesses which is peculiar to fences, highways, bridges or steamboats or to any other special subjects of investigation. Where the facts concerning their condition can not be made palpable to the jurors so that their means of forming opinions are practically equal to those of the witnesses, opinions of such witnesses may be received, accompanied by such facts supporting them as they may be able to place intelligently before the jury." This case represents the weight of authority on the point.

only to state what the records contain but also to state his opinion as to the inferences to be drawn from the records.[78]

Courts, in the case of expert testimony on value, have made an exception to the rule which prohibits a witness from giving opinionative testimony. The courts of the United States generally allow opinionative evidence concerning value. Anyone who has peculiar knowledge of the value of specific property or of a business enterprise may offer his opinion of such value before the jury. It is quite often impossible for the witness to picture to the jury all the factors that lead him to place upon specific property a certain value. Hence, from necessity, in order that the jury may utilize the expert witness' information on value, courts allow his testimonial opinion relative to the worth of specific property or of a business enterprise.[79]

In agreement with the principle admitting expert testimony generally with respect to value, several courts have broadened the scope of the admissibility of the accountant's expert testimony to include his opinion relative to the worth of property or of a business enterprise. In support of this principle the supreme court of Georgia in 1927 in the case of *Bitting* v. *State* [80] held:

"* * * It does not seem to us that any of the evidence to which objection was made was improperly admitted for any reason suggested in the exceptions or argument of counsel. It has frequently been held that proof of value is merely matter of opinion, no matter how the information of the witness may have been derived, whether based upon his own estimate, or upon an estimate accredited by the witness, but derived from the opinions of others. And while this court has decided that 'the opinions of persons cannot be proved or used in evidence this way; that is, a witness will not be permitted to prove the opinions of others on any question,' if the testimony sought to be excluded is given as the opinion of the witness himself, and vouched for by the witness as such on his oath, it is not to be excluded merely because upon cross-examination the sources of his

---

[78] Note: For a discussion of the desirability of American courts' following the English ruling permitting even lay-witnesses to state their opinions after they have presented personally observed facts see Wigmore on *Evidence*, volume IV, section 1929.

[79] Wigmore on *Evidence*, volume IV, sections 1940-1944.

[80] 139 S. E. 877.

information and the information which caused him to form the opinion testified to are discovered. The jury may discredit the opinion of the witness after they know the causes which lead to the formation of his opinion; but the opinion of the witness as to value, if it is his own opinion, is admissible as evidence for whatever it may be worth, regardless of the reliability of the data upon which he was induced to base his opinion. * * *"

Bitting v. *State,* supra, held that an expert witness' opinion with respect to value is admissible regardless of the sources of the information upon which the witness has based his opinion. Another case, *Stephens* v. *United States,*[81] decided in 1930 by the circuit court of appeals, ninth circuit, quite in agreement with the preceding case, held that an expert accountant's testimony on value may be admissible even though the witness' opinion is not based solely upon the accounting records of the business or property to be valued. A portion of the decision reads:

"Another contention in this group relates more particularly to the testimony of the witness Bryan. Referring to what appear to be annual financial statements of Stephens & Co., he criticized them as not reflecting the true financial condition of the company as of the dates to which they relate. One of the criticisms was that they exhibited as assets stocks or bonds which, as he contended the record showed, had either not been issued or of which the company had not acquired possession and ownership during the periods covered by the statements. Clearly, we think the objections made to this part of the testimony are without merit. The other criticism was that some of the statements exhibited items of stocks or bonds as assets at highly excessive overvaluations. In reaching his conclusion as to what would have been a reasonable valuation he frankly stated that he resorted to information not appearing in the books and records of the company. But it appears that he was not only a trained accountant in the strict sense, but that he had had long and wide experience in connection with business where it was necessary to observe and place valuations upon such securities, and, as he put it, he followed the same course in this case in resorting to sources of information touching value 'as I have done all my life in valuing securities.' While the propriety of receiving his testimony in this

[81] 41 F. (2d) 440.

respect is not entirely free from doubt, we are of the view that the court did not abuse its discretion in admitting it, and that there was no prejudicial error."

Closely akin to the two preceding cases is the case of *Manley v. State*,[82] decided by the court of appeals of Georgia in 1927, which held that an expert accountant's testimony as to the solvency of a business may be competent evidence. A portion of the opinion reads:

"It is true that R. E. Bentley, an expert witness in behalf of the state, testified that he had made an examination and analysis of the books of this bank, and that from such examination and analysis said bank was insolvent as far back as the first of 1915, and that such insolvency had continued from that date down to the time the bank closed its doors and went into the hands of the superintendent of banks for liquidation. This opinion of this witness is competent evidence on the question of the insolvency vel non of this bank. Such an opinion is not conclusive upon the jury. The testimony is intended to aid them in coming to a correct conclusion upon the subject; but the jury is not bound by such opinion and can disregard it. * * *"

The rule which allows an expert accountant's opinionative testimony on questions of value has the support of the well-settled common law permitting expert witnesses generally to testify with respect to value.[83] The accountant through his review and analysis of accounting records can make estimates of values in a manner not intelligible to the lay-juror. Moreover, the technique employed would be beyond the comprehension of the jury. Hence, in order that the jury may avail itself of this technical information as to value, the accountant-witness is permitted to state his conclusions as to the value of the business the records of which he has analyzed. The determination of the financial condition of a business as to solvency is a special problem of estimating values. Hence, the courts allow an accountant who has reviewed the records of a business to state whether or not he thinks the business was insolvent at the time the cause of action arose.

[82] 144 S. E. 170, 166 Ga. 563.
[83] Wigmore on *Evidence*, volume IV, secs. 1940-1944.

Accountant's Right to Refresh his Memory from Records

The supreme court of Nebraska in 1922 in the case of *Heilman* v. *State* [84] held:

"* * * An expert accountant who has examined the books of a public officer to ascertain an issuable fact and compiled a statement may refresh his memory from the compilation and testify to the result. The books, records, vouchers and documents used by the expert in making his computation were in court available to defendant, and the evidence was not objectionable on that ground."

The object of placing evidence before the court is to convey to the jury a proper understanding of the truth of the case. Since the accountant-witness is primarily concerned with conveying to the minds of the jurors a knowledge of the accounting records under consideration, certainly, any aid, such as a re-examination of the records, that would facilitate an accurate representation of the truth would be permitted by the court.

[84] 189 N. W. 303, 109 Neb. 15.

CHAPTER IV

SOME SPECIAL RIGHTS OF PUBLIC ACCOUNTANTS

CHAMPERTY

ANY comprehensive treatment of champerty must involve some attention to maintenance, for champerty is a special kind of maintenance. The common law and the statutes of both America and England are so diverse in their rulings on the two subjects that no adequate definition of either can be given. Any general statement regarding the nature of either misdemeanor must necessarily be qualified by diverse exceptions, depending upon the statutes and court precedents of the jurisdiction in which the remedy against the misdemeanor is sought.[1]

Maintenance is an officious intermeddling in a suit that in no way belongs to one, by maintaining or assisting either party with money or otherwise to prosecute or defend it. According to the early common law and statutes of England maintenance was an offense against public justice, since it kept alive strife and contention and perverted the remedial process of the law into an engine of oppression.[2]

Champerty is a species of maintenance. It is a bargain to divide the proceeds of a litigation between a party to the suit and the attorney or layman supporting the litigation. The division of the proceeds of the litigation distinguishes champerty from maintenance in general.

While maintenance and champerty were prohibited by the Roman law, the modern law on the subjects is based largely upon the developments that took place in feudal England. It was a common

---

[1] Note: Where the jurisdiction of the complaint against maintenance or champerty is different from the jurisdiction in which the cause of action arose, the suit must always be tried in accordance with the laws of the jurisdiction where the complaint is made. (Thornton on *Attorneys at Law*, volume II, p. 662.)
[2] 4 Blackstone's *Commentaries* 135.

practice during the early legal history of England for great and powerful feudal lords to take upon themselves litigation in behalf of weaker members of the community. In many instances the claims were unjust; but the feudal lords overawed the courts and obtained judgments, the benefits of which went largely to the feudal lords. Hence, to combat this pernicious practice, common-law decisions and statutes made maintenance and champerty crimes, and rendered invalid contracts tainted with those misdemeanors.

While the early law was severe on the perpetrators of maintenance and champerty, except where maintenance was extended for purely charitable purposes, there is no record that anyone was punished criminally for the commission of either misdemeanor. The effect of the laws on maintenance and champerty is to be found in the voiding of contracts. In modern times there is not the great amount of need for rigid laws on champerty and maintenance which existed in feudal Europe. The statute of limitations, the statute of frauds and the giving of costs against the unsuccessful party have contributed to prevent groundless and vexatious litigation and have caused a relaxing of the severe rules against champerty and maintenance of mediæval England. In many states the doctrine of maintenance and champerty is scarcely recognized, even by the courts. Where the laws of maintenance and champerty are recognized the many exceptions have modified their ancient severity. Neither maintenance nor champerty has been held to exist where the person maintaining and the suitor stood in some social relation, as that of relatives by consanguinity or affinity, master and servant or landlord and tenant.[3] It is well-settled law that maintenance or champerty does not exist where the one offering assistance in litigation has any interest whatever in the subject of the suit. Whether this interest is great or small, vested or contingent, certain or uncertain, it is, if honestly believed to exist, sufficient to remove the case from the rules against maintenance and champerty.[4]

By the great weight of modern authority fees charged by an attorney to a client for professional services and dependent upon

[3] *Reece* v. *Kyle,* 49 Ohio St. 475, 31 N. E. 747, 16 L. R. A. 723.
[4] 5 R. C. L., p. 274.

the amount of recovery are not within the rules against maintenance and champerty. But if the attorney agrees, not only to prosecute or defend the case for a fee contingent upon the success of the litigation, but also to bear the expense of witness fees or costs of the suit, the agreement is champertous. If, in addition to the contingent-fee stipulation, the agreement provides that the client shall not settle by compromise or otherwise without the consent of the attorney, the agreement is champertous. If the contingent fee was a reward for the attorney's services as a witness or for the quashing of a criminal prosecution, the agreement providing for such fee is champertous. Even where the attorney's contract is champertous and, therefore, void, the attorney is generally permitted to recover on a quantum meruit for the value of services rendered.[5] Some courts, including the supreme court of the United States, refuse to be concerned with all the technicalities of the common-law tests of champerty and maintenance and consider merely whether the particular contract in question is oppressive in character, and, if not, to uphold it, though the attorney agreed to bear the expenses of the litigation and contracted for a share of the proceeds.

In the main, the rules of maintenance and champerty applicable to attorneys govern in the contractual relationships between laymen. A difference lies in the fact that the attorney contributes his services while the layman generally hires the legal service necessary to prosecute or defend the suit whose court costs he has agreed to bear and in whose proceeds he has been promised a share. Not all courts require that the layman must bear the costs of the suit in addition to sharing in the proceeds of the trial before he can be said to be guilty of champerty; some courts have held agreements void for champerty where the layman was promised a share in the

[5] Note: By the weight of authority it is no defense to an action that the plaintiff has made a champertous contract for its prosecution, unless the cause of action be based upon the champertous agreement, as where the cause of action was assigned to the plaintiff by a champertous agreement. For further illustration, if a note or an account be assigned to an attorney for litigation with the understanding that the attorney is to get a percentage of the profits from litigation, the cause of action is invalid; but if no assignment is made to the attorney and the suit is brought in the name of the client, the cause of action will not be invalidated by the fact that the attorney is to bear costs of the suit and divide the proceeds of the litigation with the client. (Thornton on *Attorneys at Law*, volume II, p. 684.)

recovery in consideration of his rendering services to the litigant or securing evidence to sustain the suit or attending to the prosecution or defense of the suit.[6]

Some of the more important general characteristics of the laws of maintenance and champerty having been set forth, it remains to show to what extent the public accountant is subject to the rules of maintenance and champerty. The occasions on which an accountant as such might deem it necessary to enter into an agreement involving maintenance or champerty would be rare. The most probable situations inviting champertous agreements by public accountants would be in practice before the agencies for the collection of income taxes, federal and state. The accountant would, in such practice, be acting as a counselor and should be subject to the same rules of maintenance and champerty as are applicable to the attorney.

It might easily happen that an accountant would be asked to enter into a champertous agreement to furnish evidence. It seems to be the weight of authority that an agreement to furnish existing documents and information already in the hands of the promisor to a litigant for use as evidence in an action from which the promisor is to share in the recovery is not champertous.[7] On the other hand, if the one providing the existing information further stipulates that he will procure for a contingent fee other information necessary to sustain the suit, the agreement is champertous, tending to perjury and a perversion of justice.[8] By the weight of authority an agreement to pay an ordinary witness as compensation a fee in excess of the statutory amount is invalid, on the ground that the agreement lacks consideration and has a tendency to perjury. An agreement to pay a witness a fee contingent on the success of the suit is doubly vicious in that the agreement not only violates the statutory-fee bill, but also tends to induce the witness to color his testimony so as to win the suit. In common with a lay witness, the compensation of an expert witness can not be made to depend

[6] Williston on *Contracts*, volume III, sections 1711-1716; 5 R. C. L., pp. 268-286; Thornton on *Attorneys-at-law*, volume II, pp. 652-687; Note—16 L. R. A. 745.
[7] Annotation, 34 A. L. R. 1537.
[8] Ibid.; Annotation, 16 A. L. R. 1433.

upon the contingency of the successful outcome of the litigation. Likewise, by the weight of authority, an expert witness can not demand compensation in excess of the statutory witness fee before testifying to facts within his knowledge, although it may have required professional study, learning or skill to ascertain them.[9] If the expert witness has acquired knowledge of the facts through previous employment with a litigant or anyone else, he must testify without more compensation than the statutory fee. On the other hand, if the witness, after he has been summoned to testify, must make preliminary preparation or render professional services for the purpose of qualifying himself to give expert testimony, he is entitled to compensation for such preparatory services.[10] Hence, a public accountant in response to a court order to testify could not be compelled to make an audit without compensation in order that he might qualify to testify as an expert concerning certain accounting records.

An American case dealing with champerty on the part of an accountant was decided by the supreme court of Wisconsin in 1924. The facts of this case, *Miller* v. *Anderson*,[11] were as follows:

The plaintiff, who was an accountant, was employed as head accountant and credit man of the Interstate Packing Company at Winona, Minnesota, for a year beginning in February, 1922. In the early part of his employment the accountant heard the superintendent state that the company owed a stock shipper at Tomah, Wisconsin, a large sum of money and that the company remained silent about the debt because the shipper was unaware of the claim. After the accountant left the employ of the Interstate Packing Company he ascertained the name of the stock shipper, defendant in this case, and entered into a contract with the shipper for the collection of the debt.

The contract entered into between the plaintiff accountant and the defendant stock-shipper provided that the accountant, with the

---

[9] Note: The English courts and a substantial minority of American decisions have held that an expert witness can not be coerced to testify unless he has had compensation greater than the fee allowed a lay-witness.

[10] Annotation, 2 A. L. R. 1576; Annotation, 16 A. L. R. 1457; Williston on *Contracts*, vol. III, sec. 1716.

[11] 196 N. W. 869, 183 Wis. 163, 34 A. L. R. 1529.

Some Special Rights of Public Accountants 199

coöperation of the shipper, should make such investigations of shipments and sales made by the stock shipper to the Interstate Packing Company as the accountant deemed necessary to determine whether any debt was due by the Interstate Packing Company to the shipper. The contract further provided that, if it should be ascertained that a balance was due the shipper from the Interstate Packing Company and if such debt should be collected, the accountant and the shipper would share equally in all moneys thus received.

After the execution of this contract the accountant and the shipper obtained from the railroad over which the shipper had made his shipments the number of carloads of stock the shipper had sent to the Interstate Packing Company. By means of an intensive search the accountant and shipper were able to find among the shipper's possessions sales tickets issued by the Interstate Packing Company, which tallied with records of the railroad. Then the accountant and the shipper compared these tickets with the credits to the shipper's account on the books of the bank where he was accustomed to make deposits. All the sales tickets except two corresponded with the credits to the shipper's account on the bank books. After the accountant and the shipper determined the amount of the two shipments for which no payment had been made, the shipper drew a draft for that amount upon the Interstate Packing Company. The draft was returned unpaid. Then the shipper went to the Interstate Packing Company and succeeded in collecting $3,750. The shipper refused to remit half of the collection to the accountant; and the accountant brought an action for that sum against the shipper. The shipper set up the defense of champerty. The court's opinion in part follows:

> "That a champertous contract is void and will not be enforced is a trite proposition. Contracts to pay for collecting and procuring testimony to be used in evidence, coupled with a condition that the contractee's right to compensation depends upon the character of the testimony procured, or upon the result of the suit in which it is to be used, have been uniformly condemned by the courts as contrary to public policy, for the reason that such agreements hold out an inducement to commit fraud or procure persons to commit perjury. Thus, a

contract to pay a physician a percentage of the recovery for acting as an expert in a personal-injury action is against public policy.

"Likewise, it has been held * * * that an agreement to pay a witness more than the statutory witness fees for appearing and testifying to facts within his knowledge is contrary to public policy and void. This is especially true where the compensation is dependent upon the successful outcome of the litigation.

"It will be observed that these several principles involve a common element, namely, existing or contemplated litigation. Such contracts are held to contravene public policy because they tend to the perversion of justice. It is, therefore, necessary to examine the contract between the parties for the purpose of ascertaining whether it contemplated the institution of any action or proceeding and the rendition of any service or assistance on the part of the plaintiff condemned by the foregoing principles.

"It must be conceded that the contract, on its face, does not provide for the institution of any litigation, nor does any suggestion appear therefrom that either of the parties had any such thought in mind. But in cases such as this we are not confined to a consideration of the written contract. Parol evidence is competent to show that a writing valid on its face is a mere cover for an illegal transaction. * * * The answer alleges that the written contract was and is a part of an attempt to cover a simultaneous oral understanding and agreement between the parties which does offend against the foregoing principles. Parol evidence of the negotiations leading up to the written contract was therefore admitted and must be considered in this connection. But the parol evidence fails to reveal any thought at any time on the part of either of the parties that litigation with the packing company would be necessary or likely. In fact, it was not suggested by either party, so far as the parol evidence discloses. The nearest approach to such a suggestion occurred after the contract had been executed and after the draft made upon the packing company had been returned unpaid. The parties then went to a lawyer's office, and the plaintiff suggested that the account be placed with a lawyer, to be handled in the form of a collection. But the defendant did not like that. He thought he knew the vice-president and stock buyer of the packing company and that he could make a settlement with him. He went to Winona and effected a settlement with him. The record discloses a situation where the defendant had simply lost sight of the fact that he had not been paid for two carloads of stock shipped to the packing company. When he was first told that the packing company was the debtor which the plaintiff had in mind, he could not believe that the packing company owed him anything. It was plaintiff's task to get together defendant's records and accounts and the records of the railway company, for the purpose of informing defendant of the true situation of affairs. Plaintiff knew that the packing company knew that they were owing the defendant. Certainly plaintiff did not assume that litigation would be necessary to enforce collection. There was no agreement, expressed or implied, that plaintiff would bear any part of the expense of the litigation. There is no evidence to show that it was assumed by either party that, even if litigation should result, plaintiff would be a necessary witness. As we now view the case, we are at a loss to divine the character of the evidence which plaintiff could have given, had litigation resulted, that would have been in any sense substantial or material. Defendant's case would have been proved by showing that he had shipped a certain number of carloads of stock. This could have been shown by the records of the railroad company. Defendant's own testimony would have been sufficient to show that he had not been paid for two carloads so shipped. It would then have devolved upon the packing company to prove payment. Any testimony that the plaintiff might have given would have been so remote and of so little weight or materiality that it can not characterize the contract as one having for its purpose the influencing of litigation. To condemn this contract as one against public policy is to carry the principles invoked by the respondent to a prudish extreme, and would compel a holding that a business man whose accounts have become confused or involved may not employ an accountant to audit them for a compensation contingent upon the amount eventually collected. To such an extreme we are not prepared to go where the gist of the contract is not to promote successful litigation, but rather to place the client in the possession of the true facts concerning his affairs and accounts."

In the case of *Miller* v. *Anderson,* supra, there were the following conditions in the alleged champertous agreement:

(1) A compensation contingent upon collection of a debt.

(2) A promise by the plaintiff to search defendant's records to procure evidence to substantiate the claim which the plaintiff knew existed.

(3) No litigation contemplated.

(4) No mention or implication that plaintiff was to bear any cost of litigation.

The agreement was not champertous, for in every champertous agreement there must be present or contemplated litigation. Furthermore, the agreement was not champertous because the contingent remuneration was to be derived from an ordinary collection of a business debt and not from the proceeds of a law suit and also because the information was to be procured to substantiate a business debt and not to sustain litigation. Certainly, an accountant may perform an audit for a fee contingent upon certain collections where litigation is not contemplated.

While decisions generally have not been concerned with the adequacy of evidence to sustain litigation where champerty is alleged, yet the court's position in this case seems to be well taken in holding that an agreement to furnish evidence for litigation is not champertous unless the evidence affords substantial proof in the case. If there is no material or substantial proof in the evidence which the plaintiff can offer, he can do little or nothing by the production of such evidence to pervert the course of justice. This thought inclines toward the recent innovation of certain courts, including the supreme court of the United States, in brushing aside the technicalities of champerty and seeking to determine whether or not the agreement in reality tends toward oppression and perversion of justice.

While the court in this case is correct in the philosophy of the law of champerty, it appears to be erroneous in taking the position that the only evidence the plaintiff could have produced for litigation was from his knowledge of the accounts of the packing company. While the cases that have been involved with the commission of champerty through production of documentary or other evidence have been concerned with information not in the possession or control of the litigant, it would seem that, as in this case, where the evidence was in such a condition that it could not be used without the services of an accountant, even though the records were possessed or controlled directly or remotely by the litigant, courts should hold that the accountant procured evidence in making the search or audit and interpretations indispensable to the use of the records as evidence.

Ownership of Working Papers

English cases are singularly silent on the subject of ownership of papers upon which accountants base their reports to their clients.[12]

An important decision rendered in 1927 by the supreme judicial court of Massachusetts in the case of *Ipswich Mills* v. *Dillon* [13] set a precedent for American courts with respect to the rights of a public accountant to his working papers. In this case the defendants had been employed for many years prior to 1926 to conduct the audits and prepare income-tax returns for the plaintiff textile mill. The plaintiff in 1926 in order to obtain certain data for income-tax purposes demanded from the defendants "all papers in your possession belonging to Ipswich Mills." The accountants refused to give up the papers; and the plaintiff sought a court order to compel the defendants to deliver the papers.

The *Ipswich Mills* v. *Dillon* case held as property of the public accountant the following records, papers, letters and documents prepared in the course of the accountant-client relationship:

(1) Office copy of client's income-tax return, a copy of which had been sent to the client.

(2) Office copies of schedules relating to the client's income-tax returns, copies of which had been sent to the client.

(3) Carbon copies of letters from accountant to collector of internal revenue.

(4) Carbon copies of letters from accountant to his client.

(5) Original letters from client to accountant.

(6) Original letters from client's attorney to accountant.

(7) The research data, or working papers, the accountant had obtained from a review of the client's accounting records.

Since the accountant in this case conceded that the client was owner of papers that had originated in the client's office or in the

---

[12] "The Ownership of Accountants' Working Papers," *The Accountant*, London, 1927, volume 77, p. 187.

[13] 157 N. E. 604.

office of the client's selling agents, or in the office of someone associated with the client's selling agents, the court did not rule on the title to such papers. Such papers doubtless were the property of the client, since apparently the accountant had nothing to do with them except to gain custody of them for purposes of review.

The decision in the case, that the public accountant is an independent contractor and not an agent of his client, is well substantiated by reason and by precedents in other professions. The public accountant assumes none of the essential characteristics of an agent in his contract with his client. The professional accountant does not represent the mind of his client in the making, changing or cancelling of business contracts for the client with third parties. The public accountant is not subject to direction and control by the client as is an agent to his principal.

Since the public accountant acts in the capacity of an independent contractor and not as an agent in dealing with his client, the working papers he must prepare in order to render his reports to his client become his own property. He contracts with his client to furnish reports showing the condition of the accounting records of the client and does not agree to provide the client with means by which such reports are prepared.

The public accountant is responsible to his client to render efficient income-tax service. Because of the many contingencies that may arise after the return has been prepared and sent to the collecting agency, it is vital to the accountant that he retain a copy of the return, for only in this way can the client be assured of competent income-tax service. Unless the courts grant the accountant title to his copy of the income-tax return, the professional accountant can have no assurance that he will be able to retain the data necessary to cope with subsequent contingencies.

As the accountant should be allowed to retain title to copies of income-tax returns rendered for his client, so should the accountant be permitted to own carbon copies of letters sent by the accountant. In the course of accounting practice questions concerning previous audits arise and require the attention of the auditor. The continuation of the accountant's relation with his client may hinge upon the accountant's giving prompt attention to matters involving the former audit. It may easily happen that the information necessary to solve the question is contained in the carbon copy of a letter. It is essential to the practice of public accounting that the practitioner be permitted to own carbon copies of letters relating to audits he has performed. Only in this way can the accountant give to his client continued and trustworthy service.

Courts uniformly allow to the recipient of a letter complete title for all purposes except publication. The paper and the manuscription upon it constitute a gift by the sender to the recipient. Of course, a public accountant should not be permitted to reveal to third parties confidential information received by letter from his client; but he should be permitted to own the letters he receives.

While the *Ipswich Mills* v. *Dillon* is the only case on the ownership of the public accountant's letters, documents and working papers prepared in the course of the accountant-client relation, the principles of the case are sound and should be followed in future decisions.

Virginia has a statute which entitles a public accountant to ownership of his working papers:[14]

"All statements, records, schedules and memoranda made by a certified public accountant or a public accountant, or by an employee or employees of a certified public accountant, or public accountant, incident to or in the course of professional service to clients by such certified public accountant, or public accountant, except reports submitted by a certified public accountant, or public accountant, to a client, shall be and remain the property of such certified public accountant, or public accountant, in the absence of a written agreement between the certified public accountant, or public accountant, and the client, to the contrary."

Florida has a similar statute.[15] No cases have arisen under these statutes of Virginia and Florida.

THE ACCOUNTANT'S LIEN UPON HIS EMPLOYER'S BOOKS

Prior to a consideration of the subject of the accountant's lien upon his employer's records as a security for the payment of service

[14] Acts of assembly, Virginia, 1928, chapter 454, section 572a.
[15] *Certified Public Accountant Laws of the United States*, American Institute Publishing Co., Inc., p. 41.

fees, it is well to devote some attention to the nature of a lien. A lien is a legal claim or charge on either personalty or real estate as security for the payment of some debt or obligation. On the basis of source of creation liens are divisible into common-law, equitable, maritime and statutory. On the basis of the scope of the claims, liens are divided into general and specific.

A common-law lien is a right originating from a contract implied in law by which possession of personal property may be retained until some debt due on or secured by such property is paid or satisfied.[16] A common-law lien will be implied where a lien in a particular set of circumstances has received immemorial recognition at common-law or is uniformly and generally allowed by trade custom or practice. When the custom is first proved to establish a lien, the lien arises from the intentions of the parties as interpreted from the facts within the custom; but after common-law courts have repeatedly held a lien to exist in accordance with the particular trade custom or usage, the type of lien becomes so well established that it is implied in law. The common law makes a contract in the circumstances in order to afford a sure remedy to a person who has performed services for another. The claimant has neither title nor a right to obtain title to the property; he simply has a right of detainer for use as an effectual agency for inducing or compelling a settlement of a just claim. It necessarily follows, then, that a common-law lien can exist no longer than the duration of possession by the claimant. Furthermore, the party claiming the lien must show the just possession of the thing held; the lien can not be founded upon an illegal or fraudulent act or breach of duty.

An equitable lien is a charge or encumbrance placed upon personal or real property by a contract expressed, or implied in fact, to insure payment of a debt or performance of an obligation.[17] The charge or encumbrance is not a conveyance of title to the creditor, nor is it a right to obtain title, but rather a right to have a certain obligation settled through sale of identified property under court order. An equitable lien is created by the intentions of the parties.

[16] Jones on *Liens*, volume I, secs. 1-26.
[17] Jones on *Liens*, volume I, secs. 27-96.

An equitable lien is a means of affording justice where it may be deduced from an express contract or surrounding circumstances that the parties must have intended that a charge be maintained upon specific property to insure performance of some obligation. While at common law a lien means merely the right of possession until a pecuniary recovery is made from the general resources of the debtor, in equity a lien affords a way of satisfying rights and obligations out of identified property even though the chattel is not possessed by the creditor. As between the debtor and creditor the lien may be effectual even though possession of the property is retained by the debtor. The kinds of equitable liens are as varied as the possibilities of forming contracts creating them. An example of an equitable lien arising from an express contract is to be found in an agreement of a merchant to permit the sale of his stock of merchandise under court order to satisfy a claim of purchase money in case of default. An implied equitable lien arises when a debtor gives an order to a third person to pay a creditor out of a specific fund under the control of the third person.

By legislation in America practically all the common-law liens and many of the equitable liens have been enlarged in their scope or have been made more effectual by provisions for their enforcement.[18] In many instances the statutes have gone beyond the liens previously recognized at common law or in equity and have created a number of new liens. The tendency of legislation is to extend the protection afforded by liens to all persons who supply labor or materials for others. A common form of remedy in a statutory lien is a legal attachment. But in some states the statutes provide for equitable action as a remedy for the statutory lien. The equitable action is usually in the form of a decree for a sale of the property in order to obtain funds to satisfy the debt upon which the lien is based.

A specific lien is a right which attaches to specific property as security for some demand for the unpaid price of work done or materials furnished in repairing or constructing the identical chattel. While a specific lien may be created by common law, a contract or a statute, the origin of this type of lien is to be found in the com-

[18] Jones on *Liens*, volume I, secs. 97-112.

mon law. The specific or particular lien was made necessary to protect tradesmen and artisans for the price of work done on goods in their possession. The principal specific liens upon personal property at common law are those of mechanics and artisans, innkeepers, carriers, sellers or vendors and landlords under the process of distress. The specific lien has been adopted by equity and statutes to include situations where possession is not in the creditor. The specific or particular lien is favored by the decisions and legislation. It adds confidence to business and does not place any unconscionable restraint upon property.

A general lien is a right attached to a particular chattel to serve as security for a general balance of account due from the owner. While the general lien is generally confined to common law, it may be equitable or statutory. General liens are looked at with jealousy by courts, because such liens encroach upon the common law and destroy the equal distribution of the debtor's estate among his creditors. The principal general liens are those of factors and brokers, bankers, lawyers upon their clients' papers and moneys, warehousemen and wharfingers.[19]

Two cases have defined, though inadequately, the rights of an accountant to a lien on his employer's books. Each case appeared in 1901. *Burleigh* v. *Clark, Lim.*,[20] was decided by the chancery division of England:

"The accountant now took the view that he had a lien on the books of the company for work done, and he refused to deliver up the books except on payment by the receiver of his account, £137. The way in which he got possession of the books was this: He asked leave of the directors and the secretary to take away the books to his own office, as he said the company's office was small and inconvenient for him, and he could do the work better in his own office.

"His lordship said that the affidavits filed showed that the respondent claimed a lien, not as auditor, but as accountant. In his opinion the question of an auditor's lien did not arise and had it done so, he considered that an auditor had no such lien; but that point he did not now decide. In respect of the share register, the accountant had no possible lien on that, but he held that he was entitled to a lien

[19] Jones on *Liens*, vol. I, secs. 1-152; 37 *Corpus Juris*, pp. 306-323.
[20] *The Accountant*, London, 1901, volume 27, law reports section, p. 65.

on such books only as he had actually worked upon, in respect of his proper remuneration for work upon those books only."

Scott Shoe Machinery Co. v. Broaker,[21] the other opinion, was rendered by the city court of New York. In this case an action of replevin was brought by a client to recover possession of books in the hands of certain public accountants who held the books in an effort to enforce payment for services rendered to the client. The decision reads:

> "At common law, liens were given to attorneys, warehousemen, wharfingers and to other special classes of persons. There was no such thing as an accountant's lien. And, except in the case of these favored classes, the only persons having a lien at common law are bailees employed to change, alter, repair or do work upon some article, and who by their services have added something to its value. In this latter class are the liens of tailors, carpenters, etc. This class appears to be the same as is provided for by section 70 of the New York lien law. The defendants certainly do not come within this class. They have done nothing to the books but have merely made an examination of them. After their examination the books remained as they were before, nothing whatsoever having been added to their value. The object of the examination made by an accountant is the preparation of a report. The report may be something of value, or it may not, but the books themselves are not the least changed or improved by the investigation."

These two reported cases, dealing with the accountant's lien upon his client's books, are doubtless correctly decided in the light of the well-established law of liens. In the two cases the only semblance of a lien was a specific lien at common law, and that had necessarily to be predicated upon the possession of the records by the accountant and also upon the improvement of the records by the accountant's labors. In other words, an accountant's lien upon his client's books must be based on a possession lawfully obtained and an improvement of the records effected by the accountant through recording entries or otherwise. Generally the accountant will not obtain possession of his client's records, nor will he usually improve the records themselves. Hence, in most instances the two

[21] 71 N. Y. S. 1023, 33 Misc. Rep. 382, 10 N. Y. Ann. Cas. 130.

most essential elements of the common-law lien would be absent from the accountant's dealings with his client. Even where the elements of possession and improvement of the books are present it cannot be expected that courts will allow more than the common-law specific lien. It can not be expected that courts will allow to the accountant the common-law general lien upon his client's books to ensure collection of his service fees, in view of the jealous attitude courts usually assume towards general liens.

The occasions upon which an accountant might acquire an equitable lien to secure payment for services, indeed, would be rare. Any demand on the part of the accountant for an express contract giving him a lien upon his client's records would probably mean the termination of relations with the client. However, it is conceivable that an implied equitable lien may arise in favor of the accountant. It might happen that a client would give an order to a collecting agency to pay out of funds collected from the client's accounts receivable a certain sum as compensation to an accountant for auditing services. In such circumstances the accountant would have an implied equitable lien upon the collection fund to secure payment for auditing services.

No state seems to have a statute giving the public accountant a lien upon any property of his client to secure payment for auditing services. In fairness to accountants, state legislation might well provide for a lien upon the records or other property of clients to secure payment for auditing services. Of course, any such statute should be coupled with an appropriate remedy such as impounding of records or the sale of property to effect payment of the debt.

Rights of the Public Accountant Under United States Bankruptcy Act

A proper understanding of the public accountant's rights under the United States bankruptcy act must be based upon a general concept of the section dealing with priorities and, then, upon a survey of the court interpretations dealing specifically with public accountants. With this end in view the statute is quoted and discussed generally and then the cases pertaining to accountants are presented and reviewed.

"United States bankruptcy act of 1898, as amended, section 64: Debts which have priority. (a) The court shall order the trustee to pay all taxes legally due and owing by the bankrupt to the United States, state, county, district or municipality, in the order of priority as set forth in paragraph (b) hereof: provided, that no order shall be made for the payment of a tax assessed against real estate of a bankrupt in excess of the value of the interest of the bankrupt estate therein as determined by the court. Upon filing the receipts of the proper public officers for such payments the trustees shall be credited with the amounts thereof, and in case any question arises as to the amount or legality of any such tax the same shall be heard and determined by the court.

"(b) The debts to have priority, in advance of the payment of dividends to creditors, and to be paid in full out of bankrupt estates, and the order of payment shall be (1) the actual and necessary cost of preserving the estate subsequent to filing the petition; (2) the filing fees paid by creditors in involuntary cases, and, where property of the bankrupt, transferred or concealed by him either before or after the filing of the petition, shall have been recovered for the benefit of the estate of the bankrupt by the efforts and at the expense of one or more creditors, the reasonable expense of such recovery; (3) the cost of administration, including the fees and mileage payable to witnesses as now or hereafter provided by the laws of the United States, and one reasonable attorney's fee, for the professional services actually rendered, irrespective of the number of attorneys employed, to the petitioning creditors in involuntary cases while performing the duties herein prescribed, and to the bankrupt in voluntary and involuntary cases, as the court may allow; (4) where the confirmation of composition terms has been refused or set aside upon the objection and through the efforts and at the expense of one or more creditors, in the discretion of the court, the reasonable expenses of such creditors in opposing such composition; (5) wages due to workmen, clerks, traveling or city salesmen or servants which have been earned within three months before the date of the commencement of the proceeding, not to exceed $600 to each claimant; (6) taxes payable under paragraph (a) hereof; and (7) debts owing to any person who by the laws of the states or the United States is entitled to priority: provided, that the term 'person' as used in this section shall include corporations, the United States and the several states and territories of the United States. * * *"

It is established law that where state statutes giving priority of claims against a bankrupt are in conflict with the priorities laid down in section 64 of the United States bankruptcy act, the federal statute is given precedence under constitutional authority conferred upon the national government to enact and enforce national bankruptcy laws.[22]

Interpretations of the act may be gleaned from decisions of the federal courts. The priorities recited in section 64 apply merely to the general assets of the estate. They are superior only to the rights of general or unsecured creditors. A mortgage or other lien given and accepted in good faith and for a present consideration, which is not voidable as a preference or otherwise in fraud of the bankruptcy act, is, with respect to property subject to such liens, superior to the prior claims enumerated in section 64 of the act. The courts interpret section 64 to mean priority over other claims, not out of the funds derived from the sale of the bankrupt's property, but out of such sum as remained after the satisfaction of the debts duly secured by liens lawfully existing when the bankruptcy proceedings were instituted. Courts have taken the position that it was the plain intent of congress, in framing the bankruptcy act, not to impair but to protect and preserve statutory, common-law and equitable liens as well as mortgages, thought to be indispensable to the protection of business transactions and commercial prosperity of the country.[23] The federal courts have also justified the priority of statutory liens over the priorities set forth in section 64 on the ground that a contrary holding would operate as an undue encroachment upon rights reserved to the states. While a number of cases have relegated certain statutory liens to the position of 64b(7) providing for the priority of debts due persons entitled to priority under the laws of the United States or the states, statutory liens, with other liens and mortgages, are generally given first claim on the bankrupt's assets.[24]

[22] *In re Rodgers & Garrett Timber Co.* (D. C., Md. 1927) 22 F. (2d) 571; *In re Glover Casket Co.* (D. C., Ga., 1932) 1 F. Supp. 743; *In re Inland Dredging Corporation* (C. C. A., N. Y., 1932) 61 F. (2d) 765, certiorari denied (1933) 53 S. Ct. 403.

[23] *In re Proudfoot*, 173 F. 733 (1909).

[24] *United States Code Annotated*, title 11, bankruptcy, sec. 104, p. 73 (1927); Ibid., p. 4 of 1933 cumulative pocket part.

Some Special Rights of Public Accountants 213

The actual and necessary cost of preserving the bankrupt's estate subsequent to the filing of the petition is next in priority following liens. While the determination of what items shall be included in the actual and necessary cost of preserving the bankrupt's estate is within the sound discretion of the court in control of the proceedings, it may well be expected that the judicial discretion will follow other cases in allowing items of expense as costs of preserving the estate. Debts resulting from the following expenditures have been held, apparently by the weight of authority, to come within the preferred claims as costs of preserving the estate: receiver's salary; [25] receiver's current expenses incurred for the estate; [26] rent to landlord for storage of bankrupt's property during receivership; [27] receiver's expenses incurred to preserve bankrupt's stock of fish; [28] wages of guards to protect property of estate subsequent to filing of petition whether during receivership or trusteeship; [29] assignee's expenses of appraisal for sale prior to filing petition in bankruptcy; [30] audit services after common-law assignment prior to bankruptcy adjudication; [31] wages of laborers who operated factory during receivership; [32] fire-insurance premiums during period of common-law assignment preceding filing of bankruptcy petition and period between time of filing of petition and appointment of trustee.[33]

Let us now consider some of the claims which courts have held to be included in the second group of priorities described in section 64b. Fees paid by creditors for filing the petition in bankruptcy have been uniformly held to come within the second group

[25] *In re Scott* (D. C., N. C., 1900) 99 F. 404.
[26] *In re Veler* (C. C. A., sixth circuit, 1918) 249 F. 633.
[27] *In re Erlich* (D. C., Pa., 1924) 297 F. 327. Note: It is well-settled law that where a landlord has a statutory lien on bankrupt's property for rent at the time of commencement of bankruptcy proceedings the claim has precedence over the priorities of section 64 of the bankruptcy act. See: *In re Menzies* (D. C., Arizona, 1932) 60 F. 1064; U. S. C. A. 11, bankruptcy, section 104, p. 18 of 1933 cumulative pocket part.
[28] *In re Alaska Fishing & D. Co.* (D. C., Wash., 1909) 167 F. 875.
[29] *In re Mitchell* (C. C. A., 2nd. circuit, 1914) 212 F. 932.
[30] *In re Cooper* (D. C., Mass., 1917) 243 F. 797.
[31] *In re Hanson Co.* (D. C., Iowa, 1922) 283 F. 850.
[32] *In re Erie Lumber Co.* (D. C., Ga., 1906) 150 F. 817.
[33] *In re South Bend Lumber Co.* (D. C., Wash., 1924) 2 F. (2d) 783.

of priorities of section 64b.[34] Debts incurred by a trustee or expenditures made by creditors for the purpose of recovering to the estate property concealed or transferred before or after the filing of the petition in bankruptcy, where the transfer or concealment was made in actual or constructive fraud, by the weight of authority have been included in the second class of priorities of section 64b.[35]

What items shall be included in costs of administration, the third group of section 64b, is within the reasonable discretion of the court in control of the proceedings. In the absence of abuse the court's discretion will not be questioned upon appeal. Items generally interpreted by the courts as coming within costs of administration are these: office expenses of trustee; care and custody of bankrupt's property while in hands of trustee; rent during trusteeship; commissions of receiver and referee; expenses incurred in carrying out bankrupt's contracts; accountant's services; attorney's fees.[36]

The discussion of the fourth class of priorities of section 64b, which gives priority to the cost of successful resistance to confirmation of creditors' composition agreement, should be preceded by some attention to the meaning of confirmation of creditor's composition agreement under the act. Section 12 of the bankruptcy act provides that "a bankrupt may offer, either before or after adjudication, terms of composition to his creditors, after, but not before, he has been examined in open court, or at a meeting of his creditors, and has filed in court the schedule of his property and the list of his creditors required to be filed by bankrupts." The court may compel dissentient creditors to join in the agreement. On confirmation by the court and distribution of the consideration the case is settled. Section 64b(4) which provides for priority of creditors' claims for expenses incurred in successful resistance to confirmation of a composition agreement was added in 1926. It seems that no court has ruled upon the new provision. Hence, we have not a court interpretation of this fourth group of prior claims. However, the

---

[34] *In re Silverman* (D. C., N. Y., 1899) 97 F. 325.
[35] U. S. C. A., title 11, bankruptcy, sec. 104.
[36] U. S. C. A., title 11, bankruptcy, secs. 102 and 104.

Some Special Rights of Public Accountants 215

wording of this added provision makes it clear that the judge, in his discretion, in the order named in section 64b, may give priority to creditors' claims for reasonable expenses for attorney's fees, witness fees, and other costs incident to a successful opposition to a confirmation of a composition agreement between the bankrupt and his creditors.

The fifth group of claims under section 64b, which gives priority to wages, has been interpreted by a long line of decisions. The wages must have been earned within the period of three months preceding the commencement of bankruptcy proceedings. The wage earner must have been a servant, not an independent contractor, in order that his claim may receive priority under this fifth provision. Generally, high executives have been held not entitled to priority with respect to their salaries. Presidents, general managers and treasurers of corporations have been held to be without the preferred group of section 64b(5). On the other hand, the salary of a manager of a branch of a chain-store system has been held to come within this fifth group of prior claims. Generally, this provision of section 64b has been interpreted to apply to wages of common laborers, clerks, salesmen, stenographers and bookkeepers. A foreman's salary is a preferred claim under the fifth group if the foreman did the same kind of work as his subordinates were doing.[37]

Prior to 1926, under section 64, courts generally placed taxes second only to liens; but, under the amended section, taxes, federal and state, have been relegated to sixth place in the priorities set forth in section 64b.[38]

The seventh set of claims in order of priority, which consists of debts to persons entitled to priority under state or federal laws, is really an adoption of such laws so far as they do not conflict with the intent and purposes of the bankruptcy act. Claims under this seventh provision do not include specific liens and mortgages, but they do include freight charges of railroads under federal control, bank receiver's claim against bankrupt for double liability as stock-

[37] U. S. C. A., title 11, bankruptcy, sec. 104.
[38] Ibid.

holder, landlord's prior claim under state statute and mechanics' liens which are given preference by state laws.[39]

The enumeration of items in the seven groups of prior claims of the bankruptcy act is not intended to be exhaustive but sufficient to show how the public accountant's claims for services may be properly placed.

Apparently only two cases have dealt with the public accountant's claims for services rendered before the time of adjudication in bankruptcy, as a part of the first group of preferred claims under section 64b, which provides for priority of debts incurred to preserve the estate. *In re Hanson & Tyler Auto Co.*,[40] the first of the two cases, involved the following facts:

The Hanson & Tyler Auto Company in 1920, at the request of certain creditors, authorized the plaintiff accountants to make an audit of its business but later refused the auditors access to the books. The creditors then held a meeting for the purpose of having a general assignment of the bankrupt Hanson & Tyler Auto Company made under the laws of Iowa. The creditors also employed the plaintiff accountants to perform the audit. The estimated cost of the audit was $1,500; but the actual cost was $3,337.99. The accountants began the audit before the state-law assignment became effective and completed the audit thereafter. The completed audit was used by the trustee under the state-law assignment, and later by the trustee in bankruptcy after the case was taken to the federal district court of Iowa. After ruling that the court would protect "an assignee under state laws and under provision of a state court to the extent of the service or expense which is beneficial to the estate," the court held in regard to the preference of the accountants' claim for their services as follows:

> "With respect to the matter under consideration, it does not appear that an audit was in fact made for the assignee under the general assignment. The audit was made under an arrangement with the bankrupt itself and certain creditors of the bankrupt and largely completed before the assignment under the state law was made. It is claimed, however, that it was not completed, and that some of the

[39] U. S. C. A., title 11, bankruptcy, sec. 104.
[40] D. C., Iowa, 1922) 283 F. 850.

Some Special Rights of Public Accountants 217

work overlapped the period of the assignee's administration, but how much does not appear. The estimated cost at the time the arrangement was made is said to have been $1,500. The complete audit for which the charge is made is certified by the referee with the record and evidence, and the court is fully convinced that the estimated sum is very ample compensation for the making of the audit in question. There is an item in the bill of $865.49 for traveling and subsistence expenses. This item is a very unusual one to be included without explanation.

"Now, on this 31st day of July, 1922, said matter comes on for final determination and order in the premises, and, after carefully considering the claim as filed, the summary of evidence certified, and the entire record in the case, the court is convinced that $1,500 is very ample compensation for the services performed, and especially when the item for traveling and subsistence expenses is allowed in addition, which the court reluctantly includes, making an aggregate allowance of $2,365.49. From this should be deducted the $250 paid on November 18, 1920. The court is further of the opinion that the sum of $500, of the $1,500 service item, may be allowed as preferred, on account of having been rendered to the assignee under the state law and being beneficial to the estate.

"It is therefore ordered and adjudged that the order of the referee, which is now reviewed, be modified, and that said claim be established in the sum of $2,115.49, and that said claim to the extent of $500 only be established and allowed as a preferred claim, the balance to be established as a general claim only, and that the order of the referee, petitioned from, as so modified, be approved and affirmed."

In the *Hanson & Tyler Auto Co.* case the court ruled that the claims for audit services rendered after the assignment under state laws was made and before the bankruptcy adjudication took place were preferred under section 64b of the bankruptcy act. In the first place the court held that the auditors' claims should be preferred on the ground that proper recognition of the assignment under state laws should be made. This policy on the part of federal courts is in effect an adoption of the state laws into the bankruptcy proceedings so far as such laws do not conflict with the bankruptcy act. This ruling would place the auditors' claims within group 7 of the preferred claims under section 64b, which provides for priority of claims preferred under state and federal laws. The court, however, went further and held that the auditors' claims were entitled to priority because their services were instrumental in preserving the bankrupt's estate during the period of assignment. Under this ruling the auditors' claims were advanced to the position of the first group of prior claims under section 64b, which provides for priority of claims on account of services rendered to preserve the bankrupt's estate. Claims for services rendered the assignee under the state laws prior to adjudication in bankruptcy should receive the same status with respect to priority as claims for services rendered during receivership. Generally, expenses incurred during receivership are classed as costs of preserving the estate. Certainly an audit rendered to ascertain the property and debts during receivership partakes of the nature of services to preserve the estate. *In re Hanson & Tyler Auto Co.* should be a guide for future decisions.

In re Cabel Upholstering Co.[41] is the second of the two cases dealing with the placing claims for auditing services rendered during receivership within the first group of preferred claims under section 64b. The decision follows:

"The involuntary petition in bankruptcy was filed February 28, 1924. An examination of the statement rendered by the attorney shows that all services, with the exception of two items, were rendered prior to bankruptcy. The statement rendered by the auditor does not show what part of the services were rendered prior to bankruptcy and what were rendered after, but the referee finds that for the most part the services were incurred prior to the filing of the petition, and that whatever services were rendered afterwards did not tend to preserve the estate."

The court in the *Cabel Upholstering Co.* case gave little consideration to the accountant's services to the bankrupt. The court was correct in refusing to give priority to claims for auditing services rendered prior to the time of filing the petition in bankruptcy. Such claims are construed as debts to general unsecured creditors. It is possible that the public accountant's services subsequent to filing the petition were slight and could not have been material

[41] (D. C., Mass., 1925) 6 F. (2d) 1019.

in preserving the estate. If so, the court was correct in refusing to give preference to claims for such services; but if the audit had been performed in any considerable proportion during receivership the court should have included the claims for that proportion as costs of preserving the estate.

The decision *In re M. E. Smith & Co.*,[42] a case placing the accountant's claim for services rendered during trusteeship under section 64b(2) which gives priority to costs of administration of the estate of the bankrupt was in part as follows:

"I find, therefore, as a finding of fact, that the claimant did perform accounting (auditing) services for the former trustee herein, with the consent and approval of the referee during the years 1927 to and including a part of the year 1930, and that the reasonable value of the unpaid balance due said claimant is the sum of $1,029.75; that said claim was, and is, a valid claim against said bankrupt estate as an administration expense, and should have been paid before the declaration of any dividend, or at least before the declaration of a final dividend to the creditors, * * * (claim ordered paid out of unclaimed dividends)."

The *M. E. Smith & Co.* decision is sound in holding that audit services rendered during trusteeship are costs of administration. Generally, cases have held that current expenses incurred for the estate during the trusteeship are costs of administration. Though it might be argued that an audit helps preserve the estate during the trusteeship, as in checking cash and inventories, yet, generally the ascertainment of property will be effected through an audit during the receivership, and the audit during the trusteeship will serve largely the interests of administration. *In re M. E. Smith & Co.* should be of controlling importance to courts in future decisions.

When, in the case of the bankruptcy of a stockbroker, it becomes necessary for the trustee to engage accountants to unravel the details of the bankrupt's books in order to trace securities of creditors, expenditures for such services are chargeable to the claimants of the securities, except those who were able to trace their securities with-

---

[42] (D. C., Neb., 1931) 52 F. (2d) 212.

out the aid of accountants. This principle was established by *In re J. C. Wilson & Co.*[43] as follows:

"It was necessary for the trustee to engage accountants to unravel the details contained in the Harris books. An order has been made apportioning this expense among various claimants including the trustee. * * * No question has been raised as to the reasonableness of the charges. While it is true that the trustee represented general creditors, and doubtless has done everything in his power in their interest, nevertheless it is also true that the work on these accounts was for the benefit of the claimants, and work which it would have been necessary for them to have done, if this arrangement had not been made. These disbursements, in my opinion, were therefore chargeable to each claimant in the amounts set forth in the petition of M. & L. W. Scudder. In a case such as that of Mrs. Conant, who was able to trace her securities without the aid of accountants, no charge for that service should be made."

The decision in the case of *J. C. Wilson & Co.,* that security owners who were not able to trace their securities which had been pledged by the broker with money lenders and who availed themselves of the services of public accountants in the employ of the trustee should be charged individually with the costs of the accountants' services incurred in discovering their securities is beyond question sound. Since the securities were owned by the customers (claimants) of the bankrupt, the expense of tracing them would not constitute a charge against the estate of the bankrupt. As to the mode of enforcing the order the case is silent, and there seems to be no other case in point; but a court, sitting in equity, would probably give priority to the accountants' claims over other claims against the securities, in view of the fact that the accountants' services were rendered at the instance of the trustee in bankruptcy.[44]

---

[43] (D. C., N. Y., 1917) 252 F. 631.
[44] Note: As to the reasonableness of charges for services of public accountants in bankruptcy proceedings see: *In re Weisman* (D. C., Conn., 1920) 267 F. 588; *Kennedy v. Nathan* (C. C. A., Pa., 1930) 43 F. (2d) 71; *In re Kroeger Bros. Co.* (C. C. A., Wis., 1921) 276 F. 8.

Expenses of Audit in Addition to Personal Services of Accountant

Where it is clear from the contents and circumstances of an auditing contract that only the personal services of the public accountant are engaged, additional cost such as traveling expenses and compensation for necessary assistance and the like incurred in making the audit must be paid for by the client. The supreme court of Montana in 1925 in the case of *Callan* v. *Hample* [45] gave a clear justification of the rule:

"* * * The character and effect of the employment of an expert accountant does not differ materially from the employment of a doctor, a lawyer or other professional man. He is retained to perform services requiring his personal skill and technical knowledge not common to the one employing him, and therefore to proceed with the work in accordance with his own methods and ideas without being subject to direction or orders from his employer as to details. Such an employment does not constitute the relation of master and servant and is not governed by the rules applicable to such relation. (26 Cyc. 970; *Eldred* v. *Mackie*, 178 Mass. 1, 59 N. E. 673; *Groesbeck* v. *Pinson*, 21 Tex. Civ. App. 44, 50 S. W. 620.) Such employment of professional men and skilled workers may necessarily entail the employment of others to attend to certain details, and the outlay of incidental expense money, and a contract to pay the expenses thus necessarily incurred, as well as and in addition to the reasonable value of the services of such an one, may be inferred from the nature of the employment and the surrounding circumstances.

"The expert accountant could not be required to pay for necessary assistance, toll charges and traveling expenses, out of the reasonable compensation for his personal services any more than a doctor could be required to pay nurses' wages, drug bills and hospital expenses out of his compensation, or a lawyer to pay filing fees, witness fees and necessary traveling expenses out of the reasonable compensation for his services."

The bankruptcy courts regularly allow public accountants' claims for clerical and stenographic expenses necessary in bankruptcy audits. While reasonable amounts of traveling and hotel expenses

[45] 236 P. 550, 73 Mont. 321.

of the accountants have generally been allowed in bankruptcy audits, the courts make such allowances with no little reluctance.[46] The allowance for expenses in addition to the cost of the auditors' services should be made unless it can be shown that it was the clear intent of the auditing agreement that the accountants should bear all costs of the audit.

NATURE OF ACCOUNTANT'S SERVICES AFFECT REASONABLENESS OF CHARGES

Two decisions, one by the Louisiana supreme court [47] in 1928 and the other by the Louisiana court of appeals [48] in 1929, placed high values upon accountants' income-tax services, which the judges classed as legal as compared to values placed upon the usual auditing work which the judges thought was clerical. Perhaps the courts have been correct in attaching a higher value to income-tax services than to mere routine of reviewing records and making up working papers; but time spent in the preparation of the business reports from the working papers, in analyzing the financial and operating condition of the business, in designing an accounting system or in installing a budgetary control system should be compensated by fees on a parity with those for legal services rendered in income-tax matters.

AUDITING CONTRACTS WITH CORPORATIONS AND GOVERNMENTAL AGENCIES

The validity of public accountants' contracts for audits entered into with corporations and governmental agencies is dependent upon the authority of the representative or representatives, of the corporation or governmental subdivision. The authority of the corporate representative is generally dependent upon the resolutions of the directors, the corporate charter and the laws designed to regulate corporations. Likewise, the contracting authority of a governmental agency is dependent upon the statutes and ordinances applying to the particular subdivision of government.

[46] *In re Weisman* (D. C., Conn., 1920) 267 F. 588; accountant's unusual hotel bills and Pullman fares were not permitted as claims for bankruptcy audit, *Matter of Marks* (D. C., Ga., 1909) 22 *Am. Bankr. Rep.* 54.
[47] *Robinson & Co. v. Connell*, 117 So. 774, 166 La. 685.
[48] *Derbes v. Dixie Mill Supply Co.*, 124 So. 316, 11 La. App. 522.

Two cases before the supreme court of New York, one [49] in 1907 and the other [50] in 1915, illustrate the complexities which may arise over the authority of corporate representatives to employ public accountants to make audits.

An example of the complexities which may affect the authority of governmental agencies to contract appears in a decision rendered by the supreme court of Kansas in 1908.[51] The court ruled that a foreign corporation of accountants was eligible, even though the corporation had not obtained a permit to do business in Kansas, to contract with the governor of Kansas to audit the records of state departments. The reason advanced by the court was that the corporation of accountants was not doing business in Kansas as long as the employees of the corporation prepared only the working papers in Kansas and made up the reports outside of Kansas.

Public accountants who care to enter into auditing contracts with corporations or governmental subdivisions should have their contracts approved by competent attorneys.

Power of Practitioners of Public Accountancy to Incorporate

The public accountancy statutes of the various states and the District of Columbia differ considerably in their provision for the incorporation of public accounting firms. Most of the state public accountancy statutes are silent on the matter. Illinois and Michigan provide specifically in their public accountancy statutes that public accounting firms may incorporate.[52] It is probable that in many more states authority for public accountants to incorporate is to be found in the general laws of incorporation. Accounting firms have been chartered in the state of New York.[51]

Delaware, the District of Columbia, Massachusetts, New Mexico, South Dakota and Wisconsin prohibit by statute a corporation from assuming the certified public accountant's title.[52] An Iowa statute forbids the incorporation of accounting firms.[52] Florida has

---

[49] *Teele* v. *Consolidate Amusement Co.*, 102 N. Y. S. 666.
[50] *Bartels* v. *Ferncliff Cemetery Association*, 155 N. Y. S. 322, 169 App. Div. 421.
[51] *Haskins & Sells* v. *Kelly*, 93 P. 605, 77 Kan. 155.
[52] *Certified Public Accountant Laws of the United States*, American Institute Publishing Co., Inc.

a statute which prohibits the practice of public accountancy by a corporation whether domestic or foreign.[53]

The American Institute of Accountants holds that "audit companies and similar organizations are detrimental to the best interests of the accounting profession." [54]

The very essence of the public accountant's work is personal service. He renders his services in a position of trust in which he owes to his client a duty to exercise skill, efficiency and good faith and to the public a duty to certify only business reports free from the taints of fraud. The corporate form of organization may make it possible for accountants to shift the individual responsibilities which they owe their clients and the public in some circumstances. Hence, in the interest of the client, the public and the accountant, the corporation as a form of organization for accountants should not be favored.

[53] *Certified Public Accountant Laws of the United States,* American Institute Publishing Co., Inc.

[54] See appendix, page 227.

APPENDIX

RULES OF PROFESSIONAL CONDUCT
OF
THE AMERICAN INSTITUTE OF ACCOUNTANTS

(1) A firm or partnership, all the individual members of which are members of the Institute (or in part members and in part associates, provided all the members of the firm are either members or associates), may describe itself as "Members of the American Institute of Accountants," but a firm or partnership, all the individual members of which are not members of the Institute (or in part members and in part associates), or an individual practising under a style denoting a partnership when in fact there be no partner or partners or a corporation or an individual or individuals practising under a style denoting a corporate organization shall not use the designation "Members (or Associates) of the American Institute of Accountants."

(2) The preparation and certification of exhibits, statements, schedules or other forms of accountancy work, containing an essential misstatement of fact or omission therefrom of such a fact as would amount to an essential misstatement or a failure to put prospective investors on notice in respect of an essential or material fact not specifically shown in the balance-sheet itself shall be, ipso facto, cause for expulsion or for such other discipline as the council may impose upon proper presentation of proof that such misstatement was either wilful or the result of such gross negligence as to be inexcusable.

(3) No member or associate shall allow any person to practise in his name as a public accountant who is not a member or an associate of the Institute or in partnership with him or in his employ on a salary.

(4) No member or associate shall directly or indirectly allow or agree to allow a commission, brokerage or other participation by the laity in the fees or profits of his professional work; nor shall he accept directly or indirectly from the laity any commission, brokerage or other participation for professional or commercial business turned over to others as an incident of his services to clients.

(5) No member or associate shall engage in any business or occupation conjointly with that of a public accountant, which in the opinion of the executive committee or of the council is incompatible or inconsistent therewith.

(6) No member or associate shall certify to any accounts, exhibits, statements, schedules or other forms of accountancy work which have not been verified entirely under the supervision of himself, a member of his firm, one of his staff, a member or an associate of this Institute or a member of a similar association of good standing in a foreign country which has been approved by the council.

(7) No member or associate shall take part in any effort to secure the enactment or amendment of any state or federal law or of any regulation of any governmental or civic body, affecting the practice of the profession, without giving immediate notice thereof to the secretary of the Institute, who in turn shall at once advise the executive committee or the council.

(8) No member or associate shall directly or indirectly solicit the clients or encroach upon the business of another member or associate, but it is the right of any member or associate to give proper service and advice to those asking such service or advice.

(9) No member or associate shall directly or indirectly offer employment to an employee of a fellow member or associate without first informing said fellow member or associate of his intent. This rule shall not be construed so as to inhibit negotiations with any one who of his own initiative or in response to public advertisement shall apply to a member or an associate for employment.

(10) No member or associate shall render or offer to render professional service, the fee for which shall be contingent upon his findings and the results thereof.

(11) No member or associate of the Institute shall advertise his or her professional attainments or service through the mails, in the public prints, by circular letters or by any other written word except that a member or an associate may cause to be published in the public prints what is technically known as a card. A card is hereby defined as an advertisement of the name, title (member of American Institute of Accountants, C. P. A., or other professional affiliation or designation), class of service and address of the advertiser, without any further qualifying words or letters, or in the case of announcement of change of address or personnel of firm the plain statement of the fact for the publication of which the announcement purports to be made. Cards

permitted by this rule when appearing in newspapers shall not exceed two columns in width and three inches in depth; when appearing in magazines, directories and similar publications cards shall not exceed one quarter page in size. This rule shall not be construed to inhibit the proper and professional dissemination of impersonal information among a member's own clients or personal associates or the properly restricted circulation of firm bulletins containing staff personnel and professional information.

(12) No member or associate of the Institute shall be an officer, a director, stockholder, representative, an agent, a teacher or lecturer, nor participate in any other way in the activities or profits of any university, college or school which conducts its operations, solicits prospective students or advertises its courses by methods which in the opinion of the committee on professional ethics are discreditable to the profession.

RESOLUTIONS

Adopted by the American Institute of Accountants, September 16, 1919:

Resolved, That it is the sense of this meeting that audit companies and similar organizations are detrimental to the best interests of the accounting profession.

Adopted by the council of the American Institute of Accountants, April 11, 1932:

Whereas, Estimates of earnings contingent upon future transactions should always be clearly distinguished from statements of actual earnings evidenced by definite records, and

Whereas, An accountant may properly assist a client in estimating the results of future transactions, so long as no one may be led to believe that the estimates represent certainties,

Be it resolved, That no public accountant should permit his name to be used in conjunction with such an estimate in a manner which might lead anyone to believe that the accountant could vouch for the accuracy of the forecast; and

Be it further resolved, That violation of this dictum by a member or an associate of the American Institute of Accountants be considered by the committee on professional ethics as cause for charges under the provision of article V, section 4 (c) of the bylaws, or rule 2 of the rules of professional conduct of the American Institute of Accountants, or both.[1]

[1] Note: For a detailed treatment of the ethics of the accounting profession, see: A. P. Richardson, *Ethics of a Profession*, New York, American Institute Publishing Co., Inc., 1931.

TABLE OF CASES

	Page
Aetna Casualty & Surety Co. v. *Wilmington,* 157 A. 208	161, 182
Allgeyer v. *Louisiana,* 165 U. S. 578	138
Annotation, 2 A. L. R. 1576	198
Annotation, 16 A. L. R. 1433, 1457	197-8
Annotation, 34 A. L. R. 1537	197
Bartels v. *Ferncliff Cemetery Association,* 155 N. Y. S. 322	223
Bell v. *Tackett,* 272 P. 461	173
Bertie v. *Beuumont,* 146 English reports 105	172
Bitting v. *State,* 139 S. E. 877	190
Board v. *Reynolds,* 44 Ind. 509	52
Boston and Worcester Railroad Corporation v. *Dana,* 67 Mass. 83	153-4
Brookfield Co. v. *Mart,* 4 P (2d) 311	168
Brown v. *First National Bank,* 113 P. 483	161
Burleigh v. *Clark,* "The Accountant," London, 1901, vol. 27, law reports section, p. 65	208
Bush v. *Board of Education,* 37 S. W. (2d) 849	161, 174
Callan v. *Hample,* 236 P. 550	221
Camp v. *State,* 122 S. E. 249	161
Campbell v. *McIntyre,* 52 S. W. (2d) 162	134
Carter v. *Towne,* 103 Mass. 507	11
Chapman v. *Walton,* 131 Reprint 826	6
Chatham Furnace Co. v. *Moffatt,* 147 Mass. 403	72, 89
Citizens Bank of Tifton v. *Timmons,* 84 S. E. 232	183
Craig v. *Anyon,* 208 N. Y. S. 259	57-60
Crawford v. *State,* 138 So. 589	154-5
Crusoe v. *Clark,* 59 P. 700	154
Cuff v. *London and County Land and Building Company, Ltd.,* (1912) 1 Ch. 440	40
Davis v. *Sexton,* 207 N. Y. S. 377	111, 113
Deaderick v. *Wilson,* 8 Baxter 107	52
Delaney v. *Framingham Gas, Fuel and Water Co.,* 88 N. E. 776	171
Derbes v. *Dixie Mill Supply Co.,* 124 So. 316	222
Derry v. *Peek,* 14 App. Cas. 117	73, 76
Diamond Alkali Co. v. *Henderson Coal Co.,* 134 A. 386	186

	Page
East Grand Forks v. *Steele*, 141 N. W. 181	42, 45, 47, 53
Eberle v. *State Board of Certified Public Accountants*, 171 La. 318	118
Eckert v. *Long Island R. R. Co.*, 43 N. Y. 502	6
Edwards v. *State*, 111 So. 765	188
Flagg v. *U. S.*, 233 Fed. 481	152
Fox and Son v. *Morrish, Grant, & Co.*, 35 T. L. R. 126	40, 41
Frazer v. *Shelton*, 150 N. E. 696	134
Glanzer v. *Shepard*, 135 N. E. 275	94-5
Goldsmith v. *Clabaugh*, 6 F. (2d) 94	113
Goldsmith v. *Jewish Press Publishing Company*, 195 N. Y. S. 37	129
Grand Trunk Railway Co. v. *Ives*, 144 U. S. 408	59
Hankins v. *State*, 213 N. W. 344	160
Haskins & Sells v. *Kelly*, 93 P. 605	115, 223
Henry Squire, Cash Chemist, Ltd. v. *Ball, Baker & Co.*, 28 T. L. R. 81	34, 55
Henry v. *State*, 260 S. W. 190	126, 141
Herberg v. *State*, 222 S. W. 559	161
Hill v. *Winsor*, 118 Mass. 251	10
Hitchcock v. *Gothenburg Water Power & Irr. Co.*, 95 N. W. 638	91
Holcombe v. *Noble*, 69 Mich. 396	90
Home Building and Loan Association v. *Blaisdell*, 54 S. Ct. 231	139
Hopkins v. *People*, 1 P. (2d) 937	182
Hubble v. *Hubble*, 279 P. 550	166
Huntress v. *Blodgett*, 206 Mass. 318	89
Independent Medical College v. *People*, 55 N. E. 345	125
In re Alaska Fishing & D. Co., 167 F. 875	213
In re Cabel Upholstering Co., 6 F. (2d) 1019	218
In re City Equitable Fire Insurance Co., Lim., 40 T. L. R. 853	35, 38
In re Cooper, 243 F. 797	213
In re Erie Lumber Co., 150 F. 817	213
In re Erlich, 297 F. 327	213
In re Fisher, 51 F. (2d) 424	175-6, 180
In re Glover Casket Co., 1 F. Supp. 743	212
In re Hanson Co., 283 F. 850	213, 216-8
In re Inland Dredging Corporation, 61 F. (2d) 765	212
In re Kingston Cotton Mill Company, (No. 2), (1896) 2 Ch. D. 279	29, 33-4
In re Kroeger Bros. Co., 276 F. 8	220
In re London and General Bank, (1895) 2 Ch. 673	19, 31, 33

Table of Cases

Page

In re Menzies, 60 F. 1064 213
In re Mitchell, 212 F. 932 213
In re Polemis & Furness, Withy & Company, (1921) 3 K. B. 560.. 64
In re Proudfoot, 173 F. 733 212
In re Republic of Bolivia Exploration Syndicate, Ltd., (1914) 1
   Ch. D. 139 54-5
In re Rodgers & Garrett Timber Co., 22 F. (2d) 571 212
In re Scott, 99 F. 404 213
In re Silverman, 97 F. 325 214
In re M. E. Smith & Co., 52 F. (2d) 212 219
In re South Bend Lumber Co., 2 F. (2d) 783 213
In re Veler, 249 F. 633 213
In re Weisman, 267 F. 588 .... 220, 222
In re J. C. Wilson & Co., 252 F. 631 220
Institute of Chartered Accountants in England and Wales v. Hardwick, 34 T. L. R. 584 122
Insurance Co. v. Randall, 74 Ala. 170 13
Ipswich Mills v. Dillon, 157 N. E. 604 .... 203, 204, 205-7
Johnstone v. Morris, 292 P. 970 .... 157, 182
Junker v. Forbes, 45 Fed. 840 13
Kay v. Federal Rubber Co., 60 F. (2d) 454 166
Kennedy v. Nathan, 43 F. (2d) 71 220
Kersh v. State, 153 So. 284 186
Kountze v. Kennedy, 41 N. E. 414 .... 73, 75, 92
Landell v. Lybrand, 107 A. 783 66-8
Lane v. Atlantic Works, 111 Mass. 136 10
Leeds Estate Building and Investment Company v. Shepherd,
   (1887) 36 Ch. D. 787 .... 17, 22
Lehmann v. State Board of Public Accountancy, 94 So. 94 ...130-1, 141
Le Roy State Bank v. Keenan's Bank, 169 N. E. 1 168-9
Litchfield v. Hutchinson, 117 Mass. 195 89
Manley v. State, 144 S. E. 170 192
Matter of Marks, 22 Am. Bankr. Rep. 54 222
McCullogh v. Scott, 109 S. E. 789 127
McNaughton v. Presbyterian Church, 172 N. E. 561 .... 154, 161
Meyerson v. New Idea Hosiery Co., 115 So. 94 67
Miller v. Alabama State Board of Public Accountancy, 98 So. 893 131-2
Miller v. Anderson, 196 N. W. 869 .... 198, 201
Minnesota Rate Case, 134 U. S. 418 138

	Page
Munn v. *Illinois*, 94 U. S. 113	139
National Association of Certified Public Accountants v. *United States*, 292 F. 668	123, 126
Newton Auto Salvage Co. v. *Herrick*, 212 N. W. 680	4
Newton v. *Birmingham Small Arms Company, Ltd.*, (1906) 2 Ch. 378	48-51
Newton v. *State*, 127 A. 123	161
Nichols v. *Clark*, etc., 184 N. E. 729	96-7
Note—16 L. R. A. 745	197
Oliver v. *Oliver*, 45 S. E. 232	53
Palmer v. *Goldberg*, 107 N. W. 478	91
Payne v. *Franklin County*, 116 S. E. 627	186
Pelton v. *Nichols*, 62 N. E. 1	14
People v. *Hatfield*, 208 N. W. 682	161, 186
People v. *Marlowe*, 203 N. Y. S. 474	126, 141
People v. *National Association of Certified Public Accountants*, 197 N. Y. S. 775	125
Peterson v. *Gales*, 210 N. W. 407	68
Pierce Pet. Co. v. *Osaga Coal Co.*, 271 P. 675	161
Pioneer Lumber Co. v. *Van Cleave*, 279 S. W. 241	164, 187
Quigley v. *De Haas*, 98 Pa. 299	156
Railroad Co. v. *Schulz*, 1 N. E. 324	189
Reece v. *Kyle*, 31 N. E. 747	195
Respess v. *Rex Spinning Co.*, 133 S. E. 391	114-5
Rex v. *Kylsant*, 48 T. L. R. 62	100-9
Rex v. *Kylsant & Morland*, London, "The Accountant," 1931, new series, vol. 85, p. 109	100-9
Robinson & Co. v. *Connell*, 117 So. 774	222
Royce v. *Oakes*, 38 A. 371	13
Ruth v. *State*, 122 N. W. 733	161
Scott Shoe Machinery Co. v. *Broaker*, 71 N. Y. S. 1023	209
Shine v. *Nash Abstract & I. Co.*, 117 So. 47	67
Slaughter House Case, 16 Wall. 36	137, 139
Smith v. *London Assurance Corporation*, 96 N. Y. S. 820	42, 45
Society of Accountants and Auditors v. *Goodway and London Association of Accountants, Ltd.*, (1907) 1 Ch. 489	120-1
Southern Development Co. v. *Silva*, 125 U. S. 247	88
State v. *De Verges*, 95 So. 805	128, 141
State v. *Maslin*, 143 S. E. 3	156

TABLE OF STATUTES 233

	Page
State v. *Matkins*, 34 S. W. (2d) 1	164, 182
State v. *Olson*, 287 P. 181	161
State v. *Perry*, 90 So. 406	160
State v. *Riedell*, 233 P. 684	134
State v. *Williams*, 111 A. 701	161
Stephen v. *United States*, 41 F. (2d) 440	162, 168, 191
Stewart v. *Harris*, 77 P. 277	53
Strong v. *Repide*, 213 U. S. 419	53
Taylor v. *Hearst*, 40 P. 392	64
Teele v. *Consolidate Amusement Co.*, 102 N. Y. S. 666	223
Thoman v. *State Board of Public Accountants*, 113. So. 757; 134 So. 85	116-7
Thomas v. *The Corporation of Devonport*, (1900) 1 Q. B. 16	39, 40
Thomas v. *Railroad Co.*, 101 U. S. 71	124
Thompson v. *Walker*, 234 N. W. 144	186-7
Ultramares Corporation v. *Touche*, 174 N. E. 441	68-76, 93
Union Traction Co. v. *Berry*, 121 N. E. 655	5
United States v. *Porter*, 9 F. (2d) 153	183
Weeks v. *United States*, 232 U. S. 383	152
Weld-Blundell v. *Stephens*, (1919) 1 K. B. 520	11, 60-4
Wilson v. *Jones*, 45 S. W. (2d) 572	91
Wright v. *Alabama Board of Public Accountancy*, 123 So. 33	133-4
Wynne v. *Tyrwhitt*, 106 English reports 975	172
Young v. *State*, 103 S. E. 804	161

TABLE OF STATUTES

Acts of assembly, Virginia, 1928, chap. 454, sec. 572a	205
Certified Public Accountant Laws of the United States, 1930	109, 113, 130, 133, 180, 205, 223, 224
Laws of Arizona, regular session 1933, chap. 45, secs. 8, 9	109, 180
Laws of New York, 1929, chap. 261, art. 57	111
Rules of practice before the United States board of tax appeals, 1931, rule 2	140-1
Skillman, H. B., *1934 Cumulative Supplement to the Compiled General Laws of Florida*, chap. 50, sec. 3935 (13)	181
Session laws of Colorado, 1929, chap. 185, sec. 1 (6)	181
United States Code Annotated, title 11, bankruptcy, 1927-1934	211-2
United States securities act of 1933, as amended in 1934	76-86, 109-10
United States securities exchange act of 1934	86-8, 110

BIBLIOGRAPHY

American Institute of Accountants, *Certified Public Accountant Laws of the United States,* New York, The Century Company, 1930

American Law Institute, *Restatement of the Law of Torts,* Tentative Draft No. 4, 1929

Berle, A. A., "For Whom Corporate Managers are Trustees," 45 *Harvard Law Review* 1365

Blackstone's *Commentaries,* London, A. Strahan, 1787, Volume 4, p. 135

Bohlen, F. H., "Misrepresentation as Deceit, Negligence, or Warranty," 42 *Harvard L. Rev.* 733

Bohlen, F. H., "Should Negligent Misrepresentation be Treated as Negligence or Fraud?" 18 *Va. L. Rev.* 704

Burdick's *Law of Torts,* Albany, Banks & Co., 1926

Cooley on *Torts,* Chicago, Callaghan & Co., 1906, Volumes I, II

Corpus Juris, New York, The American Law Book Company, 1917, Volumes 22, 35, 37

Cyclopedia of Law and Procedure, New York, The American Law Book Company, 1908, Volume 29

"Directors' Liability to Individual Shareholders and to the Corporation," 45 *Harvard L. Rev.* 1389

Essert, F. H., "What is Meant by 'Police Power'?" 12 *Neb. L. B.* 208

Gordon, Spencer, "Accountants and the Securities Act," New York, *The Journal of Accountancy,* 1933, Vol. 56, p. 440

Grainger, W. H., "The Duties, Obligations and Liabilities of Auditors," London, *The Accountant,* 1923, Vol. 68, p. 521

Gregory, T., "The Responsibilities of Auditors," London, *The Accountant,* 1894, Vol. 20, p. 957

Harper on *Torts,* Indianapolis, The Bobbs-Merrill Company, 1933

Harrington, Harry M., "Torts—Liability for Negligent Language," 12 *Texas Law Review* 67

Hildebrand, I. P., "Contracts for the Benefit of Third Parties in Texas," 9 *Texas Law Review* 125

Jones on *Liens,* Indianapolis, The Bobbs-Merrill Company, 1914, Vol. I

McKelvey on *Evidence,* St. Paul, West Publishing Company, 1932

Montgomery, R. H., *The Auditor's Responsibility in Relation to Balance-sheets and Profit-and-loss Accounts,* International Congress on Accounting, London, Gee & Co., 1933, p. 3

Morgan, H., *The Auditor's Responsibility in Relation to Balance-sheet and Profit-and-loss Accounts,* International Congress on Accounting, London, Gee & Co., 1933, p. 11

Ruling Case Law, Rochester, The Lawyers Coöperative Publishing Company, 1917, Volumes 5, 15

Terry, H. T., "Negligence," 29 *Harvard L. Rev.* 40

Terry, H. T., "Negligence," Harvard Law Review Association, *Selected Essays on the Law of Torts,* Norwood, Mass., The Plimpton Press, 1924, p. 263

"The Ownership of Accountants' Working Papers," London, *The Accountant,* 1927, Vol. 77, p. 187

Thornton on *Attorneys at Law,* Northport, Long Island, N. Y., Edward Thompson Company, 1914, Vol. II

Walsh on *Equity,* Chicago, Callaghan and Company, 1930, Sec. 39

Wigmore on *Evidence,* Boston, Little, Brown & Company, 1923, Volumes I-V

Williston, Samuel, "Liability for Honest Misrepresentation," 24 *Harvard L. Rev.* 429

Williston on *Contracts,* New York, Baker, Voorhis & Co., 1931, Volume III

Willoughby on the *Constitution,* New York, Baker, Voorhis & Co., 1910, Volume II, Sec. 759

Words and Phrases (2nd Series), St. Paul, West Publishing Company, 1914, Volume 2, p. 167

DIMENSIONS OF ACCOUNTING THEORY AND PRACTICE

An Arno Press Collection

The American Association of University Instructors in Accounting. **Papers and Proceedings of the American Association of University Instructors in Accounting.** 1916-1925

Baily, Francis. **The Doctrine of Interest and Annuities.** 1808

Beckett, Thomas. **The Accountant's Assistant.** 1901

Blough, Carman G. **Practical Applications of Accounting Standards.** 1957

Bray, F[rank] Sewell. **Precision and Design in Accountancy.** 1947

Brief, Richard P., editor. **Dicksee's Contribution to Accounting Theory and Practice.** 1980

Brinton, Willard C. **Graphic Methods For Presenting Facts.** 1914

Brooks, Collin, editor. **The Royal Mail Case.** 1933

Burns, Thomas J. and Edward N. Coffman, editors. **Ohio State Institute of Accounting Conferences: Collected Papers, 1938-1963.** 1980

By a Chartered Accountant and William A. Vawter Foundation on Business Ethics. **The Etiquette of the Accountancy Profession and The Ethical Problems of Modern Accountancy.** 1927/1933

Carey, John L. **Professional Ethics of Public Accounting.** 1946

Cerboni, Giuseppe. **Primi Saggi Di Logismografia Presentati All' XI Congresso Degli Scienziati Italiani In Roma.** 1873

Cleveland, Frederick A. **Chapters on Municipal Administration and Accounting.** 1909

Cocke, Sir Hugh. **A Summary of the Principal Legal Decisions Affecting Auditors.** 1946

Cotter, Arundel. **Fool's Profits.** 1940

Courcelle-Seneuil, J.G. **Traité Élémentaire de Comptabilité.** 1869

Daniels, Mortimer B. **Corporation Financial Statements.** 1934

DeMond, C.W. **Price, Waterhouse & Company in America.** 1951

Devine, Carl Thomas. **Inventory Valuation and Periodic Income.** 1942

Dicksee, Lawrence Robert. **Business Methods and the War** with **The Fundamentals of Manufacturing Costs;** and **Published Balance Sheets and Window Dressing.** 1916/1927, 1928

Dicksee, Lawrence Robert. **Business Organisation.** 1910

Dicksee, Lawrence Robert and Editor of the Accountant's Library. **Fraudulent Accounting** and **Fraud in Accounts.** 1909/1924, 1925

Edwards, J.R., editor. **British Company Legislation and Company Accounts, 1844-1976.** 1980

Ficker, Nicholas Thiel. **Shop Expense.** 1917

Goldberg, Louis. **An Inquiry Into the Nature of Accounting.** 1965

Green, David, Jr. **Accounting for Corporate Retained Earnings.** 1980

Greene, Catharine De Motte. **The Dynamic Balance Sheet.** 1980

Hain, Hans Peter. **Uniformity and Diversity.** 1980

Hawawini, Gabriel A., and Ashok Vora, editors. **The History of Interest Approximations.** 1980

Hepworth, Samuel Richard. **Reporting Foreign Operations.** 1956

The Herwood Library of Accountancy. 1938

The Institute of Chartered Accountants in England and Wales *Library Catalogue, 1913.* 1913

The Institute of Chartered Accountants in England and Wales **Library Catalogue, 1937.** 1937

Het Internationaal Accountantscongres, Amsterdam 1926. 1927

Johnson, H. Thomas, editor. **System and Profits: Early Management Accounting at DuPont and General Motors.** 1980

King, George. **The Theory of Finance.** 1882

Langenderfer, Harold Q. **The Federal Income Tax: 1861-1872.** 1980

Leake, P.D. **Commercial Goodwill.** 1921

Leautey, Eugene and Adolfe Guilbaut. **La Science Des Comptes Mise A La Portée De Tous.** 1889

Levy, Saul. **Accountants' Legal Responsibility.** 1954

Lubell, Myron Samuel. **The Significance of Organizational Conflict on the Legislative Evolution of the Accounting Profession in the United States.** 1980

Marchi, Francesco. **I Cinquecontisti.** 1867

Merino, Barbara, editor. **Business Income and Price Levels.** 1980

Norris, Harry. **Accounting Theory.** 1946

O'Neill, Michael T., editor. **A.P. Richardson: The Ethics of a Humanist.** 1980

Parker, R.H., editor. **Bibliographies for Accounting Historians.** 1980

Parker, R.H., editor. **British Accountants: A Biographical Sourcebook.** 1980

Perera, M.H.B. **Accounting for State Industrial and Commercial Enterprises in a Developing Country.** 1980

Previts, Gary John. **A Critical Evaluation of Comparative Financial Accounting Thought in America 1900 to 1920.** 1980

Rich, Wiley Daniel. **Legal Responsibilities and Rights of Public Accountants.** 1935

Richardson, A[lphyon] P[erry], editor. **The Influence of Accountants' Certificates on Commercial Credit.** 1913

Roberts, Alfred R., editor. **Selected Papers of Earle C. King.** 1980

Saliers, Earl A. **Principles of Depreciation.** 1915

Schiff, Michael, editor. **The Hayden Stone Accounting Forums 1962-1967.** 1980

Schmalenbach, Eugen. **Dynamic Accounting.** 1959

Scovell, Clinton H. **Cost Accounting and Burden Application.** 1916

Sprague, T[homas] B[ond]. **A Treatis on Life Insurance Accounts** and **A Treatise on Insurance Companies' Accounts** 1874/1911

Stacey, Nicholas A.H., **English Accountancy 1800-1954.** 1954

Stamp, Edward, G.W. Dean, and P.W. Wolnizer, editors. **Notable Financial Causes Célèbres.** 1980

Staubus, George J. **An Accounting Concept of Revenue.** 1980

Taylor, R. Emmett. **No Royal Road.** 1942

Todhunter, Ralph. **Institute of Actuaries' Text-Book of the Principles of Interest, Life Annuities, and Assurances, and Their Practical Application.** 1901

Wells, Murry C., editor. **Controversies on the Theory of the Firm, Overhead Allocation and Transfer Pricing.** 1980

Wildman, John R. and Weldon Powell. **Capital Stock Without Par Value.** 1928